BURBANK

Personal Typewriting

FOURTH EDITION

S. J. WANOUS Professor of Education, Emeritus
University of California, Los Angeles

BERLE HAGGBLADE Professor of Office Administration
Chairman, Office Administration Department
California State University, Fresno

Copyright © 1980
by South-Western Publishing Co.
Cincinnati, Ohio

ISBN: 0-538-20690-X
Library of Congress Catalog Card Number: 78-58012

678H7

Published by

T69 SOUTH-WESTERN PUBLISHING CO.

CINCINNATI   WEST CHICAGO, ILL.   DALLAS   PELHAM MANOR, N.Y.   PALO ALTO, CALIF.

PREFACE

The Fourth Edition of PERSONAL TYPEWRITING, which may be used in either a one-semester or a two-semester course, is designed especially for junior high school and middle school students. The topics covered in both skill building and problem copy are therefore geared to the interests, experiences, and reading abilities of learners at this age level. Materials on capitalization, punctuation, and footnotes, as well as outlines, book reviews, and other commonly prepared school papers, are correlated with similar materials in language arts books.

Drill and timed writing copy is easy in the early lessons and advances in gradual stages to average difficulty. After the introduction of the home row, only two new keys are introduced in any one lesson. Keyboard drills concentrate on only one new key at a time. All keys taught are reviewed vigorously and frequently.

OBJECTIVES

Students who complete PERSONAL TYPEWRITING should accomplish several major objectives:

- Achieve sufficient touch typewriting skill to use the typewriting as a basic communication tool in the preparation of personal and school papers.
- Attain optimum typewriting skill according to their individual abilities.
- Acquire the ability to transfer thoughts from their heads to typewritten copy.
- Review and improve basic English skills of punctuation, spelling, and proofreading.
- Gain an acquaintanceship with the kinds of materials prepared in vocational applications of typewriting.

ORGANIZATION

The book contains 140 lessons plus an office simulation. The first 70 lessons are devoted to skill development and basic personal typewriting operations. The second 70 lessons review materials covered in the first 70 lessons and present advanced work. In the first half of the book, for example, themes without footnotes are covered. In the second half, the students type longer themes with footnotes and bibliographies. Extra-credit problems and alternate suggestions for composing activities are included to accommodate students with varying needs.

Basic Skill. The view is firmly held that personal typing students must learn to type so well that they can forget the machine in order to focus their attention on the wording and form of the papers they must prepare. To this end, technique drills with goals to be achieved are included in almost every lesson. Speed and control aids are generously placed throughout the entire book. The copy appears in print, rough draft, and script in order to enable students to develop typing skill under realistic conditions.

Personal and School Papers. Once an acceptable level of basic skill has been developed, the book covers the form and preparation of personal notes, personal business letters, themes, outlines, book reviews, speech notes, class notes, minutes of meetings, agendas, and other personal papers. The students type first from model copy containing detailed reminders. Later, they type from unarranged copy.

Composing on the Typewriter. The development of composing skill on the typewriter is a major aim of this book. Short composing drills are started in Lesson 36, after the students have fixed desirable technique patterns. These drills lead gradually to the composing of letters and short papers.

NEW FEATURES

Approximately half of the drill and problem copy in this edition is new, ensuring students an adequate amount of fresh, timely material.

Introduction of symbol keys has been delayed until Lessons 31-35, with the intervening lessons devoted to further development of basic skills.

To provide for dependable skill measurement, 5-minute timed writing copy in Units 15-17 has been triple controlled according to syllable intensity, average word length, and word frequency level.

For convenience, a reference section containing frequently needed explanations and illustrations appears in the preliminary pages of the book.

The final unit consists of an office simulation which gives sudents an opportunity to apply the typewriting skills to the production of jobs required in a typical school office.

ACKNOWLEDGEMENTS

We sincerely appreciate the aid of many teachers and students who have helped collect, organize, and write the materials for this book. A special note of thanks is due to Walter L. Shell for his thorough and constructive analysis of the preceding edition.

S. J. Wanous
Berle Haggblade

CONTENTS

OPERATING PARTS OF THE TYPEWRITER

All typewriters have similar parts. These parts are identified on the photographs of the manual typewriter shown below and on the electric typewriter on page v. The exact location of the parts on the illustrated typewriters may be slightly different from the location on your typewriter, but the differences are, for the most part, few and slight.

To identify the parts of the typewriter, locate the numbered part on the illustration. Refer to the same number in the list below for the name of the part. The function of each part is explained in the textbook. Learn to operate each part correctly as it is explained to you.

Extra parts peculiar to your typewriter can be identified by reference to the instructional booklet prepared especially for your typewriter.

Manual Typewriter

1	Carriage return lever (line space regulator)	12	Card and envelope holders	24	Tabulator
2	Left cylinder knob	13	Printing point indicator	25	Tab set key
3	Variable line spacer	14	Paper bail roll	26	Backspace key
4	Left carriage release	15	Right margin set	27	Right shift key
5	Line-space regulator	16	Paper table	28	Space bar
6	Rachet release (automatic line finder)	17	Cylinder (platen)	29	Left shift key
7	Paper guide	18	Paper release lever	30	Shift lock
8	Paper guide scale	19	Right carriage release	31	Ribbon control
9	Left margin set	20	Right cylinder knob	32	Margin release key
10	Paper bail roll	21	Aligning scale	33	Tab clear key
11	Paper bail	22	Cylinder scale (line-of-writing scale)		
		23	Ribbon carrier		

Electric typewriters are available with either a movable carriage as on the manual typewriter on page iv or with a rotating element which moves across the paper as the characters are typed. The model shown below is a single-element typewriter.

All of the parts identified on the manual typewriter except the carriage release lever and the left and right carriage releases can be found on the electric model. Some additional parts have also been identified on the electric.

Electric Typewriter

1	Carriage return lever (not on electric—see number 34)	**11**	Paper bail	**23**	Ribbon carrier (not shown—under cover)
2	Left cylinder knob	**12**	Card and envelope holders	**24**	Tabulator
3	Variable line spacer	**13**	Printing point indicator	**25**	Tab set key
4	Left carriage release (only on electrics with movable carriage)	**14**	Paper bail roll	**26**	Backspace key
		15	Right margin set	**27**	Right shift key
		16	Paper table	**28**	Space bar
5	Line-space regulator	**17**	Cylinder (platen)	**29**	Left shift key
6	Rachet release (automatic line finder)	**18**	Paper release lever	**30**	Shift lock
		19	Right carriage release (only on electrics with movable carriage)	**31**	Ribbon control (not shown—under cover)
7	Paper guide			**32**	Margin release key
8	Paper guide scale	**20**	Right cylinder knob	**33**	Tab clear key
9	Left margin set	**21**	Aligning scale	**34**	Carriage return key
10	Paper bail roll	**22**	Cylinder scale (line-of-writing scale)	**35**	ON/OFF switch

MACHINE ADJUSTMENTS

Operating a typewriter involves more than learning to stroke the keys. This page and page vii contain information regarding machine adjustments which you must know for the particular typewriter you are using.

Pica and Elite Type

Some typewriters are equipped with pica type; some with elite type. Pica type is larger than elite type. Note the difference.

- *The cylinder scale (No. 22) range is from 0 to about 90 on pica machines; from 0 to about 110 on elite machines.*

Pica: fjfjfjfjfj   **(10 letters)**

|← 1 inch →|

Elite: fjfjfjfjfjfj   **(12 letters)**

Paper Guide and Centering Point

On every typewriter, there is at least one scale, usually the cylinder scale (No. 22), that reads from 0 at the left to 85 or more at the right, depending on the width of the carriage and style of type—either pica or elite. The spaces on this scale are matched to the spacing mechanism on the typewriter.

To simplify direction giving, your instructor may ask you to insert paper into your machine so that the left edge corresponds to 0 on the carriage scale. The center point on 8½″ x 11″ paper will then be 42 on the carriage scale for pica machines and 51 (or 50 for convenience) on elite machines.

If this procedure is adopted, adjust the paper guide to the left edge of your paper after it is inserted with the left edge at 0 on the carriage scale. Note the position of the paper guide. Move it to this point at the beginning of each class period.

Setting the Margin Stops

You may set the margin stops for any length of line desired, such as a 50-, 60-, or 70-space line. To have equal left and right margins, take these two steps.

Step 1—Subtract half the line length from the center point of the paper. Set the left margin stop at this point.

Step 2—Add half the line length, plus 5 to 8 spaces for the end-of-line bell, to the center point. Set the right stop at this point.

The best margin balance is achieved when the right margin stop is set so the bell will ring about 3 spaces before the point at which you want the line to end.

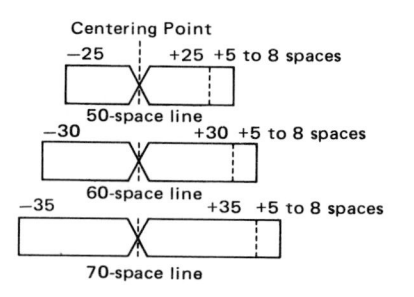

Four types of margin stops are described below. Determine which type of margin set your typewriter has, then follow the appropriate directions.

Key-Set Margins

1. With the carriage at the left margin, depress and hold the margin set key while moving the carriage to the desired position.
2. Release the margin set key.
3. Set the right margin in the same manner.

Magic Margins

1. Pull the left magic margin forward; hold it while moving the carriage to the desired position.
2. Release the magic margin.
3. Set the right margin in the same manner.

Push-Button Margins

1. Push down on the left margin button, and slide it to the desired position.
2. Set the right margin in the same manner.

Push-Lever Margins

1. Push in on the left margin lever, and slide it to the desired position.
2. Set the right margin in the same manner.

Clearing and Setting the Tabulator Stops

Tab Clear—To clear the tabulator mechanism, depress the tab clear key as you move the carriage its full width. To move an individual stop without canceling other stops, tabulate to the stop, and operate the tab clear key.

Tab Set—To set tabulator stops, move the carriage to the desired position; then depress the tab key. Repeat this operation to set as many tabulator stops as are needed.

- *Some typewriters have a total tab clear key which clears all tabulator stops at one time without moving the carriage.*

Changing the Ribbon

- *In general, the instructions given here apply to standard and electric typewriters. Consult the manufacturer's pamphlet accompanying your machine for special instructions.*

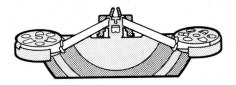

Path of the ribbon as it winds and unwinds on the two spools

1. Wind the used ribbon on one spool. Usually it is best to wind it on the right spool.
2. Study the route of the ribbon as you wind. Note especially how the ribbon winds and unwinds on the two spools. Note, too, how the ribbon is threaded through the ribbon-carrier mechanism.

3. Lift the right spool slightly off its hub to see if both sides are the same. Study both sides of the spool so you will replace it properly.
4. Remove the ribbon from the carrier, and remove both spools. Note how the ribbon is attached to the empty spool. The new ribbon must be attached in the same manner.
5. Fasten the new ribbon to the empty spool, and wind several inches of the new ribbon on it.
6. Place both spools on their hubs, and thread the ribbon through the carrier. Make sure the ribbon is straight.

BASIC TECHNIQUES

Position of Hands

When typing, keep your fingers deeply curved. Fingernails should be neatly trimmed. You can't type with long nails.

Do not permit your hands to turn over on the little fingers. Hold the hands directly over the keys. Turn the hands inward slightly to get straight strokes.

Don't buckle your wrists upward. Hold your wrists down near, but not resting on, the front frame of the typewriter. The forearms should form a parallel line with the slope of the keyboard.

Don't rest your fingers heavily on the home keys. Barely touch them with your fingertips. Feel the keys; don't smother them.

When a finger makes a reach from its home position to strike another key, the other fingers remain on or near their home keys. Such reaches are made by the finger without twisting the wrist or moving the arm or elbow.

Posture

Good posture is vital in learning to type well. Given here are 10 guides of good form. Study the guides carefully. Observe them whenever you work at your typewriter.

1. Book at right of machine on bookholder or with something under top for easier reading.

2. Table free of unneeded books and papers.

3. Front frame of the typewriter even with the edge of the desk.

4. Body centered opposite the **h** key, 6 to 8 inches from front frame of typewriter.

5. Sit back in chair. Hold shoulders erect with body leaning forward slightly from waist.

6. Elbows held near the body.

7. Wrists held low with forearms parallel to the slant of the keyboard. Do not rest lower hand on frame of typewriter.

8. Feet on the floor, one just ahead of the other.

9. Head turned toward book with eyes on copy.

10. Fingers curved and held over second row of keys.

Typing Rhythm

Strike the keys at a steady pace, without breaks or pauses. At first, you will think each letter as you type it. Later, you will think and type short, easy-to-type words and phrases as a whole. You will type longer, hard-to-type words by letters or syllables. You will combine whole word typing with letter or syllable typing into a smooth, fluent, steady rhythm.

Stroking

Center the stroking action in your fingers. Keep elbows, arms, and wrists quiet as you type. Your fingers should be deeply curved. Use quick sharp strokes. Release the keys quickly by snapping the fingers toward the palm of the hand. Hit the keys squarely with short, quick, straight strokes.

Each key should be struck with a firm, sharp stroke and released quickly.

The finger is snapped slightly toward the palm of the hand as the key is released.

Spacing Between Words

Almost one in every five strokes is made with the space bar. To operate the space bar correctly:

1. Hold the right thumb curved under the hand just over the space bar.

2. Strike it with a quick down-and-in motion of the thumb.

3. Keep the right wrist low and quiet as you strike the bar.

4. Keep the left thumb out of the way.

Shift Keys

Use a one-two count:

One—Depress the shift key and hold it down.

Two—Strike the capital letter; then quickly release the shift key and return the little finger to its typing position.

Returning the Carriage

Manual Typewriter

Return the carriage following these steps:

1. Move the left hand, palm down, to the carriage return lever (No. 1). Keep your right hand in home position and your eyes on the book.
2. Move the lever forward to take up the slack.
3. With the fingers bracing one another, return the carriage with a flick of the wrist.
4. Quickly return your left hand to its home position and continue typing at once.

Electric Typewriter

1. Reach the little finger of your right hand to the carriage return key (No. 34).
2. Tap the return key quickly.
3. Quickly return the finger to its home-key position and continue typing at once.

Typewriter Care

Do Daily

1. Brush the dirt and dust from the typebars.
2. Keep desk free of dust, especially the area under the machine.
3. Cover the machine when it is not in use.
4. Shut off power on an electric typewriter after each use.

Do Weekly

1. Clean type faces, using approved cleaner.
2. Move the carriage to extreme end positions. With cloth moistened with oil, clean the carriage rails on each side.
3. Clean platen, feed rolls, and paper bail rolls with cloth moistened with cleaning fluid.

REFERENCE GUIDE

Vertical Centering

Centering material so that it will have uniform top and bottom margins is called *vertical centering*.

1. Count the lines in the copy to be centered. If your copy is to be double spaced, remember to count the spaces between the lines. There is only one line space following each line of copy when material is double spaced.

2. Subtract the total lines from the lines available on the paper you are using. (There are 33 lines on a half sheet, 66 on a full sheet.)

3. Divide the number of lines that remain by 2. The answer gives you the number of lines in the top and bottom margins. If the result contains a fraction, disregard it.

4. Insert your paper so that the top edge is exactly even with the aligning scale (No. 21). Bring the paper up the proper number of line spaces. Start typing on the next line space.

Vertical Centering Shortcut

1. Insert paper to Line 33, the vertical center. Roll the cylinder back (toward you) once for each two lines in the copy to be typed. This will place the copy in *exact vertical center*.

2. To type a problem in *off-center* or *reading position*, roll the cylinder back three more times.

3. If you wish, you can square the edges of the paper from top to bottom and make a slight crease at the right edge. The crease will be at the vertical center (Line 33). Insert the paper to the crease, roll back once for each two lines to the position for typing.

Horizontal Centering

Centering headings and paragraph material so that there will be equal left and right margins is called *horizontal centering*.

1. Check the placement of the paper guide. Turn to page vi, and read the directions for adjusting the paper guide.

2. Move the carriage to the center point.

3. Backspace once for each 2 spaces in the line to be centered. If there is one letter left, do not backspace for it. Begin to type at the point where the backspacing is completed.

Finding the Horizontal Center Point on Odd-Size Paper or Cards

In order to center headings on paper or cards of different sizes, you must learn how to find the center point of these papers or cards.

1. Insert paper or card into the machine.

2. Add the numbers on the cylinder scale at the left and right edges of the paper or card.

3. Divide the sum obtained in Step 2 by 2. The resulting figure gives you the center point of the paper or card.

Steps in Arranging Tables Horizontal Placement

1. Center the paper in the machine.

2. Move the left and right margin stops to the ends of the scale. Clear the tabulator rack.

3. Find how many spaces are to be used between the columns.

4. Move the carriage to the center of the machine.

5. Spot the longest word or entry in each column.

6. Backspace once for each two spaces in the longest word or entry in each column.

7. Backspace once for each two spaces *between* the columns.

8. Set the left margin stop at the point at which you stop backspacing. This is the point where the first column will start.

9. From the left margin, space forward once for each letter, digit, and space in the longest entry in the first column and once for each space between Columns 1 and 2. Set a tab stop for the second column. Continue in this way until all stops have been set for all columns.

10. Return the carriage. Operate the tab bar or key to determine whether or not all the tab stops have been set.

Centering Columnar Headings

Follow these steps to center headings over the columns of a table:

1. Set the carriage at the point a column is to begin.

2. Space forward 1 space for each 2 spaces in the longest line in that column.

3. From that point, backspace once for each 2 spaces in the columnar heading.

4. Type the heading. It will be centered over the column.

Typing Left-Bound Reports

Move the center point 3 spaces to the right to allow for the wider left margin.

1. Set margin stops for a 1½-inch left margin (pica, 15 spaces; elite, 18 spaces) and a 1-inch right margin (pica, 10 spaces; elite, 12 spaces).

2. On all but the first page, leave 1-inch top and bottom margins.

3. Type the title in all capital letters 2 inches from the top of the first page. Triple-space after it.

4. Long quotations (4 line spaces), footnotes, and bibliographical items should be single spaced. Long quotations should be indented 5 spaces from each margin. Double-space the remainder of the report.

5. If the first page is numbered, center the number ½ inch from the bottom. The following pages are numbered ½ inch (4 line spaces) from the top of the page and aligned with the right margin. Triple-space after typing the page number; type the body of the report.

6. At least 2 lines of a paragraph must appear at the bottom of a page, and at least 2 lines of a paragraph should be carried forward to a new page.

Typing Footnotes

All important statements of fact or opinion and all direct quotations that are taken from books or articles for use in a theme must have footnotes. Footnotes give complete information about the references from which materials were taken.

1. Make a light pencil mark in the margin to indicate where the divider line will be typed.

2. After typing the last line of a full page of copy, change from double spacing to single spacing. Space once, then use the underscore key to type a 1½-inch divider line.

3. After typing the divider line, space twice; then type the footnote reference.

4. Single-space footnotes; double-space between them.

Although footnotes vary in length, in general the following system works well for determining where the divider line should be typed: (a) make a light pencil mark for the 1-inch bottom margin, (b) from this pencil mark space up 3 line spaces for each footnote and once for the divider line, (c) make a second light pencil mark—the point at which the divider line should be typed.

On a page only partially full, the footnotes appear at the bottom of the page.

Typing a Bibliography

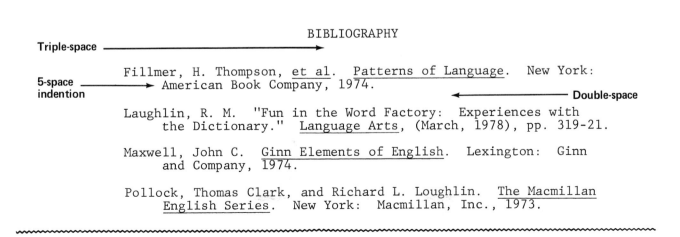

BIBLIOGRAPHY

Triple-space

Fillmer, H. Thompson, et al. *Patterns of Language*. New York: American Book Company, 1974.

5-space indention

Double-space

Laughlin, R. M. "Fun in the Word Factory: Experiences with the Dictionary." *Language Arts*, (March, 1978), pp. 319-21.

Maxwell, John C. *Ginn Elements of English*. Lexington: Ginn and Company, 1974.

Pollock, Thomas Clark, and Richard L. Loughlin. *The Macmillan English Series*. New York: Macmillan, Inc., 1973.

First Page of Theme with Footnotes

2 inches
(13th line space)

LEARNING TO LISTEN

Triple-space ⟶

The fact that communication is a two-way process means both people in a conversation must listen as well as talk before real understanding can be achieved.

Experts in the field remind us that we spend more of our waking hours listening than we spend in any of the other basic communication activities. According to Miller, each of us can expect to spend more of our lives hearing and listening than doing anything else except breathing.[1]

1 inch left margin   1 inch right margin

Listening is much more than just hearing, however. Hearing involves only the ears; listening requires the use of both the ears and the mind. Unless our minds are tuned in to what the other person is saying, communication will not take place.

One of the keys to good listening is to learn to concentrate on the ideas the speaker is trying to convey and not be distracted by other sounds or thoughts. Because our minds are capable of going much faster than anyone can talk, we have to work at keeping our attention focused on what the other person is saying.

We can help keep our minds from wandering off the subject by speaking to the point occasionally or by asking questions which will help the other person expand on some point which may not have been clear.

Single-space ⟶
_____

Double-space ⟶
[1]Dorothy Miller, Ginn Elementary English (Lexington: Ginn and Company, 1972), p. 55.

Approximately 1 inch

Erasing and Correcting Errors

1. Move the carriage to the extreme right or left so that the eraser crumbs will not fall into the typewriter.

2. To avoid moving the paper out of alignment, turn the cylinder forward if the erasure is to be made on the upper two thirds of the paper; backward, if on the lower third of the paper.

3. To erase on the original sheet, lift the paper bail out of the way and place a 5- by 3-inch card in back of the original copy and in front of the first carbon sheet. Use an eraser shield to protect the letters that are not to be erased. Use a hard typewriter eraser. When you complete the erasure, brush the eraser crumbs away from the typewriter.

4. Move the card in front of the second carbon sheet if more than one copy is being made. Erase the errors on the carbon copy with a soft (or pencil eraser) first, then use the hard typewriter eraser used in erasing on the original copy.

5. When the error has been neatly erased on the original and all the carbon copies, remove the card, position the carriage to the proper point, and type the correction.

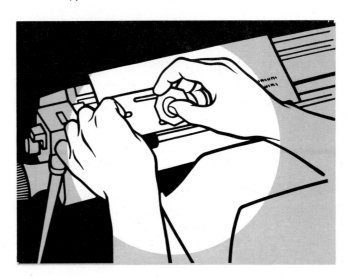

Typing and Addressing a Postal Card

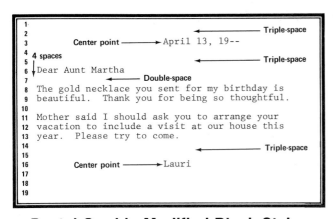

Postal Card in Modified Block Style

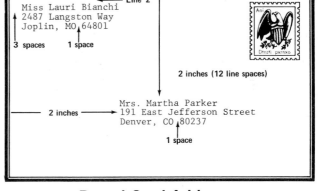

Postal Card Address

Two-Letter ZIP Code Abbreviations

Alabama	AL	Indiana	IN	Nebraska	NE	South Carolina	SC
Alaska	AK	Iowa	IA	Nevada	NV	South Dakota	SD
Arizona	AZ	Kansas	KS	New Hampshire	NH	Tennessee	TN
Arkansas	AR	Kentucky	KY	New Jersey	NJ	Texas	TX
California	CA	Louisiana	LA	New Mexico	NM	Utah	UT
Colorado	CO	Maine	ME	New York	NY	Vermont	VT
Connecticut	CT	Maryland	MD	North Carolina	NC	Virginia	VA
Delaware	DE	Massachusetts	MA	North Dakota	ND	Washington	WA
Florida	FL	Michigan	MI	Ohio	OH	West Virginia	WV
Georgia	GA	Minnesota	MN	Oklahoma	OK	Wisconsin	WI
Hawaii	HI	Mississippi	MS	Oregon	OR	Wyoming	WY
Idaho	ID	Missouri	MO	Pennsylvania	PA		
Illinois	IL	Montana	MT	Rhode Island	RI		

Typing Personal/Business Letters

The most commonly used form for a personal business letter is illustrated below. The typewritten name of the sender below the complimentary close is optional.

1. Set the machine for single spacing.

2. Set the margins. (The margins vary according to the length of the letter.)

3. Start typing the return address on the 18th line space. (The number of line spaces varies with the letter size. The longer the letter, the fewer the number of spaces.) For a modified block letter, start the return address at the center point of the paper. For a block style letter, start the return address at the left margin.

4. Space down 4 times for the address.

5. Type the salutation a double space below the address.

6. Start the body a double space below the salutation. Double-space between paragraphs.

7. Type the complimentary close a double space below the body. For a modified block style letter, start at the center point. For a block style letter, type it at the left margin.

8. Type the name of the writer on the 4th line space from the complimentary close.

Personal/Business Letter in Modified Block Style

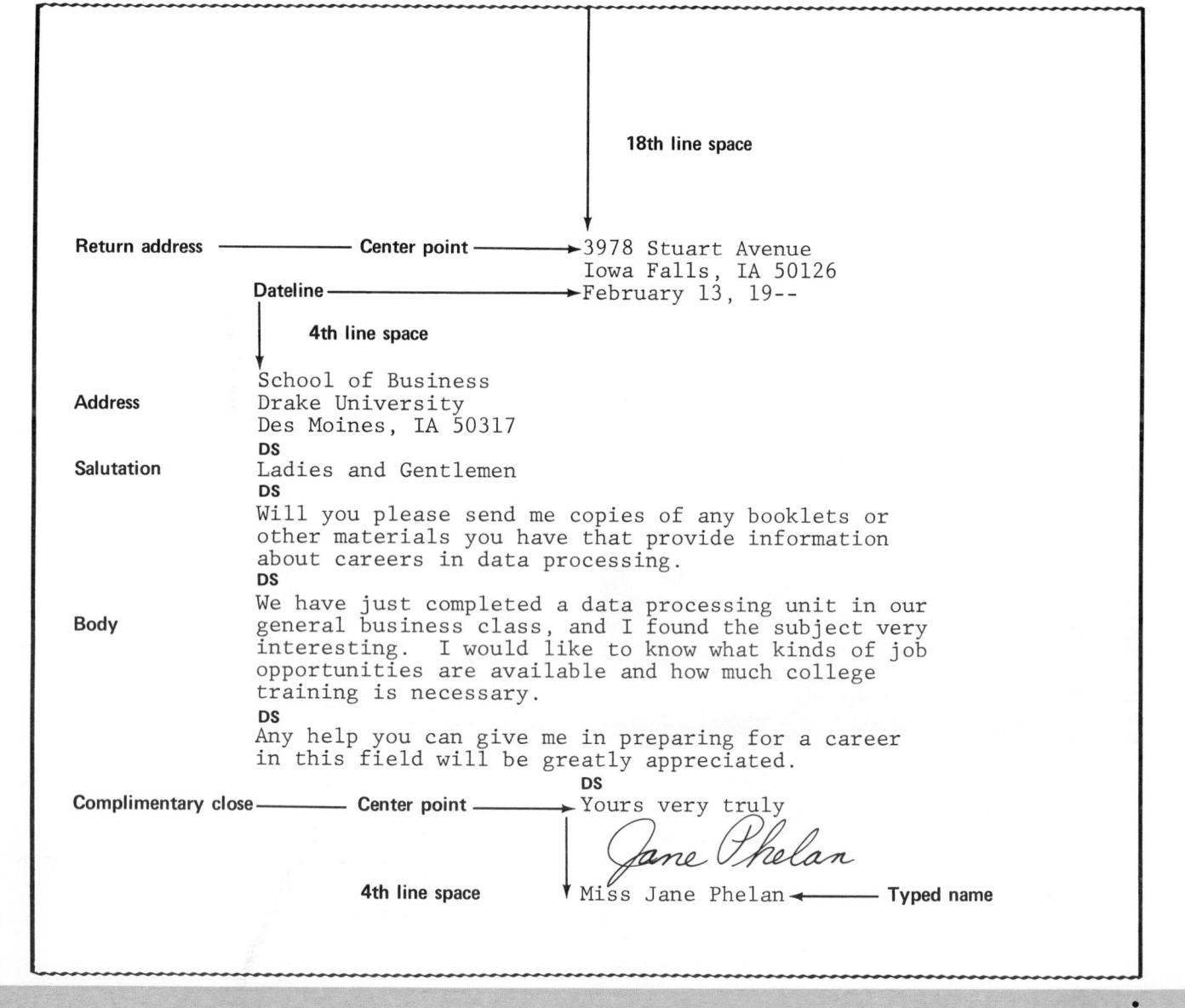

Addressing a Small Envelope

1. Type the writer's name and return address in the upper left corner as shown in the illustration below. Begin on the second line space from the top edge and 3 spaces from the left edge.

2. Type the receiver's name about 2 inches (12 line spaces) from the top of the envelope. Start about 2½ inches from the left edge.

3. Use the block style and single spacing for all addresses. City and state names and ZIP Code must be typed on one line in that order.

4. The state name may be typed in full, or it may be abbreviated by using the 2-letter state abbreviation or the standard abbreviation.

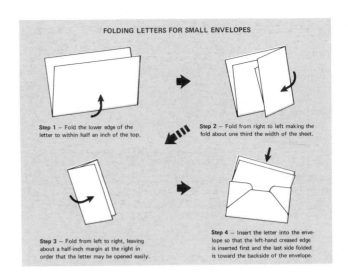

FOLDING LETTERS FOR SMALL ENVELOPES

Step 1 — Fold the lower edge of the letter to within half an inch of the top.

Step 2 — Fold from right to left making the fold about one third the width of the sheet.

Step 3 — Fold from left to right, leaving about a half-inch margin at the right in order that the letter may be opened easily.

Step 4 — Insert the letter into the envelope so that the left-hand creased edge is inserted first and the last side folded is toward the backside of the envelope.

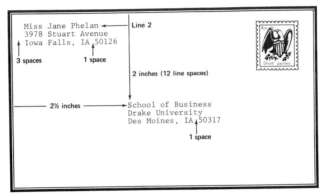

Miss Jane Phelan ← Line 2
3978 Stuart Avenue
Iowa Falls, IA 50126

↑ 3 spaces   1 space

2 inches (12 line spaces)

2½ inches →

School of Business
Drake University
Des Moines, IA 50317

1 space

Addressing a Large Envelope

A large envelope is usually typed for business letters or for letters of more than one page. Type the address 2½ inches from the top and 4 inches from the left edge of the envelope. Directions for spacing the address and using abbreviations for the state name and the ZIP Code are the same as listed above for addressing a small envelope.

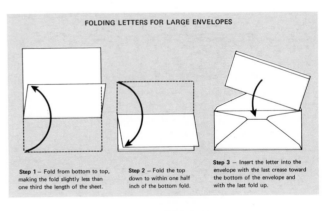

FOLDING LETTERS FOR LARGE ENVELOPES

Step 1 — Fold from bottom to top, making the fold slightly less than one third the length of the sheet.

Step 2 — Fold the top down to within one half inch of the bottom fold.

Step 3 — Insert the letter into the envelope with the last crease toward the bottom of the envelope and with the last fold up.

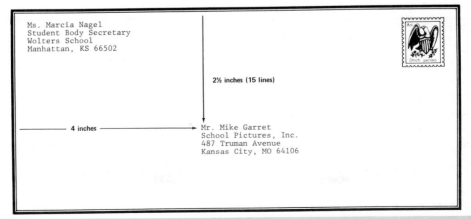

Ms. Marcia Nagel
Student Body Secretary
Wolters School
Manhattan, KS 66502

2½ inches (15 lines)

4 inches →

Mr. Mike Garret
School Pictures, Inc.
487 Truman Avenue
Kansas City, MO 64106

Information About Business Letters

Letter Styles—With slight variations, the modified block style shown on page xix is used in almost all business letters. Another style that is growing in usage is the block style illustrated on page xx.

Punctuation Styles—Two commonly used punctuation styles are open and mixed. In *open* punctuation, no punctuation marks are used after the salutation or the complimentary close. In *mixed* punctuation, a colon is placed after the salutation and a comma after the complimentary close.

Vertical Placement of Dateline—Vertical placement of the date varies with the length of the letter. However, in the majority of business letters the date is typed on line 18. The address is typed on the 4th line space (3 blank spaces) below the date.

Abbreviations—Excessive abbreviations should be avoided. It is acceptable, however, to abbreviate the state name in an address when using a ZIP Code. Leave one space between the state name and the ZIP Code.

Titles in Address—As a mark of courtesy, always use a personal or professional title on a letter, envelope, or card addressed to an individual: *Mr. Robert Wertz, Dr. Ann Hendricks.* When a woman's preferred title is unknown, use *Ms.* as the personal title.

Titles in Closing Lines—In the closing lines of a letter, a personal or professional title should not be used before the name of a male writer. A female may use a personal title if she wishes.

Reference Initials—Reference initials of the typist should always be typed two line spaces below the typed name of the writer of the letter.

Stationery Size—Most business letters are typed on 8½- by 11-inch stationery that is imprinted with the name and address of the company.

Envelopes—Use large or small envelopes for one-page letters and large envelopes for two-page letters or when enclosing materials within a letter.

Carbon Copies

To make carbon copies, place the carbon paper (with glossy side down) on a sheet of plain paper. The paper on which you will prepare the original is then laid on the carbon paper, and all the sheets are inserted into the typewriter. The dull surface of the carbon sheet should be toward you when the sheets have been rolled into the typewriter. Erasing on carbon copies is explained on page xv.

Enclosure Notation

An enclosure notation is used when a paper (or papers) is sent with the letter. Type the notation at the left margin a double space below the reference initials. Use the plural, **Enclosures**, if two or more items will be enclosed.

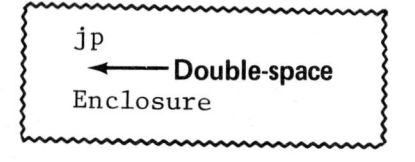

Attention Line

An attention line is used to direct a letter to a particular person. It is usually typed on the second line below the address. In addressing the envelope, type the attention line immediately below the company name.

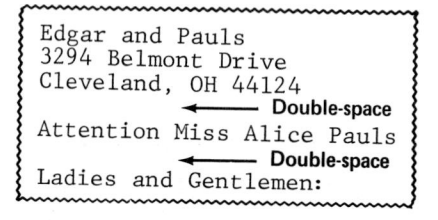

Subject Line

When a subject line is used in a letter, it may be typed on the second line below the salutation and centered; or it may be typed at the left margin.

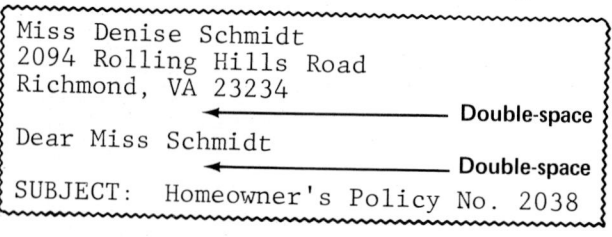

Postscript

Type a postscript a double space below the reference initials. It need not be preceded by the letters P. S.

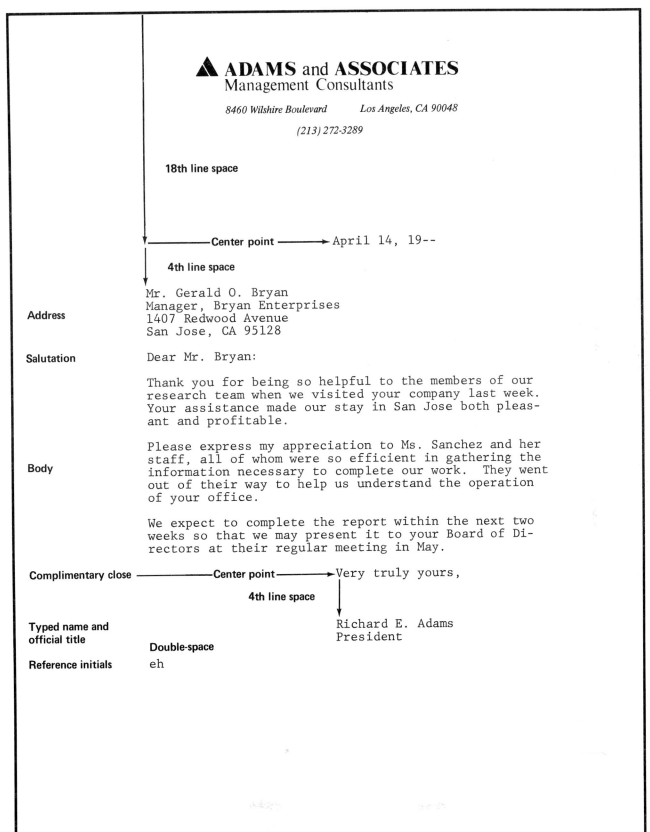

▲ ADAMS and ASSOCIATES
Management Consultants

8460 Wilshire Boulevard   Los Angeles, CA 90048

(213) 272-3289

18th line space

———————Center point ——————→ April 14, 19--

4th line space

Address
Mr. Gerald O. Bryan
Manager, Bryan Enterprises
1407 Redwood Avenue
San Jose, CA 95128

Salutation
Dear Mr. Bryan:

Body
Thank you for being so helpful to the members of our research team when we visited your company last week. Your assistance made our stay in San Jose both pleasant and profitable.

Please express my appreciation to Ms. Sanchez and her staff, all of whom were so efficient in gathering the information necessary to complete our work. They went out of their way to help us understand the operation of your office.

We expect to complete the report within the next two weeks so that we may present it to your Board of Directors at their regular meeting in May.

Complimentary close ———————Center point——————→ Very truly yours,

4th line space

Typed name and official title
Richard E. Adams
President

Double-space

Reference initials   eh

Business Letter in Block Style

ADAMS and ASSOCIATES
Management Consultants

8460 Wilshire Boulevard   Los Angeles, CA 90048

(213) 272-3289

18th line space

April 16, 19--

4th line space

Address

Ms. Janet Miller
1401 McKinley Avenue
Houston, TX 77088

Salutation

Dear Ms. Miller

Body

Brent Whitten has just informed me that the Finance Committee will hold its annual meeting in Houston on June 5. Therefore, I need a motel reservation for the evenings of the 4th and 5th.

Will you please take care of this matter for me, either at the Hacienda or some comparable motel convenient to the meeting site. I think the Hacienda offers three different rates for single rooms. As all of their facilities are excellent, the least expensive rate available will be fine with me.

Perhaps we can get together for a short while on Monday evening to discuss the agenda.

Complimentary close   Sincerely yours

← **Double-space**

Company name in closing   ADAMS AND ASSOCIATES

4th line space

Typed name and official title

Miss Kay Wiley
Vice-President

Reference initials   eh

SUMMARY OF RELATED LEARNINGS

Capitalization Guides (pp. 80, 99, 114, 220)

Capitalize:

1. The first word of a complete sentence.
2. The first word of a quoted sentence. (Do not capitalize fragments of a quotation resumed within a sentence.)
3. Languages and numbered school courses, but not the names of other school subjects.
4. The pronoun *I*, both alone and in contractions.
5. Titles of organizations, institutions, and buildings.
6. Days of the week, months of the year, and holidays, but not seasons.
7. Names of rivers, oceans, and mountains.
8. *North, South,* etc., when they name particular parts of the country, but not when they refer to directions.
9. Names of religious groups, political parties, nations, nationalities, and races.
10. All proper names and the adjectives made from them.
11. The names of stars, planets, and constellations, except the sun, moon, and earth, unless these are used with other astronomical names.
12. A title when used with a person's name.
13. First words and all other words in titles of books, articles, periodicals, headings, and plays, except words which are articles, conjunctions, and prepositions.
14. The first and last words, all titles, and all proper names used in the salutation of a business letter.
15. Only the first word of the complimentary close.
16. All titles appearing in the address of a letter.
17. The title following the names of the dictator in the closing lines of a business letter.

Spacing Guides (pp. 23, 49, 51, 52, 54, 56, 57, and 125)

1. Space twice after a period that ends a sentence, except when the period comes at the end of the line. When it does, return the carriage without spacing.
2. Space once after a question mark within a sentence; twice after a question mark at the end of a sentence.
3. Space twice after an exclamation point at the end of a sentence.
4. Space twice after a colon except in stating time.
5. Space once after a semicolon or comma.
6. Space once after a period that ends an abbreviation; twice if that period ends a sentence. (Do not space after a period within an abbreviation.)
7. Space once between a whole number and a "made" fraction.

8. Do not space between the $ and the number which follows it.
9. Do not space before or after the diagonal.
10. Do not space between a number and a following % sign.
11. Do not space between parentheses and the material they enclose.
12. Do not space before or after the apostrophe.
13. Do not space between quotation marks and the material they enclose.
14. Do not space before or after a dash.
15. Do not space before or after the hyphen in a hyphenated word.

Number Expression Guides (pp. 59, 96, 194, 204, 223)

1. Type even sums of money without decimals or zeros.
2. Type distances in figures.
3. Use figures to type dates. When the day comes before the month, use a figure and follow it with *th, st,* or *d.*
4. Spell a number beginning a sentence even though figures may be used later in the sentence.
5. Use figures with *a.m.* and *p.m.* Use words with *o'clock.*
6. Amounts of money, either dollars or cents, should be typed in figures.
7. Type policy numbers without commas.

Word-Division Guides

Do not:
1. Divide words of one syllable, such as *thought, friend,* or *caught.*
2. Separate a syllable of one letter at the beginning of a word, such as *across.*
3. Separate a syllable of one or two letters at the end of a word, such as *ready, greatly,* or *greeted.*
4. Divide words of five or fewer letters, such as *also, into, duty,* or *excel.*
5. Separate a syllable that does not contain a vowel from the rest of the word, such as *wouldn't.*
6. Divide the last word on a page.

Divide:
1. Words only between syllables.
2. Hyphened compounds at the point of the hyphen; for example, *self-control.*
3. Words so that *cial, tial, cion, sion,* or *tion* are retained as a unit.
4. A word that ends in double letters after the double letters when a suffix is added, such as *fill-ing.*
5. A word in which the final consonant is doubled when a suffix is added between the double letters, such as *control-ling.*

Punctuation Guides

Apostrophe (p. 193)

1. Use an apostrophe in writing contractions.
2. *It's* means *it is. Its,* the possessive pronoun, does not take an apostrophe.
3. Use the contraction o'clock (of the clock) in writing time.
4. Add 's to form the possessive of any singular noun.
5. Add 's to plural nouns that do not end in s.
6. If a plural noun does end in s, add only an apostrophe after the s.
7. The apostrophe denotes possession. Do not use it merely to form the plural of a noun.
8. Use 's to form the plural of figures, letters, signs, and words referred to as words.

Colon (p. 169)

1. Use a colon to introduce a list of items or expressions.
2. Use a colon to separate the hours and minutes when they are expressed in figures.
3. Use a colon to introduce a question or long quotation.

Comma (pp. 136 and 160)

1. Use a comma after each item in a series, except the last.
2. Use a comma to separate consecutive adjectives when the *and* has seemingly been omitted. Do not use the comma when the adjectives do not apply equally to the noun they modify.
3. Use a comma to separate a dependent clause that precedes the main clause.
4. Use a comma to separate the independent parts of a compound sentence joined by *and, but, for or, neither, nor.*
5. Use a comma to prevent misreading or confusion.
6. Use a comma to set off a direct quotation from the rest of the sentence.
7. Do not set off an indirect quotation from the rest of the sentence.
8. Use commas to set off parenthetic expressions that break the flow of a sentence. If the parenthetic expression begins or ends a sentence, use one comma.
9. Use a comma to set off *yes, no, well, now.*
10. Use commas to set off the name of the person addressed.
11. Use commas to set off appositives that give additional information about the same person or object and that can be omitted without changing the meaning of the sentence.
12. Do not use a comma to separate two nouns, one of which identifies the other.
13. Use commas to separate the date from the year and the name of a city from the name of the state.

Dash and Parentheses (p. 174)

1. Use a dash to show a sudden break in thought.
2. Use a dash before the name of an author when it follows a direct quotation.
3. Use parentheses to enclose an explanation.

Period, Question Mark, Exclamation Point (p. 132)

1. Use a period after a sentence making a statement or giving a command.
2. Use a period after each initial.
3. Use a period after most abbreviations. (Nicknames are not followed by periods.)
4. Use a question mark after a question.
5. After requests and indirect questions, use a period.
6. Use an exclamation point to express strong or sudden feeling.

Quotation Marks (p. 178)

1. Place quotation marks around the exact words of a speaker.
2. When the quotation is broken to identify the speaker, put quotation marks around each part. If the second part of the quotation is a new sentence, use a capital letter.
3. Use no quotation marks with an indirect quotation.
4. Use quotation marks around the titles of articles, songs, poems, themes, short stories, and the like.
5. Always place the period or comma inside the quotation mark.

Semicolon (p. 162)

1. Use a semicolon between the clauses of a compound sentence when no conjunction is used. (If a conjunction is used to join the clauses, use a comma between them.)
2. Use a semicolon between the clauses of a compound sentence that are joined by such words as *also, however, therefore,* and *consequently.*
3. Use a semicolon between a series of phrases or clauses that are dependent upon a main clause.

INDEX TO SPECIAL DRILLS

INDEX

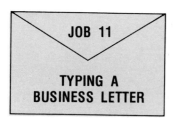

JOB 11

TYPING A BUSINESS LETTER

Student Council / Columbia School / 5590 North Milbrook / Fresno, CA 93706 / Dear Student Council Members: / On behalf of all our players and coaches, I want to thank you for your fine support this year. Your many efforts and ideas assured us a successful season. I know the students, faculty, and staff here at Columbia are proud of the leadership you have provided. (¶) Congratulations for an outstanding job. / Sincerely, / Coach Johnson

1. Type this letter for Coach Johnson. Use a 50-space line.

JOB 12

TYPING AN ANNOUNCEMENT

1. Type this announcement on a half sheet of paper.

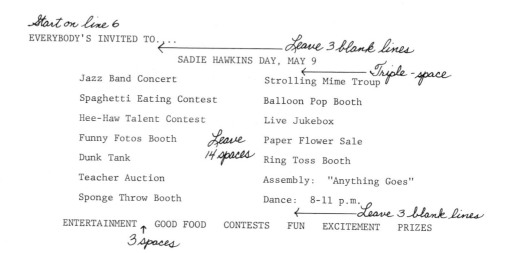

JOB 13

TYPING AN INTEROFFICE MEMORANDUM

TO: All Organization Sponsors / FROM: Greg Pelton, Director of Student Activities / DATE: *Current date* / SUBJECT: Fund-Raising Information / In order to aid the Boosters Club in planning our fund raising projects for next year, we need to have the following information from your group: (1) an estimate of how much money you will need, and (2) a list of your planned fund-raising activities. (¶) Please remember that any fund raiser in which the community is involved must have Board approval. Campus fund raisers require approval only from this office. (¶) Information should be sent to me no later than May 1 so the proposed student body budget can be submitted by May 15.

1. Type this memorandum using a 60-space line.

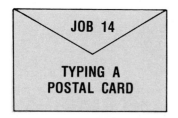

JOB 14

TYPING A POSTAL CARD

Dear Ray: / Thank you for your continued support of our Columbia Boosters Club. (¶) We're looking forward to seeing you at the annual Boosters Barbecue in the school cafeteria on May 16 at 6:00 p.m. / Greg Pelton

1. Type the following message on a postal card as illustrated on page 77.
2. Address the card to Mr. Ray Eggebraaten. His address appears in Job 7.

Cycle 1

Learning To Operate
Your Typewriter

JOB 8

TYPING AN INTEROFFICE MEMORANDUM

1. Type this memorandum using a 60-space line.

2. Refer to page 215 for proper form.

TO: All Advisory Period Teachers / FROM: Greg Pelton, Director of Student Activities / DATE: *Current date* / SUBJECT: Student Body and Class Officer Elections / Our Activities Handbook states that elections for student body and class offices must take place no later than the third Thursday in May preceding the school year in which they are to serve. We have therefore designated May 16 as election day. (¶) Please remind your advisory group that anyone wishing to be a candidate for any office must present a petition to the student body vice-president no later than May 2. The petition must be signed by ten members of the candidate's class. No person may sign more than one petition for the same student body or class office.

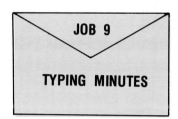

JOB 9

TYPING MINUTES

1. Type these student council minutes in the form illustrated on page 166.

2. Set your machine for a 1½-inch left margin and a 1-inch right margin.

COLUMBIA SCHOOL STUDENT COUNCIL MEETING

Minutes of Meeting

Date: Current date
Time: 11:05 a.m.
Place: Room 14, C Building
Present: L. Bishop, G. Brandon, C. Brower, M. Bruno, P. Erni, M. Folcarelli, Mr. Pelton, E. Quesada, R. Robles, J. Savala

1. The meeting was called to order by Eric Quesada, ASB President.

2. John Savala presented a proposed policy concerning the use of radios on campus. It was moved by Cynthia Brower that the policy be approved. The motion was seconded by Mark Bruno. It passed unanimously.

3. The Drama Club constitution was submitted for Student Council approval. After a brief discussion, Mr. Pelton suggested that the petition be sent back for some minor adjustments.

4. Pat Erni reported on the CASC meeting held April 5 in Santa Clara.

5. The meeting was adjourned at 11:40 a.m.

Marty Folcarelli, Secretary

JOB 10

TYPING A BUSINESS LETTER

1. Type this letter using a 50-space line.

Mr. Art Petrucci / Stanton Office Equipment / 384 Olive Avenue / Fresno, CA 93706 / Dear Mr. Petrucci: / Thank you for taking the time to demonstrate your duplicating equipment to our student council members and our newspaper staff. We now have a much better understanding of the type of machine we need. (¶) I have recommended the purchase of your Model A6 to Dr. Denin. She has assured me that this equipment will have a high priority on our next year's budget. As soon as formal approval has been received, one of us will be in touch with you. / Very truly yours, / Greg Pelton / Director of Student Activities

Lesson 1

1a ■ Find the Home Keys and Space Bar

1. Place the fingers of your left hand on **a s d f.**

2. Place the fingers of your right hand on **j k l ;.**

3. Take your fingers off the home keys. Replace them. Say the keys of each hand as you touch them. Repeat several times to get the "feel" of these keys.

4. Hold your right thumb over the middle of the space bar. Strike it with a quick, inward motion of your right thumb. Keep the left thumb out of the way.

5. Curve your fingers. Hold them very lightly over the home keys.

6. Type the line below. Say and think each letter as you strike it.

```
ff jj dd kk ss ll aa ;; fj dk sl a; fj dk sl a; fj
```

1b ■ Return the Carriage

Manual Typewriter

2. Check that the fingers of the right hand are on their home keys.

3. Move the lever forward to take up the slack.

1. Move the left hand, palm down, to the carriage return lever (No. 1).

4. With the fingers bracing one another, return the carriage with a flick of the wrist.

5. Return your left hand at once to its home position.

Electric Typewriter

1. Reach the little finger of your right hand to the carriage return key (No. 1).

2. Tap the return key quickly.

3. Return the finger at once to its home-key position.

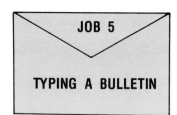

JOB 5

TYPING A BULLETIN

1. Type these items for tomorrow's Daily Bulletin on a full sheet of paper.

2. Use a 60-space line.

3. Center the main heading on line 13. Double-space between headings; triple space after the secondary heading.

4. Single-space the items; double-space between them.

DAILY BULLETIN

Tomorrow's date   or 5th

1. All participants in the "charlie brown" play who have 4th period lunch are to meet in K Building during the morning break.

2. The ∧seventh grade soccer team plays Kerman today at 3:00 p.m. The bus will leave from the gym parking lot ∧ at 1:30 p.m.

3. Decorations committee members should report to Ms. Jasutis in the cafeteria immediately after school today.

4. Our third annual District coral Sing will be held this evening in Clark Auditorium. The program will begin at 7:30 p.m.

5. Mrs. Chavez would like to see any member of the student library staff who have not yet been assigned working hours *for this month.*

6. Students who plan 5th to participate in the Carnation sale will meet during 4th period in Mr. Pelton's office.

7. The C.S.F. meeting scheduled for tonight has been canceled. *Our meeting will be held during the regular time next week.*

JOB 6

TYPING A BUSINESS LETTER

1. Type this letter using a 50-space line.

2. Refer to page 205 for typing an enclosure notation.

Miss Jill Regentz / Student Activities Director / Easterby Middle School / 49 East Portals Drive / Los Banos, CA 93635 / Dear Jill: / Enclosed is a copy of our proposal for the Interscholastic Council that I mentioned to you at the meeting on Saturday. (¶) After many hours of discussion, our school council members voted unanimously to accept this final draft. It also has the approval and support of our principal, Dr. Mary Denin. (¶) I hope this proposal will be helpful to you in furthering the aims of the Council. If you have any questions, please call me. / Cordially yours, / Greg Pelton / Director of Student Activities

JOB 7

ADDRESSING ENVELOPES

1. Address a large envelope to each Boosters Club member shown on this list.

2. Refer to page 87 for assistance in correct placement of envelope addresses.

Mrs. Kelly J. Black
6069 North Harrison
Fresno, CA 93711

Mr. R. T. Jayapalan
18 West Ida, Apt. 6
Fresno, CA 93726

Dr. Bertha Ching
769 Almond Drive
Fresno, CA 93710

Mr. J. C. Jimenez
3966 Norwich Avenue
Fresno, CA 93726

Mr. Ray Eggebraaten
7328 North Tamera
Fresno, CA 93711

Ms. Olga Nunes
3045 Adler Way
Fresno, CA 93710

1c ■ Home-Key Practice

Directions—Type each line with your teacher at least once.

Technique Goal—Think and say each letter as you strike it.

1   ff jj ff jj ff jj ff jj ff jj fj fj fj fj fj fj fj

2   dd kk dd kk dd kk dd kk dd kk dk dk dk dk dk dk dk

3   ss ll ss ll ss ll ss ll ss ll sl sl sl sl sl sl sl

     Home keys

4   aa ;; aa ;; aa ;; aa ;; aa ;; a; a; a; a; a; a; a;

5   fj dk sl a; fj dk sl a; fj dk sl a; fj dk sl a; fj

6   fj dk sl a; fjdk sla; fjdk sla; fjdk sla; fj dk sl

Think and say each letter

1d ■ Technique Builder—Stroking

Directions—Type each line once with your teacher. Type the lines a second time by yourself.

Technique Goal—Curve your fingers. Use quick, sharp strokes.

1   all all fall fall all all fall fall all fall falls

2   ad lad ad lad ad lad all a lad all a lad all a lad

3   as ask as ask as ask all all lass lass as all lass

     Home keys

4   ask a lass; ask all lads; a lad asks; a lass asks;

5   a lass; as a lass; as a lass falls; as a lad falls

6   a lad; a lass; a lass asks; a lad asks; ask a lass

Quick, sharp strokes

1e ■ Remove the Paper

1. Pull the paper bail (No. 11) out from the cylinder (No. 17).

2. Pull the paper release lever forward (No. 18).

3. Remove the paper with your free hand.

4. Return the paper release lever to its original position.

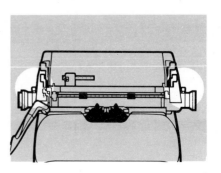

1f ■ Center the Carriage

Before leaving your typewriter, center the carriage. To do so, depress the right or left carriage release lever (No. 4 or 19), and move the carriage to the approximate center of your typewriter.

Also, pick up all paper and dispose of it.

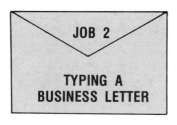

JOB 2

TYPING A BUSINESS LETTER

1. Type this letter for Mr. Pelton's signature. Place his title on the line below his typed name.

2. Use a 60-space line.

3. Refer to page 200 for assistance.

Mr. James Coiner, Principal / Hoover Junior High School / 2835 North Peach Avenue / Modesto, CA 95351 / Dear Jim: / I'll be glad to explain our new field trip policy to you. We believe it will eliminate some of the problems we encountered last year. (¶) The teacher requesting the absence issues a permission slip to each participating student. This teacher, as well as all teachers whose classes the student will miss, must sign each slip. Students must also obtain a parent's signature. (¶) There are two major exceptions to this policy: (1) extremely large groups, such as those required for class pictures, and (2) athletic events which take place during the latter part of the school day. (¶) Please let me know if you need any further information. / Sincerely yours, / Greg Pelton / Director of Student Activities

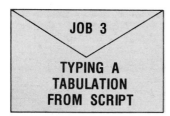

JOB 3

TYPING A TABULATION FROM SCRIPT

1. Center this list of student body officers on a half sheet.

2. Triple-space the heading; double-space the items.

3. Leave 12 spaces between columns.

STUDENT BODY OFFICERS

President	Eric Quesada
Vice-President	Robin Allen
Secretary	Marty Folcarelli
Treasurer	Marlene Miyaki
Speaker	Jerry Schultz
Assemblies	Ron Robles
Communications	Sue Lizardo
Organizations	Cynthia Brower

JOB 4

TYPING A BUSINESS LETTER

1. Type this letter for your student body president.

2. Use a 50-space line.

Miss Susan Espuda / ASB President / Jefferson School / 1800 North Cedar Avenue / Fresno, CA 93705 / Dear Susan: / On behalf of the Columbia School Student Council, I want to express my appreciation to all of you at Jefferson for your help in cosponsoring the Sharp Show with us last Tuesday evening. (¶) The program was certainly of mutual benefit to both our student bodies. The great entertainment the Sharps provided was thoroughly enjoyed by our students who attended the performance. (¶) We were pleased to cooperate with you and look forward to similar joint programs in the future. / Sincerely yours, / Eric Quesada / ASB President

Lesson 2

2a ▪ Know Your Typewriter

1. As your teacher calls the parts listed on pages iv and v, find them on your typewriter.

2. Adjust the paper guide. If necessary read the directions for your machine on page vi.

3. Set the margin stops for a 50-space line, unless this has already been done for you. If necessary, read the directions for your typewriter on pages vi and vii.

4. Set the line-space regulator at "2" for double spacing.

5. Insert paper. Adjust the paper bail rolls.

6. Check your position: Front of typewriter even with desk edge. Body centered opposite **h** key, 6 to 8 inches from front of typewriter. Sit erect; hold elbows near body. Feet on floor, one foot ahead of the other.

2b ▪ Keyboard Review

Directions—Type each line once with your teacher.

Spacing Guide—Space once after a semicolon (;) within a line.

1		`ff jj dd kk ss ll aa ;; ff jj dd kk ss ll aa ;; fj`
2		`fj dk sl a; fj dk sl a; fj dk sl a; fj dk sl a; fj`
3	Home keys	`a all all fall fall lad lad lads ask ask lass lass`
4		`a lass; as a lass falls; all lads fall; ask a lass`
5		`as; ask a; ask a lad; ask a lass; ask all lads; as`

Think each key as you strike it

Plan for Learning New Keys

1. Find new key on keyboard chart.
2. Locate key on your typewriter.
3. Place fingers over home keys.
4. Know what finger strikes key.
5. Watch your finger as you make the reach to the new key.
6. Type each short drill twice on the same line. Be sure to use the correct finger.

2c ▪ Location of G and U

Find **g** on the chart. Find it on your typewriter keyboard. Place your fingers over the home keys. Touch **gf** lightly without moving the other fingers from their typing position.

←REACH TO G   REACH TO U→

Find **u** on the chart. Find it on your typewriter keyboard. Place your fingers over the home keys. Touch **uj** lightly without moving the other fingers from their typing position.

Type g with the f finger

Type u with the j finger

`fgf fgf gf gf ag lag lag`   • Type twice on same line •   `juj juj uj uj ud dud dud`

Unit 18 ■ Working in a School Office

This unit has been designed to give you an opportunity to apply your typing skills in a simulated office. You will be doing the kinds of jobs you could expect to do if you were actually employed.

You have been asked to work as a typist one period each day in the office of Mr. Greg Pelton, Director of Student Activities at Columbia School. Most of the typing you do will be for Mr. Pelton. Occasionally, however, you may be asked to type for someone else. General instructions to be followed are given in Job 1 below. Specific instructions are also included with each job.

Since other people will be depending on the accuracy of the materials you prepare, be sure to proofread your work carefully. Remember that the one single trait valued most highly in office work is *accuracy*.

Remember, too, that *good work habits* are essential to success as an office worker. Make certain you understand the instructions for each job before you begin; then work as efficiently as you can to produce quality copy.

JOB 1

TYPING A REPORT

1. Type this report on a full sheet, using a 60-space line.

2. Center the heading on the 13th line space from the top. Triple-space after the heading.

3. Single-space the numbered items and double-space between them.

GUIDE FOR OFFICE EMPLOYEES

1. report for work at the beginning of the period to which you have been assigned. Please sign the attendance sheets each day.

2. If you are going to be absent, telephone the activities office between 7:30 a.m. and 8:00 a.m. on line 18.

3. Type all letters in the modified block style, with mixed punctuation. Type the current date. Prepare a carbon copy and address an envelope for each letter.

4. Refer to your typewriting textbook whenever you need help in placing material attractively on the page.

5. Proofread each job and correct all errors before you remove your paper from your typewriter.

6. Leave all completed jobs on my assistant's desk. You will be told whether you are to keep unfinished jobs for the next day or to leave them for someone else.

2d ■ Location Drills—G and U

Directions—Type each line once with your teacher. Type the lines a second time by yourself.

Technique Goal—Think and say each letter as you strike it.

g   fgf fgf fgf fgf gf gf gf gf lag lag flag flag flag   Type **g** with the **f** finger

       lad lad glad glad lag lag flag flag lass lass flag

u   juj juj juj juj uj uj uj uj dud dud dull dull dull   Type **u** with the **j** finger

       full full dug dug dull dull us us us fuss fuss dug

2e ■ Technique Builder—Eyes on Copy

Directions—Set the line-space regulator at "1." Type each line twice as shown.

Technique Goal—Keep your eyes on the book. Think each letter as you type.

- *To double-space between groups of lines, operate the carriage return lever or key twice. To triple-space, operate the lever or key three times.*

1   fjdk sla; fjdk sla; gf uj gf uj gf uj jug jug jugs   Single-space
     fjdk sla; fjdk sla; gf uj gf uj gf uj jug jug jugs   repeated lines

2   lug lug slug slug lad lad lass lass lag lag flags;
     lug lug slug slug lad lad lass lass lag lag flags;   Double-space when you start a new line

3   us us fuss fuss dug dug; glass glass; flask flasks
     us us fuss fuss dug dug; glass glass; flask flasks

4   a lad; a jug; a lug; a jug; a flask; a glass flask   Triple-space between parts
     a lad; a jug; a lug; a jug; a flask; a glass flask   ← of a lesson

2f ■ Fluency Practice

Directions—Type each line twice. Double-space after the second typing of a line.

Technique Goal—Use quick, sharp strokes. Release the keys instantly.

1   a lad; a lass; as a lad; as a lass; lugs; all lugs

2   a full lug; a full jug; a full glass; a full flask

3   all fall; lug lugs; jug jugs; flag flags; us fuss;   Each line twice

4   us us dusk dull dull gull gulls; a gull; all gulls

5   as a; as a lad; as a lad falls; a lass; as a lass;

Remove paper—Center carriage

LESSON 140

140a ■ Keyboard Review • Each line at least three times

5 minutes

All letters **SS** The woman gave hazy explanations for both of Judge Mackey's questions.

Figure-Symbol Miss Morse told the seventh grade students to add 5/6, 19/30, and 2/3.

Left hand and weak fingers What size quilts do you have? Sally saw six dozen square zinc plates.

Flowing, rhythmic stroking

Easy To get to the top of the oak, do not merely sit on the acorn and wait.

| 1 | 2 | 3 | 4 | 5 | 6 | 7 | 8 | 9 | 10 | 11 | 12 | 13 | 14 |

140b ■ Timed Writings

10 minutes

Directions—Type a 1- and a 5-minute writing on 136d, page 221. Circle errors. Compute *gwam*.

140c ■ Problem Measurement

30 minutes

Problem 1 ■ Interoffice Memorandum

Directions—Type the following memorandum in the form illustrated on page 215.

TO: Shirley Schramm / FROM: Robert J. Piersol / DATE: April 14, 19-- / SUBJECT: Additional Copies of Ellis Report / Please run off 35 additional copies of the Ellis Report. They are to be attached to the staff meeting minutes of April 3. I have to keep the original copy, so please do not let anything happen to it. (¶) If you do not have time to distribute this material, give Jack a call and he will get someone to help you. It would probably be a good idea to remind him that all engineers are to receive these copies, even if they were not in attendance at the last meeting. Thanks very much for your help. / (xx)

Problem 2 ■ Invoice

Directions—Type the following invoice in the form illustrated on page 217.

Sold To The Mullennix Mart, 487 North Sixth, Lincoln, NB 68520 / *Terms* 2/10, n/30 / *Date* May 15, 19-- / *Our Order No.* 4258 / *Cust. Order No.* 646 / *Shipped Via* A and M Freight / *Salesperson* Louis Mudge

Quantity	Description	Unit Price	Amount
1	S12-726 Cassette Recorder	49.95 ea.	49.95
5	M16-107 LP Record Baskets	7.50 ea.	37.50
2 doz.	E9 1.4v Portable Radio Batteries	8.25 doz.	16.50
			103.95

140d ■ Extra-Credit Typing ■ Composing a Business Letter

Directions—Compose a letter to Mr. M. E. Minich, 35 Mesa Drive, Tempe, AZ 85281. Your purpose is to let him know his schedule for the Management Development Program. Include in the body of your letter the table given in 138c, Problem 2, page 224. Use modified block style with mixed punctuation.

Lesson 3

3a ▪ Keyboard Review

Directions—Type each line once with your teacher. Type the lines again by yourself.

Posture Goal—Sit erect. Hold elbows near the body. Keep wrists low and quiet.

g   fgf fgf gf gf lad lass lad glad lag slag lag flag;

u   juj juj uj uj lug slug lug slug jug jugs jug jugs;

       us us dusk dusk fluff fluff all fall; a flag falls

All letters taught   a full lug; a full jug; a full flask; a full glass

Eyes on this copy

3b ▪ Location of E and H

Find **e** on the chart. Find it on your typewriter keyboard. Place your fingers over the home keys. Touch **ed** lightly. Move the **d** finger upward and forward without moving your hand.

Type e with the d finger

←**REACH TO E**   **REACH TO H**→ Find **h** on the chart. Find it on your typewriter keyboard. Place your fingers over the home keys. Touch **hj** lightly without moving the other fingers from their typing position.

Type h with the j finger

ded ded ed ed ed led led   ● **Type twice on same line** ●   jhj jhj hj hj ha had had

3c ▪ Location Drills—E and H

Directions—Type each line once with your teacher. Type the lines a second time by yourself.

Technique Goal—Snap the finger toward the palm of the hand after each stroke.

e   ded ded ded ded ed ed ed ed led led fled fled fled

       led lag led lag fled flag us use use less less use

       sue sue due due else else jade jade desk desk fell

h   jhj jhj jhj jhj hj hj hj hj hall hall had had half

       had a half; had a half; a half lug; had a half jug

       has gas gash lash sash flash flush hush husk shall

Type e with the d finger

Type h with the j finger

1   SS   I believe the booklet entitled <u>Your Career</u> is on the desk in Room 239.

2   Disney's "Wonderful World of Color" will be shown tonight at 7:30 p.m.

3   Pam Beck (who attended Fort Miller last year) will run the 220 for us.   Work for control

4   The old Abbott and Costello films can be rented for approximately $15.

5   Only 15% of those who invested will receive more than 9 cents a share.

| 1 | 2 | 3 | 4 | 5 | 6 | 7 | 8 | 9 | 10 | 11 | 12 | 13 | 14 |

139c ■ Problem Typing   *30 minutes*

Problem 1 ■ *Business Letter from Script*

50-space line   Date on line 18   Block style   Open punctuation   Current date   Carbon copy   Large envelope

Mrs. Ruth Grubb / 2103 Seventh Avenue / Buffalo, NY 14214 / Dear Mrs. Grubb (¶) Enclosed is our refund check for $18.50 covering the purchase price of the blender you recently returned. (¶) We hope this method of handling your order meets with your approval. Please think of us again whenever you need kitchen appliances. / Yours very truly / Martin Schmidt / Customer Services / (xx) / Enclosure

Problem 2 ■ *Interoffice Memorandum*

Directions—Type the following memorandum in the form illustrated on page 215.

TO: All Employees / FROM: Wayne Brooks, Manager / DATE: February 7, 19-- / SUBJECT: Excessive Employee Absence / During the last two weeks several supervisors have brought to my attention the fact that excessive absences among staff members have been causing some work load problems in our various departments. (¶) I realize that the majority of you are most conscientious about using your sick leave only for its intended purpose. You know that each employee was hired to do a job because that particular job has to be done. If you are not here, some others must attempt to do your work in addition to their own. Naturally, when we are considering people for promotions, we have to give a good deal of weight to past attendance records. (¶) Again, I do want to stress that the sick leave program is to be used when needed; but I want you also to be more aware of what problems continued absences cause your fellow employees and the management. I know we can count on your cooperation. / (xx)

Problem 3 ■ *Business Letter from Script*

Directions—Retype the letter in Problem 1 above, making these changes: **1.** Address the letter to Ms. C. E. Nelson, 41 Butler Street, Erie, PA 16511. **2.** Change the amount of the check to $23.75.

3d ■ Technique Builder—Finger-Action Stroking

Directions—Set line-space regulator at "1." Type each line twice.

Technique Goal—Move your fingers, not your arms or wrists.

1   fdsa jkl; fdsa jkl; gf uj ed ed hj hj led fled leg

2   sell sells fell fell dull dull seek seek feel feel ←Double-space after second typing of line

3   deal deal due due duel had had he he she she shell

4   flee flee gull gull sell sell shell shell had head Triple-space between lesson parts

5   jell jell us us use use fuse fuse age age had half ←

Finger-Action Stroking

When one of your fingers reaches from its home position to strike another key, keep the other fingers near their home keys. Make the reach without raising the wrist or moving your arm or elbow.

Reach to first row

Reach to third row

3e ■ Fluency Practice   • Each line three times

1   he had; she had; he led; she led; a lad had a half

2   he led; she led; he led us; she led us; had a dull   Type without pauses

3   he has; she has; he has a half lug; she has a full

4   a dull hue; a full glass; a full keg; she had half

Lesson 4

• *Spacing: Double.*
• *Margins: 50-space line.*

4a ■ Keyboard Review

Directions—Type each line once with your teacher. Type the lines again by yourself.

Posture Goal—Sit back in your chair with body centered opposite **h** key.

e   ded ded ed ed led led fled fled sled sled sell led

h   jhj jhj hj hj had had hall hall half half held led

u   juj juj uj uj lug dug full full sue sue fuel us us   Eyes on this copy

    keg jug she shall half glass; she had a full glass

All letters taught   jell husk dusk; a full keg; a half lug; she shall;

138c ■ Problem Measurement

30 minutes

Problem 1 ■ Business Letter in Rough Draft

50-space line
Date on line 18
Modified block
Open punctuation
Carbon copy
Small envelope

Mrs.
~~Miss~~ Donna Hudson   *June 20, 19--*
3290 Marshall (Street) *Avenue*
Scranton, PA 18519

Dear Mrs. Hudson

> We have received a copy of *your* ~~the~~ letter which you
wrote to Mr. Cords at our home office *in New Haven.*
As I explained to you in our conversation last
week, we want to assist our customers through the
local dealer *ships* when ever possible. Since we had
not heard anything further from you, we ~~had~~ assumed
that ~~everything was satisfactory.~~ *the matter*
had been settled .

Miss Diana Semrau, I have asked our service representative for your
area, to visit Norm's in Scranton. She will be in
touch with you ~~shortly~~ *soon* so that the two of you may
get together ~~at that time.~~ *to discuss the matter.*

Sincerely *yours*

Dana Simis
Manager, Consumer Relations   *Move to center*

Reference initials

Problem 2 ■ Table

Half sheet
Centered vertically
Double spacing
6 spaces between
columns

MANAGEMENT DEVELOPMENT PROGRAM

←———————— Triple-space

Topic	Date	Leader
What Is Management?	September 12	Mr. Minich
Management Decision Making	October 10	Miss Cutler
Management Communication	November 7	Mrs. Lewis
Management Policy	December 12	Mrs. Hendry

Lesson 139

● *70-space line*

139a ■ Keyboard Review ● Each line at least three times

5 minutes

All letters **SS**   My box was packed with five dozen jars of apple, fig, and quince jams.

Figure-Symbol   If I add 3,682 and 57, I certainly should not get 4,032 for an answer!   Feet on
                                                                                            the floor

Difficult reach   The executive was aware that exemptions were awarded, then taken away.

Easy   Both of the men had to ride the bus to work in the busy city each day.

| 1 | 2 | 3 | 4 | 5 | 6 | 7 | 8 | 9 | 10 | 11 | 12 | 13 | 14 |

4b ■ Location of R and I

Find **r** on the chart. Find it on your typewriter keyboard. Place your fingers over the home keys. Touch **rf** lightly. Move the **f** finger upward and forward without moving your hand.

←REACH TO R

REACH TO I→

Find **i** on the chart. Find it on your typewriter keyboard. Place your fingers over the home keys. Touch **ik** lightly. Raise the **j** finger slightly to give the **k** finger freedom of movement.

Type r with the f finger

Type i with the k finger

frf frf rf rf fu fur fur

• Type twice on same line •

kik kik ik ik id did did

4c ■ Location Drills—R and I

Directions—Type each line once with your teacher. Type the lines again by yourself.

Technique Goal—Reach to **r** and **i** without moving your hands forward. Hold the wrists low and quiet.

r   frf frf frf frf rf rf rf rf fur fur furs furs sure

surf surf rug rug drug drug rue rue rule rule jars

Type r with the f finger

i   kik kik kik kik ik ik ik ik did did slid slid dike

dike jig jig fig fig dish dish fish fish fill fill

Type i with the k finger

Hands turned sidewise

Straight, Direct Stroking

Do not permit your hands to turn sidewise on the little fingers. Hold the hands directly over the keys. Turn the hands in toward your thumbs slightly to get straight, direct strokes.

←——Wrong

Right ——→

Hands directly over keys

4d ■ Technique Builder—Straight, Direct Strokes •

Change to single spacing. Type each line two times.

1   fdsa jkl; rf rf rf ik ik ik did did dike dike ride

←——Double-space

2   rug rug rig rig field fields girls girls high high

3   aid aid air air fire fire file files feel feel kid

4   far far fair fair life life aid aid jail jail sale

5   he has; she has; he had; she had; he did; she did;

←——Triple-space

Lesson 138

138a ■ Keyboard Review ● Each line at least three times

5 minutes

All letters **SS** Elizabeth very quickly solved the sixth problem again just for Weston.

Figure-Symbol Type policy numbers without commas. My insurance policy is No. 92358.

Quiet wrists
and arms

sw Shrewd witnesses will wisely swear they saw shadows on the white snow.

Easy If you type right, you will be hitting those keys as if they were hot.

| 1 | 2 | 3 | 4 | 5 | 6 | 7 | 8 | 9 | 10 | 11 | 12 | 13 | 14 |

138b ■ Speed Stretcher ● Use Speed Stretchers for 5-minute writings, or use each paragraph for 1-minute writings.

10 minutes

All letters   1.4 si   5.3 awl   85% hfw

	GWAM
	1' | 5'

DS A recent survey of our nation's public libraries showed that a lot | 13 \| 2 51
of things checked out today won't fit on your bookshelves. What they | 27 \| 5 54
stock, in addition to the usual books and magazines, reflects the tastes | 42 \| 8 57
and needs of those who use their materials and services. Just take a | 56 \| 11 59
look at some of the items you can find there. | 65 \| 13 61

At the time this particular study was being made, for example, | 13 \| 16 64
one library had a waiting list for some of the gardening and yard tools | 27 \| 18 67
that could be checked out. No matter whether one needed to turn over | 41 \| 21 69
soil in the garden, cut some bushes, or dig a hole, the proper piece of | 55 \| 24 72
equipment could be obtained. | 61 \| 25 73

People who enjoy taking care of their own automobile repairs can | 13 \| 28 76
find help in the library too. In addition to books on this subject, | 27 \| 31 79
of course, one library lends a special kind of meter and light used to | 41 \| 33 82
time an auto engine. It also has available a creeper, the low platform | 55 \| 36 85
on wheels that lets you get under your car. | 64 \| 38 86

You can be sure that their regular job, that of helping us with | 13 \| 41 89
books and information, is still being done. In fact, the task of find- | 27 \| 43 92
ing answers to our questions has been speeded up a great deal by the | 41 \| 46 94
use of modern aids such as computers and television. | 51 \| 48 96

1' | 1 | 2 | 3 | 4 | 5 | 6 | 7 | 8 | 9 | 10 | 11 | 12 | 13 | 14 |
5' | 1 | 2 | 3 |

4e ■ Fluency Practice

Directions—Each line three times. Double-space after the third typing of a line.

Technique Goals—Return the carriage without looking from the copy. Type at a steady pace.

1   he had a disk; she hid a dish; she had a dark dish

2   he had a red sled; he did ride; he had a hard ride

3   she had a fur; she had a real fur; she sells furs;

4   he held a safe lead; she held a shelf; he hid here

Type without stopping

Lesson 5

- *Spacing: Double.*
- *Margins: 50-space line.*

Quick, Sharp Stroking

Strike each key with a quick, sharp stroke. Release it quickly.

Snap the finger slightly toward your palm as the key is released.

5a ■ Keyboard Review • Type once—then repeat

Home row   fdsa jkl; fdsa jkl; gf hj gf hj fall glad half had

r   frf frf rf rf fur fur fir rid sure sure hear heard

i   kik kik ik ik did did slid slid dike dike hid hide

All letters taught   disk rush gull ride lake jail fail; she hid a sled

she had a hard sled ride; she held a real fur sale

Quick, sharp strokes

5b ■ Location of C and N

Find **c** on the chart. Find it on your typewriter keyboard. Place your fingers over the home keys. Touch **cd** lightly. Hold the **a** finger in typing position, but let the other fingers move slightly.

←REACH TO C   REACH TO N→

Find **n** on the chart. Find it on your typewriter keyboard. Place your fingers over the home keys. Touch **nj** lightly without moving the other fingers from their typing position.

Type c with the d finger

Type n with the j finger

dcd dcd cd cd ca car car   • Type twice on same line •   jnj jnj nj nj an and and

Lesson 137

137a ■ Keyboard Review ● Each line at least three times

5 minutes

All letters **SS** We planned to move the six wagons quickly to Arizona before next July.

Figure-Symbol A total of 84 runners had cracked the 4-minute mile "barrier" by 1967.

Type steadily

Weak fingers I saw we were lax and had acquired lazy habits playing weak opponents.

Easy Write the names of all the machines you can in the blanks on the form.

| 1 | 2 | 3 | 4 | 5 | 6 | 7 | 8 | 9 | 10 | 11 | 12 | 13 | 14 |

137b ■ Building Skill on Figures and Symbols

● Type each line once. Then type two 1-minute writings on each sentence.

10 minutes

1 **SS** Sonja Henie of Norway won Olympic Gold Medals in 1928, 1932, and 1936.

2 On July 2, 1971, Robert F. May threw a Frisbee a distance of 285 feet.

Work for control

3 Lynne Cox (at only 15) swam the English Channel in 9 hours 57 minutes.

| 1 | 2 | 3 | 4 | 5 | 6 | 7 | 8 | 9 | 10 | 11 | 12 | 13 | 14 |

137c ■ Problem Typing

30 minutes

Problem 1 ■ *Business Letter in Modified Block Style*

60-space line   Modified block   Mixed punctuation   Date on line 18   Carbon copy   Small envelope

● *The opening and closing lines of this letter are in problem form. Capitalize and punctuate them correctly.*

january 5, 19-- / mr harold e lane / 1428 east chestnut avenue / atlanta ga 30342 / dear mr lane / We appreciate very much your attendance at the recent preview showing of our latest office equipment. We were glad that such a large number of people were able to come on rather short notice. (¶) It was a real pleasure for us to explain the new 110 Series family of computers. Although it was our intention to make this first session as complete as possible, we realize there may be areas of special interest to you in which you would like more information. Should you have questions about any aspect of this system, I hope you will stop in to see us at our main supply room. We will be happy to help you. (¶) Thanks again, Mr. Lane, for being with us. / sincerely yours / terry ray / sales representative / (xx)

Problem 2 ■ *Business Letter with Subject Line*

Directions—Retype the letter in Problem 1. Add this subject line:

SUBJECT: Preview Showing of 110 Series

Problem 3 ■ *Business Letter with Attention Line*

Directions—Type the letter in Problem 1 again. Omit the subject line, and address it to:

G and L Office Supply / 12 Ila Avenue / Topeka, KS 66234 / Attention Mrs. Betty Goertzen / Ladies and Gentlemen

5c ■ Location Drills—C and N

Directions—Type each line once with your teacher. Type the lines again by yourself.

Technique Goal—Strike each key with a quick, sharp stroke. Release it quickly.

c 　dcd dcd dcd dcd cd cd cd cd cud cud call call cake

Type **c** with the **d** finger

　　lick lick sick sick such such rice lace luck cluck

n 　jnj jnj jnj jnj nj nj nj nj an an and and sand end

Type **n** with the **j** finger

　　land land ran ran end end lend lend sign sign send

　　fin fin find find rain rain gain gain sun sun sung

5d ■ Technique Builder—Quick, Sharp Stroking ● Single spacing—each line twice

1 　nu nu cd cd ail fail an and land and hand end lend

2 　run rung sun sung sin sing fine find kind can hand

3 　in inch end send fire crack field us dusk rush run

Quick, sharp strokes

4 　lark lack lake cake ache arch line fine sign learn

5 　an and land sand hand end send lend ail fail sails

5e ■ Fluency Practice ● Each line three times

1 　she can run; she can slide; she can run and slide;

2 　he can lend; he can lend a hand; he can send a rug

Type steadily

3 　he he; if he is here; he hid in; he hid in a field

4 　she can find; she can find a; she can find a guide

Lesson 6

● *Spacing: Double.*
● *Margins: 50-space line.*

6a ■ Keyboard Review ● Type once—then repeat

n 　jnj jnj nj nj an an and land need need sun sun end

c 　dcd dcd cd cd cud cud cull cull call call luck can

r, i 　frf kik rf ik fur fir girl fire ride hire fir fail

Eyes on this copy

　　seen sense share clean clear class lack jack field

All letters taught

　　he and she can run; held a nail; lack a drill flag

136d ■ Speed Ladder Paragraphs ● As directed in 116d, page 189   *20 minutes*

		1'	5'

All letters   **DS**   Although there has been talk for years about moving people via   13 | 3 66

¶ 1
44 words
1.4 si

fast trains, monorails, or tubes, the automobile continues to reign   26 | 5 57

supreme. Auto makers say there may soon be as many cars in the land   40 | 8 60

as there are adults.   44 | 9 61

No one knows, of course, just what cars of tomorrow will be like.   57 | 11 64

¶ 2
48 words
1.4 si

The consumer might be able to buy a tiny shopping car for use around   71 | 14 66

town, a large cruiser to drive out on the highway, and a specialized   85 | 17 69

vehicle for any recreational needs.   92 | 18 70

Safety will be the aim of many changes in cars of the future. One   105 | 21 73

official predicts that warning lights to alert drivers to dangers such   120 | 24 76

¶ 3
52 words
1.4 si

as tires that are low on air will be common. Engineers are working on   134 | 27 79

rear-view devices that will be better than mirrors.   144 | 29 81

If the trend to more and more cars continues, there is no doubt   157 | 31 83

that some kind of traffic control systems will be required. Some now   171 | 34 86

¶ 4
56 words
1.4 si

in limited use are connected to computers that change traffic light   184 | 37 89

timing of the direction of traffic in freeway lanes to speed the flow   198 | 40 92

of cars.   200 | 40 92

Disposing of old cars as they wear out will also pose a massive   213 | 43 95

problem. About six million cars are junked every year in the United   227 | 45 97

¶ 5
60 words
1.4 si

States alone. Laid end to end they would stretch nearly around the   240 | 48 100

earth at the equator or fill an eight-lane highway bumper-to-bumper   254 | 51 103

All ¶'s
1.4 si

from New York to San Francisco.   260 | 52 104

```
1' |  1  |  2  |  3  |  4  |  5  |  6  |  7  |  8  |  9  |  10 |  11 |  12 |  13 |  14 |
5' |           1          |            2           |            3          |
```

136e ■ Creative Typing

10 minutes

Directions—Type a short paper on how you expect to use your typing skill. Give your paper a title and type the final copy in unbound manuscript style as directed on page 94.

6b ■ Location of T and . (period)

Find **t** on the chart. Find it on your ←REACH TO T   REACH TO .→ Find the period on the chart. Find it typewriter keyboard. Place your fingers over the home keys. Touch **tf** lightly without moving the other fingers from their typing position.

on your typewriter keyboard. Place your fingers over the home keys. Touch **.l** lightly, lifting the little finger only enough to give freedom of movement.

**Type t with
the f finger**

**Type . with
the l finger**

ftf ftf tf tf fi fit fit   ● Type twice on same line ●   l.l .l .l .l fell. fell.

6c ■ Location Drills—T and . (period)

Directions—Type each line once with your teacher. Type the lines again by yourself.

Technique Goal—Reach to the new keys without moving the hands out of position.

t

ftf ftf ftf ftf ftf tf tf tf it it fit fit lit lit

the the then then turn turn cut cut fit fit it its

ten tan then than hit hit jet jet let let sit sits

. (period)

l.l l.l l.l .l .l .l fill. full. sell. call. hall.

Type **t** with
the **f** finger

Type **.** with
the **l** finger

6d ■ Shifting for Capitals—Left Shift Key

The left shift key (No. 29) is used to type capital letters with the right hand.

**USE A
ONE-TWO
COUNT**

One—Depress the shift key with the **a finger**. Hold it down.
Two—Strike the capital letter; then quickly release the shift key and return the **a finger** to its typing position.

Directions—Change to single spacing. Type each line two times.

Spacing Guide—Space twice after a period that ends a sentence except when the period comes at the end of the line. When it does, return the carriage without spacing.

1   Hi Hi Hi Hill Lu Lu Luke Luke Kit Kit Kitt Jud Jud

2   Lu ran. Lu ran here. I can see. I can see Juan.

Space twice
after period

3   Jill had a hat. Hugh hid it. Lu and Lisa see it.

UNIT 17 ■ Improving Your Basic Skills—Measurement

General Directions ■ Lessons 136 - 140

Machine Adjustments—Follow the general directions given in earlier units of this cycle.

Correcting Errors—Unless your teacher directs otherwise, correct any errors you make on problem copy.

Special Forms—Type the problems on the special forms provided in the workbook or on plain paper.

Lesson 136

• *Use a 70-space line for all lessons in this unit.*

136a ■ Keyboard Review • Each line at least three times   *5 minutes*

All letters	**SS**	To move enough zinc for export would require buying trucks and a jeep.
Figure-Symbol		The stocks that sold for $104.37 in 1929 had risen to $568.60 by 1969.
Long reach		Myra was quite mystified by a myriad of mysterious symbols on my door.
Easy		You must have a goal in mind if you want to profit from your practice.

Fingers deeply curved

| 1 | 2 | 3 | 4 | 5 | 6 | 7 | 8 | 9 | 10 | 11 | 12 | 13 | 14 |

136b ■ Control Builder • Type four 1-minute writings at your control rate.   *5 minutes*

DS   When our western states were young, travel across their arid lands posed a problem. In seeking an answer, someone proposed the camel. It could carry heavy loads, move quickly across deserts, go without water, and live on prickly pears and scrub brush. Although the beasts did well, the railroads soon took their jobs away.

65 words
1.4 si

Type without pauses

136c ■ Capitalization Guides— Business Letter Parts • Read the explanations; each line three times.   *5 minutes*

Line 1—In business letters, capitalize the first and last words, all titles, and all proper names used in the salutation.

Line 2—Capitalize only the first word of the complimentary close.

Line 3—All titles appearing in the address should be capitalized.

Line 4—If a title follows the name of the dictator in the closing lines of a business letter, it must be capitalized.

1	**SS**	Dear Sir: My dear Tom: Dear Mr. Smith: Dear Dr. Johnson: Dear Fran
2		Yours truly, Sincerely yours, Yours very truly, Cordially yours, Yours
3		Ms. Doris Ewy, Manager; Miss Ellen Day, Secretary; Mr. Ben Blue, Chief
4		Lori Brown, President; Rita Hill, Attorney; John Stone, Vice-President

Quick, firm reach to the shift key

| 1 | 2 | 3 | 4 | 5 | 6 | 7 | 8 | 9 | 10 | 11 | 12 | 13 | 14 |

6e ■ Technique Builder—Shift-Key Control

Directions—Each line two times.

Technique Goal—Hold the shift key down until you strike the capital letter; then release it quickly.

1   tf .l tf .l if if it it is is the the the fit fits

2   he the then; an than thank; in thin think; at that

3   aid air fair; the their things; chief child change

4   It is here. Nan hit it. Jeff can see it. I ran.

Space twice after period

5   June can tell us. He can sell it. I can take it.

6   He has the right light. Kate can see it at night.

7   It is light. It is right. It is right and light.

Lesson 7

- *Spacing: Double.*
- *Margins: 50-space line.*

7a ■ Keyboard Review

Directions—Type once; then repeat.

Posture Goal—Hold shoulders erect with body leaning forward slightly from the waist.

t   tft tft tf tf the then than it fit fight lit light

Shift   Hi Hi Hill Lil Lil; Lil King; Kate Kate; Kate Kane

. (period)   l.l l.l Jan can sell it. Jane can fill their jug.

Space twice after period

All letters taught
Kate said she called her at night. He can see us.
Jan and Jack caught that large fish in Kiles Lake.

7b ■ Location of V and Y

Find **v** on the chart. Find it on your typewriter keyboard. Place your fingers over the home keys. Touch **vf** lightly without moving the other fingers from their typing position.

←REACH TO V   REACH TO Y→

Find **y** on the chart. Find it on your typewriter keyboard. Place your fingers over the home keys. Touch **yj** lightly without moving the other fingers from their typing position.

Type v with the f finger

Type y with the j finger

fvf fvf vf fiv five five   ● Type twice on same line ●   jyj jyj yj yj ja jay jay

135c ■ Problem Typing

Problem 1 ■ Interoffice Memorandum with Table

Directions—Type this interoffice memorandum in the form shown in 132c, page 215. Use a 60-space line. Leave 5 spaces between columns in typing the table. Double-space before and after the table. Prepare one carbon copy.

● *If necessary, see directions for arranging tables on page 108.*

TO: Terry Wetmore / FROM: Pat Murphy / DATE: June 4, 19-- / SUBJECT: Open Enrollment Period / The open enrollment period for term life insurance, written by Northern National Life Insurance Company, has been extended through June 30. This period affords our employees the rare opportunity to obtain life insurance at a reasonable rate regardless of their physical condition. (¶) I have listed below the names and social security numbers of the people in your section who enrolled in the program last year:

Lanny E. McBride	539-29-4374
Stephanie Petrucci	592-03-5748
Richard E. Tellier	487-33-2893

Please notify all of your other employees of this extended enrollment period.

Problem 2 ■ Table

Directions—Type the following table centered vertically on a full sheet. Triple-space between the heading and the first item; double-space the items. Leave 6 spaces between columns. Prepare one carbon copy.

● *If necessary, see directions for vertical centering on page 61.*

WESTERN REGION ADDRESS LIST

Mrs. Rachel Cotten	15 Carroll Drive	Logan, UT 84321
Miss Rebecca Falk	539 Almond Avenue	Los Banos, CA 93635
Dr. Laurie Groth	866 North Gearheart	Butte, MT 59701
Mr. John Highfill	901 Henning Boulevard	Boise, ID 83705
Mr. Dewey Johnson	5221 Griffith Way	Spokane, WA 99216
Mr. Jerry Kilbert	1492 Fremont Street	Flagstaff, AZ 86001
Ms. Marilyn Martino	2826 East Cedar Street	Seattle, WA 98118
Dr. D. L. Pierson	2983 Harvard Avenue	Chico, CA 95926
Ms. Caroline Rameriz	37 Keats Avenue	Redding, CA 96001
Mrs. Lupe Rodriguez	231 College Drive	Las Vegas, NV 98104
Mr. T. Hillman Willis	14 Chickadee Lane	Portland, OR 97210

135d ■ Extra-Credit Typing

Problem 1

Directions—Type the interoffice memorandum given in 132c, Problem 1, page 215. Prepare one carbon copy. Fill in the heading as follows:
TO: T. A. Young / FROM: Earle J. Moore / DATE: May 25, 19-- / SUBJECT: New Date Stamp Procedure

Problem 2

Directions—Type on a half sheet the table given in 135c, above. Center it vertically. Triple-space after the heading; single-space the items. Leave 4 spaces between columns. Prepare a carbon copy.

7c ■ Location Drills—V and Y

Directions—Type each line once with your teacher. Type the lines again by yourself.

Technique Goal—Think the letters as you type. Use quick, sharp strokes.

v   fvf fvf fvf fvf vf vf vf vf five fives lives lives

     have have five five give give dive dive hive hives   Type v with the f finger

y   jyj jyj jyj jyj yj yj yj yj jay jays lay lays slay

     sly sly fly fly try try jay jay ray ray stay stays   Type y with the j finger

     the they eye eyes try tray fry fray lay lays yells

7d ■ Shifting for Capitals—Right Shift Key

The right shift key (No. 27) is used to type capital letters with the left hand.

USE A ONE-TWO COUNT

One—Depress the shift key with the **;** finger. Hold it down.

Two—Strike the capital letter; then quickly release the shift key and return the **;** finger to its typing position.

Directions—Type each line two times. Change to single spacing.

Spacing Guide—Remember to space twice after a period that ends a sentence (except at the end of a line).

1   Ted Ted Fran Fran; Ted and Fran; Fran and I; Frank

2   Ted is here. Fran can see Ted. She can see Fran.   Quick, firm reach to the shift key

3   Frank is ill. I need Art here. She and I see it.

7e ■ Technique Builder—Shift-Key Control

Directions—Each line three times. Double-space after the third line.

Technique Goal—Hold the shift key down until you strike the capital letter; then release it quickly.

1   vf yj vf yj day day dry dry say say stay stay days

2   yes yet year the they ray gray tray sly slay style

3   She can. She can have her turn. I can give five.   Return without spacing after . at the end of the line

4   Jan and I can stay. Jan can stay there five days.

5   Ann and Karl are here. Jan left her friend there.

6   I can learn. She can get all the funds she needs.

134b ■ Typing Titles of Articles and Poems

Directions—1. The first line gives the rule; the remaining lines apply it.

2. Type each sentence three times; then take a 1-minute writing on each sentence.

1   SS   The name of a poem, article, or play should be set in quotation marks.

2   Today, each English class will read Longfellow's "Paul Revere's Ride."

Quick carriage return

3   We saw it in Leigh White's article, "Chicago's Airport of the Future."

4   Joyce and Bert were lucky to get such good tickets for "My Fair Lady."

| 1 | 2 | 3 | 4 | 5 | 6 | 7 | 8 | 9 | 10 | 11 | 12 | 13 | 14 |

134c ■ Problem Typing

30 minutes

Problem 1 ■ Interoffice Memorandum • As directed in 132c, page 215

TO: The Staff / FROM: E. R. Mead, Manager / DATE: November 12, 19-- / SUBJECT: Wrist Calendars / Many of you have commented about the excellent response you received from customers regarding the wrist calendars we provided as gifts last year. We are therefore planning to give these handy calendars to our regular customers and friends again this year. (¶) Please pick up your supply from Mark Johnson in Room 119. If you think you will need more than he has set aside for you, you can request extras after all employees have received their original supply. (¶) You will note they are printed on each side for use with either a yellow or white gold watch band. / (xx)

Problem 2 ■ Invoice • As directed in 133c, page 217

Sold to Russell and Coe, 538 East Indian Road, Fort Wayne, IN 46807 / *Terms* 2/10, n/30 / *Date* December 12, 19-- / *Our Order No.* 98736 / *Cust. Order No.* 3749 / *Shipped Via* Union Freight / *Salesperson* D. L. Bastady

Quantity	Description	Unit Price	Amount
2	M53 C-2594 Hand Mixers	15.95 ea.	31.90
10 pr.	FM-79Z Wire Cutters	4.45 pr.	44.50
8 gal.	23-60 White House Paint	8.95 gal.	71.60
			148.00

Lesson 135

• *70-space line*

135a ■ Keyboard Review • Each line at least three times

All letters   SS   Even now, a dozen more expect to qualify for those kinds of good jobs.   *5 minutes*

Figure-Symbol   A $1 bet on a race horse, "Wishing Ring," won $1,213 on June 17, 1912.

Balanced- and one-hand   if they see, if they look, if they wear, if they jump, if they address   Sit erect

Easy   When all their work is done, have them hand it in to the team captain.

| 1 | 2 | 3 | 4 | 5 | 6 | 7 | 8 | 9 | 10 | 11 | 12 | 13 | 14 |

135b ■ Timed Writings • Type a 1- and a 5-minute writing on 131d, page 214. Circle errors. Compute *gwam*.   *10 minutes*

Lesson 8

8a ■ Keyboard Review

Directions—Type once; then repeat.   **Posture Goal—**Wrists held low; elbows near body.

v   fvf fvf vf vf five five live live give give leaves   Wrists low

y   jyj jyj yj yj jay jay eye eyes say says stay stays

Shift   Al Ruth Sue Jane Gus Ken Jan and Val; Dan and Fern

        Juan and I can catch that large fish in June Lake.   Elbows near body

All letters taught   Kay Kirk says I can have the five trays Ned needs.

8b ■ Technique Builder—Stroking   • Single-spacing—each line at least two times

1   I can see the car. He has a red hat. She has it.

2   Two- and three-letter words   It is due in a day. I had a gun. She can get it.   Quick, sharp strokes

3   The lad can see us. It is in the air. I can run.

4   Ned had the red rug. The lad can hit the fat hen.

5   Three-letter words   Jan has her hat. She can get the rug and the gun.   Instant release

6   She cut her eye. Sue and she hid the gun and fur.

7   They have the red jugs. They left here last year.

8   Four-letter words   Tell Ruth they have her car. They held five kegs.   Wrists low and still

9   They sent the keys here. They had nine live fish.

10   Chuck likes large desks. Jayne takes these three.

11 Five-letter words   Clare sells signs. Frank still takes these cakes.   Fingers deeply curved

12   Keith fills eight large tanks. Grace stays there.

| 1 | 2 | 3 | 4 | 5 | 6 | 7 | 8 | 9 | 10 |

8c ■ Sentence Skill Builder

Directions—Type a 1-minute writing on the first line of each group of lines in 8b. Compute your gross words a minute (*gwam*).

In typewriting 5 strokes are counted as one word. Each line in 8b has 50 strokes, or 10 words. For each full line typed, give yourself a score of 10 words. Two full lines typed, for example, give you 20 gwam. For a partially typed line, note the scale under the sentences. Add the figure nearest the last word or letter typed to your complete sentence score. This total is your gross words a minute (gwam).

133c ■ Problem Typing

Problem 1 ■ Invoice

Directions—Type the invoice shown below. Clear your machine of tab stops; set your left margin and new tab stops at the positions indicated. Make one carbon copy. *(A form is provided in the workbook.)*

● *An invoice is a bill. It is a printed form on which are typed the quantities and items delivered, the unit prices, the extensions, and the total. Some invoices have ruled columns; some do not.*

LINDQUIST & LARSON COMPANY
2805 North Peachtree Way   Atlanta.GA 30338 (401) 631-5099

INVOICE

SOLD TO	Sunnyside Supply Shop 410 West Curtis Street Terre Haute, IN 47836	DATE	August 5, 19--
		OUR ORDER NO.	90388
		CUST. ORDER NO.	1290
		SHIPPED VIA	Rapid Transit
TERMS	2/10, n/30	SALESPERSON	R. Larson

QUANTITY	DESCRIPTION	UNIT PRICE	AMOUNT
1	S12 D-9048 12-Transistor Radio ←——Double-space——→	69.95 ea.	69.95
8 rolls	E14 X-12 "3000" Speed Film	2.35 roll	18.80
5 gal.	X60 B-9093 Insecticide	6.48 gal.	32.40
↑ Margin	↑ Tab	↑ Tab Double-space	121.15 ↑ Tab

Invoice

Problem 2 ■ Invoice ● As directed in Problem 1

Sold To Luellen Hardware, 1393 Granada Avenue, Jackson, MS 39264 / *Terms* 2/10, n/30 / *Date* June 15, 19--/ *Our Order No.* 98389 / *Cust. Order No.* 2387 / *Shipped Via* National / *Salesperson* R. Lawson.

Quantity	Description	Unit Price	Amount
4	S18 B-3570 Clock Radios	49.95 ea.	199.80
2	P19 B-3257 Car-Home Coolers	82.50 ea.	165.00
12 doz.	S61 109 "Hawkeye" Golf Balls	9.65 doz.	115.80
			480.60

Lesson 134

134a ■ Keyboard Review ● Each line at least three times

All letters SS	Pale, excited men inquired about a few objects hovering in a hazy sky.
Figure	The Pittsburgh Pirates won their 1902 pennant by a margin of 27 games.
Right hand	Look in on my nylon mill, Jill Polk; I'll hook pink poplin on my loom.
Easy	It is true that one who does not drive the auto right may not be left.

Elbows in

| 1 | 2 | 3 | 4 | 5 | 6 | 7 | 8 | 9 | 10 | 11 | 12 | 13 | 14 |

8d ▪ Indenting for Paragraphs

You will use the tabulator bar or key (No. 24) to indent for paragraphs. Find this bar or key on your typewriter. Touch lightly the tab bar (right index finger) or tab key (right little finger). Deeply curve the other fingers in making this reach.

Next, turn to page vii and read how to use the tab clear key (No. 33) and the tab set key (No. 25).

8e ▪ Paragraph Typing

Directions—Set machine for a 5-space paragraph indention and double spacing. Type twice. Repeat if time permits.

Technique Goal *(Manual)*—Hold the tab bar or key down until the carriage stops.

(Electric)—Tap the tab key lightly and immediately return to the home position.

Words

Tab⟶ The girls have a tent near the lake. They | 9

stay at the lake all day in the fall. Kay says | 18

I can use her raft if I like. | 24

Tab⟶ She can drive there in a day in their car. | 33

Ken and I can ride in it. She says that she is | 42

sure there is gas in the car. | 48

| 1 | 2 | 3 | 4 | 5 | 6 | 7 | 8 | 9 | 10 |

Lesson 9

- *Spacing:* Double.
- *Margins:* 50-space line.

9a ▪ Keyboard Review

Directions—Type once; then repeat.

Posture Goal—Sit back in chair. Eyes on copy.

t tf tf tf it it fit fit hit hit sit sit kit kit jut

n nj nj nj fan fan fun fun gun gun run run send send

v vf vf vf five five dive dives give gives live live

y yj yj yj jay jay eye eye lay lay dry dry slay slay

Eyes on this copy

All letters taught

Jane said the craft is in the shed near the field.

Sue can have Ray shut the large gate at the track.

| 1 | 2 | 3 | 4 | 5 | 6 | 7 | 8 | 9 | 10 |

Problem 2 ■ Interoffice Memorandum

Directions—Type the following memorandum according to the directions given in Problem 1.

TO: Richard Rogers, Office Manager / FROM: J. B. Ross, General Manager / DATE: July 25, 19-- / SUBJECT: Staff Meeting / Our next staff meeting will be held on Wednesday afternoon at 3:15. We shall have to meet in the committee room on the third floor because our regular committee room is being used for a sales conference. Please notify all the members in your department of the time and place. (¶) Your report will be the first item we have to consider. If you can have copies made for everyone, I think we can save quite a bit of time. Since we have a very full agenda, it looks as though the meeting will probably last until 5:00 p.m. / (xx)

Lesson 133

● *70-space line*

133a ■ Keyboard Review ● Each line at least three times

5 minutes

All letters SS I'm amazed to know the fall gym party and major banquet are exclusive.

Figure In 1884, a champion ice skater went 10 miles in 31 minutes 11 seconds.

Left hand Sweet tastes were decreased as excess treats were served as a dessert.

Easy Forms for the maps in problem six are provided for you in chapter six.

Wrists and elbows still

| 1 | 2 | 3 | 4 | 5 | 6 | 7 | 8 | 9 | 10 | 11 | 12 | 13 | 14 |

133b ■ Speed Stretcher ● Use Speed Stretchers for 5-minute writings, or use each paragraph for 1-minute writings.

10 minutes

All letters   1.4 si   5.3 awl   85% hfw

		GWAM
		1' | 5'

DS Every summer many thousands of teenagers search for jobs in which   13 \| 3 41
they can earn some money for a trip, a new fishing rod, or simply to   27 \| 5 44
help out with the family budget. Getting a paycheck of your very own   41 \| 8 47
can be fun, but there are several points that should be kept in mind   55 \| 11 50
in obtaining summer employment.   61 \| 12 51

Try to get employment that is in line with your career plans. In   13 \| 15 54
that way you can gather first-hand information about your chosen career.   28 \| 18 57
You will be able to decide whether or not you and your career make a   42 \| 21 59
good team. It's quite important that you learn this about yourself.   56 \| 23 62
This is not the only principle to keep in mind, however.   67 \| 26 64

A summer job gives you a chance to learn how to work. Capitalize   13 \| 28 67
on the opportunity to interact with other people, to take directions,   27 \| 31 70
and to put what you presently know to an acid test. This is the payoff   42 \| 34 73
for summer work—a golden opportunity to learn just what is expected,   55 \| 37 75
plus a chance to see how well you can fill the bill.   66 \| 39 78

| 1' | 1 | 2 | 3 | 4 | 5 | 6 | 7 | 8 | 9 | 10 | 11 | 12 | 13 | 14 |
| 5' | | 1 | | | 2 | | | 3 | | |

9b ■ Location of B and O

Find **b** on the chart. Find it on your typewriter keyboard. Place your fingers over the home keys. Touch **bf** lightly, allowing your **d** and **s** fingers to move slightly to give freedom of action.

←REACH TO B   REACH TO O→

Find **o** on the chart. Find it on your typewriter keyboard. Place your fingers over the home keys. Touch **ol** lightly without moving the other fingers from their typing position.

Type b with the f finger

Type o with the l finger

fbf fbf bf bf ib fib fib   ● Type twice on same line ●   lol lol ol ol ol old old

9c ■ Location Drills—B and O

Directions—Type each line once with your teacher. Type the lines again by yourself.

Technique Goals—Reach to the new keys with your fingers. Keep your wrists and elbows low.

b   fbf fbf fbf fbf bf bf bf bf buff buff job job jobs

       big big both both boy boy boys blue blue ball ball

       bus bus by by buy buy but but hub hub lab lab burn

Type b with the f finger

o   lol lol lol lol ol ol ol ol old old fold fold cold

       so so to to do do of of of got got loss loss go go

Type o with the l finger

9d ■ Technique Builder—Wrists Low and Steady

Directions—Change to single spacing. Type each line two times.

Technique Goal—Curve your fingers; not your wrists. Hold your wrists low and steady.

1   ol bf ol bf old sold cold bold hold loss lost gold

2   cold could should bond bound found ground so sound

Curve your fingers

3   by by buy buy but but book books boy boys bid bids

4   to do; to do the; to go; to go to the; to go there

5   if you; if you do; if you do so; if you can do the

6   I can be. I can be there. They can be there too.

Wrists and elbows still

7   They can buy it all right. They can buy it there.

| 1 | 2 | 3 | 4 | 5 | 6 | 7 | 8 | 9 | 10 |

Lesson 132

132a ■ Keyboard Review • Each line at least three times

5 minutes

All letters **SS** A just, quick, but exact mind will help you develop a zest for living.

Figure-Symbol All 34 eighth graders did Spelling Lesson 1-B on page 368 for Tuesday.

Double letters All room committees agreed that baggage accommodations were very good.

Wrists low
and still

Easy A few of the rogues had thrown rocks at the big signs outside of town.

| 1 | 2 | 3 | 4 | 5 | 6 | 7 | 8 | 9 | 10 | 11 | 12 | 13 | 14 |

132b ■ Technique Builder—Stroking • Type ech line twice; then type two 1-minute writings on each line.

10 minutes

1 **SS** quiz azure police apply taxes flaw hazy axe zero soap war palm was set

2 upon square zone plow lamp play flax cases quack zipper zeal possesses

Fingers
deeply
curved

3 They politely applauded the plays. The astronauts waited on the pads.

4 Samuel soon saw that I was acquitted. The lazy pupils flunked a quiz.

| 1 | 2 | 3 | 4 | 5 | 6 | 7 | 8 | 9 | 10 | 11 | 12 | 13 | 14 |

132c ■ Problem Typing

30 minutes

Problem 1 ■ Interoffice Memorandum

• The interoffice memorandum is used for correspondence between offices or departments within a company. Its chief advantage is that it can be set up quickly.

• If the workbook form is not available, type the TO:, FROM:, DATE:, and SUBJECT: in all caps at the left margin beginning on line 12.

Directions—Type the interoffice memorandum shown. Use a 60-space line.

TM Towne Management, Inc.

INTEROFFICE MEMORANDUM

Words

Personal titles omitted **TO:** Claire E. Hampton — 4

FROM: William C. Wayne — 7

DATE: July 21, 19-- — 10

SUBJECT: New Date Stamp Procedure — 15

← Triple-space

The mail room returned the attached envelope to us today with — 27
a note asking that we stop using our present stamp. The one — 39
made for our office should be thrown away as we have not used — 52
a post office box address for several years. — 61

A new stamp is being made, and we should get it next week. If — 73
it is necessary for you to use the old one during the next few — 86
days, just draw a line through the box number and write in our — 98
street address. Please tell the others in your department to — 111
follow the same procedure until you get your new stamp. — 122

xx — 122

Reference initials

Interoffice memorandum

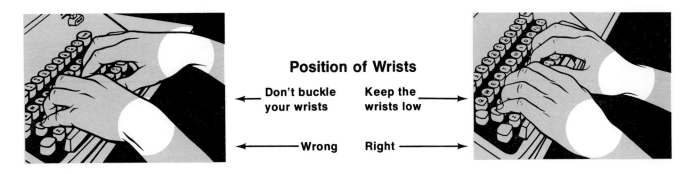

Position of Wrists

← Don't buckle your wrists   Keep the wrists low →

← Wrong   Right →

9e ▪ Sentence Skill Builder

Directions—Type two 1-minute writings on each sentence. Figure your gross words a minute (*gwam*).

1   They can do the job if I have the tools they need.

2   I can learn to do the things that need to be done.   Keep the wrists low

3   I can gain a high skill goal for the job if I try.

| 1 | 2 | 3 | 4 | 5 | 6 | 7 | 8 | 9 | 10 |

Lesson 10

• *Spacing: Double.*
• *Margins: 50-space line.*

10a ▪ Keyboard Review • Type once—then repeat

o   lol lol ol ol old bold sold folds holds so or sort

b   fbf fbf bf bf bluff be bill blue ball bad bug burn   Eyes on copy

v, y   vf yj vf yj dry try drive guy give hay have strive

Shift   Sue Black and Les Church; Nick Branch and Ann Todd   Quick, sharp strokes

    Keith can buy the stove for you if Grace sells it.

All letters taught   Jo can buy it. She can buy it for you. I had it.

| 1 | 2 | 3 | 4 | 5 | 6 | 7 | 8 | 9 | 10 |

10b ▪ Location of X and P

Find **x** on the chart. Find it on your ←REACH TO X typewriter keyboard. Place your fingers over the home keys. Touch **xs** lightly, lifting the little finger slightly to give your **s** finger freedom of movement.

REACH TO P→ Find **p** on the chart. Find it on your typewriter keyboard. Place your fingers over the home keys. Touch **;p** lightly, keeping your elbow quiet and holding the other fingers in typing position.

Type x with the s finger

Type p with the ; finger

sxs sxs xs xs ix six six   • Type twice on same line •   ;p; ;p; p; p; pa par par

LESSON 10 ▪ PAGE 17

| | | GWAM |
| | | 1' | 5' |

All letters **DS**   In the days before TV and the daily paper brought weather reports — 13 | 3 55

¶ 1
44 words
1.4 si

and farm news quickly to all our homes, one household item was thought — 27 | 5 57

to be almost as important to the good life as the Bible. That item — 41 | 8 60

was an almanac. — 44 | 9 61

According to one editor, city folks seem to like almanacs as much — 57 | 11 63

¶ 2
48 words
1.4 si

as their country cousins do. This may be so because many people have — 71 | 14 66

a love for the soil within them, and an almanac represents a link with — 85 | 17 69

life on the farms of bygone days. — 92 | 18 70

Almanac ranks have now shrunk to roughly a dozen different ones — 105 | 21 73

from the hundreds that were printed a century ago. One that claims — 118 | 24 76

¶ 3
52 words
1.4 si

to be among the oldest was founded at the time George Washington was — 132 | 26 78

President. It still has its old-time cover and type style. — 144 | 29 81

Today there are still readers who swear by almanac predictions. — 157 | 31 83

Some like to read the choice bits of homespun philosophy, the helpful — 171 | 34 86

¶ 4
56 words
1.4 si

household hints, and the stale jokes found in almanacs. Morticians, — 185 | 37 89

banks, and stores of every kind give them to their best customers each — 199 | 40 92

year. — 200 | 40 92

At the heart of each almanac is its calendar, telling about the — 213 | 43 94

daily rising and setting habits of the sun and moon and suggesting — 226 | 45 97

¶ 5
60 words
1.4 si

excellent days for planting and fishing. Many of these handy guides — 240 | 48 100

to better living come with a hole in one corner so they can be hung — 253 | 51 103

All ¶'s
1.4 si

from a nail in the kitchen wall. — 260 | 52 104

| 1' | 1 | 2 | 3 | 4 | 5 | 6 | 7 | 8 | 9 | 10 | 11 | 12 | 13 | 14 |
| 5' | | 1 | | | 2 | | | 3 | |

131e ■ Skill Comparison • Type a 1-minute writing on each sentence in 131a, page 213. Compare rates.   *5 minutes*

10c ■ Location Drills—X and P

Directions—Type each line once with your teacher. Type the lines again by yourself.

Technique Goal—Reach to the new keys with your fingers. Keep the wrists low.

x   sxs sxs sxs sxs xs xs xs xs six six fix fix ox box

      lax lax flax flax flex flex next next fox fox hoax

Type **x** with the **s** finger

p   ;p; ;p; ;p; ;p; p; p; p; p; par par part pass pass

      past past page page pay pay put put trip trip kept

Type **p** with the **;** finger

Space-Bar Control

Curve right ← thumb over space bar

Strike with quick down- → and-in motion

10d ■ Technique Builder—Down-and-in Motion of Right Thumb ● Single spacing Each line twice

1   xs p; xs p; xs p; flax flax help help cap caps six

2   fox tax fox lax six jinx box hex coax hoax vex axe

3   top stop lot lay play plan plus post nap hope ship

4   fix the step; keep the box; pay the tax; six steps

5   I can pay it. He can pay for it. She can pay it.

6   I paid six of the girls for the good job they did.

Strike space bar with quick down-and-in motion

Wrists and elbows still

| 1 | 2 | 3 | 4 | 5 | 6 | 7 | 8 | 9 | 10 |

10e ■ Paragraph Typing

Directions—Set machine for a 5-space paragraph indention and double spacing. Type twice. Repeat if time permits.

Technique Goal (*Manual*)—Hold the tab bar or key down until the carriage stops.

Words

Tab——————→ You can type at a high rate if you hold your   9

hands still as you reach for the keys. Just keep   19

your eyes on this page. These are the things you   29

need to do as you type. Try these hints and see.   39

| 1 | 2 | 3 | 4 | 5 | 6 | 7 | 8 | 9 | 10 |

UNIT 16 ■ Typing Business Forms

General Directions ■ Lessons 131 - 135

Machine Adjustments—Use a 70-space line for drills and timed writings in this unit. Single-space sentences and drill lines. Double-space between groups of repeated lines. Double-space paragraph copy. It will be necessary for you to reset your margins before typing problem copy.

Correcting Errors—Your teacher will tell you whether or not you are to correct errors on problem copy.

Special Forms—For problems, use the forms provided in the workbook or plain paper.

Lesson 131

• Use a 70-space line for all lessons in this unit.

131a ■ Keyboard Review • Each line at least three times   5 minutes

All letters	SS	Many exciting folk and jazz concerts have been played in town squares.
Figure		Wall Street had 16,410,000 shares of stock traded on October 29, 1929.
e, i		Their niece received a prize when she hiked over here in nine minutes.
Easy		They kept their goals before them during the time they were in charge.

Eyes on this copy

| 1 | 2 | 3 | 4 | 5 | 6 | 7 | 8 | 9 | 10 | 11 | 12 | 13 | 14 |

131b ■ Control Builder • Type four 1-minute writings at your control rate.   5 minutes

	Words
DS Gerbils are little rodents of Old World origin. They make fine,	13
active pets. A hamster can be an introvert, but not a gerbil. They	27
drink tiny amounts of water, so their cages don't need much cleaning.	41
Because of their good nature and ease of care, gerbils are in growing	55
demand for use in medical research these days too.	65

65 words
1.4 si

131c ■ Speed Ladder Sentences   10 minutes

Directions—Type each sentence for 1 minute with the call of the guide at 15-, 12-, or 10-second intervals.

Technique Goal—Return the carriage quickly.

			GWAM		
			15"	12"	10"
1	SS	Be sure your feet are flat on the floor.	32	40	48
2		One foot should be placed ahead of the other.	36	45	54
3		Proper position of the feet will aid your balance.	40	50	60
4		Remember to hold your elbows in close to your body too.	44	55	66
5		Hold your wrists down low, just above your typewriter frame.	48	60	72
6		Keep the hands quiet; do not bound them in the air when you type.	52	65	78
7		Make quick, sharp strokes with your fingers well curved over the keys.	56	70	84

| 1 | 2 | 3 | 4 | 5 | 6 | 7 | 8 | 9 | 10 | 11 | 12 | 13 | 14 |

Lesson 11

11a ▪ Keyboard Review

Directions—Type once; then repeat.

Posture Goal—Body centered opposite the **h** key, 6 to 8 inches from front frame of typewriter.

x   sxs sxs xs xs six six lax flax next next flex flex

p   ;p; ;p; p; p; par part pal pail plan pain rip trip

b, o   bf ol bf ol bold bolt boil rob robe job born board   Quick carriage return

th   there then their thin these they than thanks those

All letters taught   I can ask every girl there to try to learn a part.

All six boys just have to find out if they can go.

```
|  1  |  2  |  3  |  4  |  5  |  6  |  7  |  8  |  9  | 10  |
```

11b ▪ Location of W and M

Find **w** on the chart. Find it on your typewriter keyboard. Place your fingers over the home keys. Touch **ws** lightly, lifting the little finger slightly to give your **s** finger freedom of movement.

←REACH TO W

REACH TO M→

Find **m** on the chart. Find it on your typewriter keyboard. Place your fingers over the home keys. Touch **mj** lightly without twisting your hand or moving the other fingers from their typing position.

Type w with the s finger

Type m with the j finger

sws ws ws wish wish wish   • Type twice on same line •   jmj jmj mj mj ja jam jam

11c ▪ Location Drills—W and M

Directions—Type each line once with your teacher. Type the lines again by yourself.

Technique Goal—Keep your fingers deeply curved. Reach with your fingers; keep wrists still.

w   sws sws sws sws ws ws ws ws wish wish win win wind   Type **w** with the s finger

wall wall walk walk well well how how way way laws

m   jmj jmj jmj jmj mj mj mj mj jam jam make make made

men men mean mean them them come come much much am   Type **m** with the j finger

same same game games more more most most from from

130b ■ Timed Writings • Type a 1- and 5-minute writing on 126c, page 207. Circle errors. Compute gwam.   *10 minutes*

130c ■ Problem Typing   *30 minutes*

Problem 1 ■ Business Letter in Modified Block Style

60-space line   Date on line 18   Modified block   Mixed punctuation   Current date   Carbon copy   Large envelope

Miss Monica Johnson / 3978 North Fifth Street / Baltimore, MD 21204 / Dear Miss Johnson: / We have enclosed the charge slip from Weinstock's Automotive Service for the recent towing of your car. (¶) Since claims of this type are always handled on a reimbursement basis, we will need a receipted bill before your claim can be processed. When you pay the bill, please ask for a receipt which you can submit to us. We shall then reimburse you up to the amount our nearest service garage would have charged under their contract rules. (¶) I have also enclosed an Information Request Form which you will need to complete and return with your receipt. It will assist our Service Department in promptly considering your claim. (¶) Thank you for your cooperation, Miss Johnson. We hope to hear from you soon./ Cordially yours, / James R. Castenada / Claims Manager / (xx) / Enclosures

Problem 2 ■ Composing a Personal/Business Letter

Directions—Compose and type an answer to the letter typed in Problem 1. Tell Mr. Castenada that you have paid your towing bill, and you are sending him the receipt. Also mention that you are enclosing the completed Information Request Form. Use the letter style you prefer. Use your own return address. With your teacher's permission you may type the **Alternate Suggestion** below instead of this problem.

Alternate Suggestion

60-space line   Block style   Date on line 18   Mixed punctuation   Carbon copy   Large envelope

September 4, 19-- / Ms. Shirley Panico / 639 East Portals Drive / Greeley, CO 80639 / Dear Ms. Panico: / We are planning to open a child care center for small children, ages three through five. The center will endeavor to provide a happy and wholesome schedule of activities for children during the day when their parents cannot care for them. (¶) We are hopeful that the opening date will be November 1. The facilities will operate Monday through Friday from 7 a.m. to 6 p.m. every month of the year. Fees will be $18 per week. (¶) In order to determine the need and desire for such a day care program, we should like your cooperation in completing and returning the enclosed form. If you want to be informed when the center is opened, please place a check mark in the space indicated. / Very truly yours, / CHILD CARE CENTER / Robin Cresto / Manager / (xx) / Enclosure

130d ■ Extra-Credit Typing

Problem 1

Type Problem 1, page 205, in block style, open punctuation. Address the letter to Mr. Gene Davis / 39 Doyle Avenue / Nashville, TN 37208.

Problem 2

Type Problem 2, page 211, in modified block style, mixed punctuation. Add an appropriate subject line.

Problem 3

Type the problem you did not type for 130c, Problem 2, above.

11d ■ Technique Builder—Quick, Sharp Stroking

Directions—Change to single spacing. Type each line two times.

Technique Goal—Don't rest your fingers heavily on the home keys. Barely touch them with your fingertips. Feel the keys; don't smother them. Make short, direct reaches. Strike the keys; don't push them.

Strike, don't push!

1 ws mj ws mj ws mj two town who whom when now known

2 shy what how show we well went want much mail main   Light touch

3 me met mad made so some low slow win wind aim fame

4 will win; will take; will make; will move; will be

5 who may; who makes; who must; some walk; some show   Quick, sharp strokes

6 Meet each new day with a smile if you wish to win.

   | 1 | 2 | 3 | 4 | 5 | 6 | 7 | 8 | 9 | 10 |

11e ■ Sentence Skill Builder

Directions—Type a 1-minute writing on each sentence. Figure your *gwam* on each sentence.

Technique Goal—Barely touch the keys with your fingertips. Strike the keys quickly; don't push them.

1 Type in the right way if you want to do good work.

2 They can go to the town to get the film they need.   Quick, crisp, short strokes

3 I can learn to like to do the things I need to do.

   | 1 | 2 | 3 | 4 | 5 | 6 | 7 | 8 | 9 | 10 |

11f ■ Paragraph Skill Builder

Directions—Five-space paragraph indention; double spacing. Type three 1-minute writings on the paragraph. Figure your *gwam* on the best writing.

● *To figure your gwam on paragraph copy, note the figure at the end of the last complete line typed in the column at the right. To it, add the words in a line partially typed by noting the scale at the bottom. Use the figure nearest the last stroke typed. The total is your gross words a minute (gwam).*

                                                            Words

Tab———————► Plan your work if you want to make the best   9

             use of your time. This is true for your work at   19

             home as well as for what you do at school.   27

   | 1 | 2 | 3 | 4 | 5 | 6 | 7 | 8 | 9 | 10 |

129c ■ Problem Typing

Problem 1 ■ Business Letter with Enumerated Items

60-space line   Modified block   Date on line 18   Current date   Mixed punctuation   Carbon copy   Large envelope

• *Indent the enumerated items 5 spaces from each margin. Double-space before and after each of the items.*

Miss Mary Miller / 3197 Cornell Drive / Flint, MI 48505 / Dear Miss Miller: / As one of our best customers, you are eligible for the Superior Chargecard that is enclosed. (¶) Here are just a few of the card's many advantages:

1. It is honored throughout the state by over 50,000 merchants.

2. It identifies you to merchants as a person of good standing.

3. There are no dues and no interest charges when you pay within 30 days.

If you wish, Miss Miller, you may extend your payments by paying as little as 5% of your outstanding balance or $10 each month, whichever is greater. (¶) Your signature on the back of the card is sufficient. Need we say more?/Cordially yours, / Robert Pengilly / Sales Representative / (xx) / Enclosure

Problem 2 ■ Business Letter in Rough Draft

50-space line
Block style
Date on line 18
Open punctuation
Carbon copy
Large envelope

April 14, 19- -

Mr. Jeff Bakkedahl
287 Lawton Ave. *spell out*
Casper, WY 82601
Dear Mrs. Bakkedahl:

Enclosed with this letter is a new set of cards. *Please* for you use in making your *monthly* land payments. *Destroy* any old cards you may have and use the new ones beginning July 1st.

We *have* made this change because our recordkeeping *has been* *converted* ~~changed~~ from a service bureau to an in-house computer.

Sincerely yours
Lelie Delara Controller *move to next line*

xx

Enclosure *Your prompt payments are surely appreciated!*

Lesson 130

• *70-space line*

130a Keyboard Review • Each line at least three times

5 minutes

All letters SS   Wendy bought an exquisite Navajo necklace for me on a trip to Arizona.

Figure-Symbol   I said the famous Dempsey-Tunney fight was held on September 22, 1927.

Feet on the floor

4th finger   All the people we saw appeared happy with the apparatus at the bazaar.

Easy   We also wish to thank all eight of them for returning their own signs.

| 1 | 2 | 3 | 4 | 5 | 6 | 7 | 8 | 9 | 10 | 11 | 12 | 13 | 14 |

LESSON 130 ■ PAGE **211**

Lesson 12

12a ■ Keyboard Review

Directions—Type once; then repeat.

Posture Goal—Elbows near body; wrists held low and steady.

w	sws sws ws ws wish wise win wind wall walk who how
m	jmj jmj mj mj jam jam me met melt mad made arm sum
x, p	xs p; xs p; xs p; par part lax flax lap slaps coax
in	fine find kind line think thing since spring bring

Elbows in

Wrists low

I think all six girls did a good job at the games.

A few of you will have to put the chairs in place.

All letters taught

| 1 | 2 | 3 | 4 | 5 | 6 | 7 | 8 | 9 | 10 |

12b ■ Location of Q and , (comma)

Find **q** on the chart. Find it on your ←**REACH TO Q** typewriter keyboard. Place your fingers over the home keys. Touch **qa** lightly without moving the elbow in or out. Hold the elbow steady.

Type q with the a finger

REACH TO ,→ Find the **comma** on the chart. Find it on your typewriter keyboard. Place your fingers over the home keys. Touch **,k** lightly, lifting the **j** finger slightly to give you freedom of action.

Type , with the k finger

aqa qa qa quit quit quit   • Type twice on same line •   k,k k,k ,k rk, irk, irk,

12c ■ Location Drills—Q and , (comma)

Directions—Type each line once with your teacher. Type the lines again by yourself.

Spacing Guide—Space once after a comma.

q	aqa aqa aqa qa quit quite quiet quills quips equip
	pique quilt square quench queen quart quote quotes
	quaint quake quick queue squid squeak equal plaque
, (comma)	k,k k,k k,k ,k ,k work, rock, broke, trick, truck,
	fork, forks, sock, socks, dock, dike, lock, clock,
	kick, choke, steak, rake, kale, king, chock, soak,

Type **q** with the a finger

Type **,** with the k finger

128c ■ Problem Typing

30 minutes

Problem 1 ■ Business Letter with Table

50-space line	Modified block	Date on line 18
Mixed punctuation	Carbon copy	Small envelope

● *Indent the first column of the table 5 spaces from the left margin. Leave 5 spaces between the columns. Double-space before and after the table.*

May 9, 19-- / Cords Clothiers / 2018 Carmel Avenue / Pocatello, ID 83217 / Ladies and Gentlemen: / SUBJECT: Advertising Plans / It is always a pleasure to participate with our customers in a cooperative advertising program. (¶) According to the terms of our agreement, it is necessary for us to receive from you two full tear sheets covering each advertisement. Will you please send us another tear sheet to cover the following advertisements:

Twin Falls News-Dispatch	April 23
Idaho Falls Telegram	April 25
Pocatello Journal	May 1

We look forward to continued cooperation with you in your advertising plans. / Very truly yours, / LENNAN MANUFACTURING COMPANY / Ms. Martha W. Nelson / Advertising Director / (xx)

Problem 2 ■ Business Letter with Table

Directions—1. Type the letter in Problem 1 in block style, with open punctuation, and address it to:

Jack's Men's Wear
1867 Moroa Avenue
Modesto, CA 95350

2. Insert the following table in place of the one used in Problem 1:

Sacramento Bee	April 18
Monterey Herald	May 1
San Francisco Chronicle	May 3

Lesson 129

● *70-space line*

129a ■ Keyboard Review ● Each line at least three times

5 minutes

All letters **SS** John and William quickly packed the five dozen very big express boxes.

Figure-Symbol They reported (in 1980) that 265 of the 1,743 names were listed there.

Quick, sharp strokes

Long reach I joined in their annual hunting fun with the gun snugly under my arm.

Easy All eight of them were so tired they slept right on through the night.

| 1 | 2 | 3 | 4 | 5 | 6 | 7 | 8 | 9 | 10 | 11 | 12 | 13 | 14 |

129b ■ Speed Builder

10 minutes

Directions—1. Type a 1-minute writing to determine your goal word.

2. Type a 5-minute writing. At the end of each minute the return will be called. Try to reach your goal.

	Words
DS Years ago some unsung hero realized that when a large group of	13
people faced the same kind of risks, only a few really suffered a	26
loss. This person then came up with the idea that if all would agree	40
to share the losses of a few, the threat of total disaster would be	53
removed. Thus it was that the idea of insurance was born.	65

65 words
1.3 si

12d ■ Technique Builder—Eyes on Copy

Directions—Single spacing. Type each line twice; then type 1-minute writings on the last three lines.

Technique Goal—Don't look from the copy to your typewriter and back again. Type right! Keep your eyes on the copy at all times.

1   qa ,k qa ,k qa ,k quit, qualm, quip, quite, squeal

2   quick, quill, queen, quotes, qualms, quilt, quench

3   to quote, to quit, the quick, the queen, the quilt

4   I was quick to quote the girls with the red quilt.   Space once after comma

5   Drive right, as the life you save may be your own.

6   As you type, use quick, short, firm, sure strokes.

7   We can gain the high skills we need for this work.

     | 1 | 2 | 3 | 4 | 5 | 6 | 7 | 8 | 9 | 10 |

12e ■ Paragraph Skill Builder

Directions—Five-space paragraph indention; double spacing. Type the paragraph once for practice; then type three 1-minute writings on it. Figure your *gwam* on the best writing.

	Words
Tab ⟶ It is said that they who sling mud must give	9
ground. There is much truth in these words. You	19
will lose more than you gain when you give way to	29
the use of words and thoughts that are too harsh.	39

     | 1 | 2 | 3 | 4 | 5 | 6 | 7 | 8 | 9 | 10 |

Lesson 13

● *Spacing: Double.*
● *Margins: 50-space line.*

13a ■ Keyboard Review ● Type once—then repeat

q   aqa aqa qa qa quit quits quote quotes quart quarts

, (comma)   k,k k,k ,k ,k work, all, fork, fill, dark, squall,

w, m   ws mj ws mj ws mj warm warm mow mow whom whom home   Sit erect

an   an and can man change chance plan plant stand want

     Type with a fixed goal in mind; use quick strokes.   Wrists low

All letters taught   A job will give you the chance to test your skill.

     | 1 | 2 | 3 | 4 | 5 | 6 | 7 | 8 | 9 | 10 |

Lesson 128

128a ■ Keyboard Review • Each line at least three times

5 minutes

All letters   **SS**   Their own quaint jujitsu expert amazed folks on the block every night.

Figure-Symbol   The 27 students in Room 139 raised a total of $46.85 during the drive.

Reach with your fingers

Right hand and weak fingers   Opal paid for the opera tickets. I will oppose the plan to supply it.

Easy   The flies that make the loudest noise are the ones that get hit first.

| 1 | 2 | 3 | 4 | 5 | 6 | 7 | 8 | 9 | 10 | 11 | 12 | 13 | 14 |

128b ■ Speed Stretcher •

Use Speed Stretchers for 5-minute writings, or use each paragraph for 1-minute writings.

10 minutes

All letters   1.4 si   5.3 awl   85% hfw

	GWAM 1'	5'

DS   Try this little test. First, type your name in full; then type it | 13 | 3 53 |

again. The second time, however, skip every other letter. Which was | 27 | 5 56 |

easier and faster—the first or the second typing? The first one was | 41 | 8 59 |

likely a bit easier and quicker, even though you typed twice as many | 55 | 11 62 |

letters. Why was this true? What did the test prove? | 66 | 13 64 |

When you typed your full name the first time, you typed it from | 13 | 16 66 |

habit. This, however, did not help you on your second typing. You had | 27 | 19 69 |

to concentrate on each letter separately as you typed it. As a result, | 42 | 22 72 |

you typed slowly. Good habits are a valuable aid in typing as well as | 56 | 24 75 |

in almost everything else you do. They often save you time. | 68 | 27 77 |

There are only two things to remember about building good habits. | 13 | 29 80 |

First, when you type, type correctly. If you realize that the right | 27 | 32 83 |

way is the easy way, this rule will not be too hard to follow. Next, | 41 | 35 85 |

practice with zeal! You certainly cannot expect to type well if you | 55 | 38 88 |

waste part of the practice session every day. | 64 | 40 90 |

Have you ever attempted to break a bad habit? Everyone says the | 13 | 42 93 |

job is not easy. Although it might not seem like it, good habits are | 27 | 45 96 |

no easier to eliminate than bad ones. Once you learn to type correctly, | 42 | 48 98 |

you are on the way because your good habits will take over for you. | 55 | 51 101 |

1' | 1 | 2 | 3 | 4 | 5 | 6 | 7 | 8 | 9 | 10 | 11 | 12 | 13 | 14 |
5' | 1 | 2 | 3 |

13b ▪ Location of Z and ?

Find **z** on the chart. Find it on your typewriter keyboard. Place your fingers over the home keys. Touch **za** lightly, keeping the other fingers in typing position.

←REACH TO Z   REACH TO ?→

Find **?** on the chart. Find it on your typewriter keyboard. Place your fingers over the home keys. Touch **?;** lightly several times. Remember to shift to type **?**

Type z with the a finger

Type ? with the ; finger

aza za za zone zone zone   • Type twice on same line •   ;?; ?; ?; Why? Why? Why?

13c ▪ Location Drills—Z and ?

Directions—Type each line once with your teacher. Type the lines again by yourself.

Spacing Guide—Space once after a question mark within a sentence; twice after a question mark at the end of a sentence.

z
aza aza aza za za za zone zones zero zip zeal zinc   Type z with the a finger

zoo size maze maze gaze graze doze quiz quiz froze

?
;?; ;?; ;?; ?; ?; ?; Is it? Can they go? Why go?   Type ? with the ; finger—Note spacing guide above

Can he tell them how? or why? Whom will she take?

13d ▪ Technique Builder—Shift-Key Control • Single spacing; each line two times. Type 1-minute writings on the last three lines.

1 za ?; za ?; What zinc? Who froze it? Whose zone?

2 Does Jorge know? When can Pam come? Is Kim sure?   Hold shift key down; release it quickly

3 Can we go? Is this the zone? Was the prize here?

4 Will the Jets play the Rams on their field? When?

5 Do you want Steve to get the prize in May or June?

| 1 | 2 | 3 | 4 | 5 | 6 | 7 | 8 | 9 | 10 |

13e ▪ Paragraph Skill Builder • Double spacing; three 1-minute writings

Words

Tab———————→ Now that you know where to find each of the   9

keys, your job is to work hard and learn to type   18

well. This is a goal that all of you can reach.   28

| 1 | 2 | 3 | 4 | 5 | 6 | 7 | 8 | 9 | 10 |

Lesson 127

127a ▪ Keyboard Review • Each line at least three times
5 minutes

All letters **SS** We looked up at a majestic flag flying in the quiet breeze over Texas.

Figure-Symbol The 1,256 scouts marched 38 blocks before more than 24,970 spectators.

Long words Periodically, specimens of fish never before identified are recovered.

Type with your fingers

Easy Turn to the division problems if you are through with your other work.

| 1 | 2 | 3 | 4 | 5 | 6 | 7 | 8 | 9 | 10 | 11 | 12 | 13 | 14 |

127b ▪ Paragraph Guided Writings • As directed in 116b, page 188
10 minutes

DS

Very few foods are more American than the hot dog. The billions
eaten each year prove it. Still, there are two other sandwiches that
rank ahead of the famous weiner and bun. Would you believe that peanut
butter and jelly is first and the hamburger second? Because of this,
those who sell hot dogs will have to try harder.

65 words
1.4 si

Words
13
27
41
55
65

127c ▪ Problem Typing
30 minutes

Problem 1 ▪ Business Letter with Postscript

• *Type a postscript a double space below the reference initials. It need not be preceded by the letters P. S.*

50-space line   Carbon copy   Modified block
Mixed punctuation   Date on line 18   Small envelope

```
lg
◄──────────── Double-space
I'm having an examination copy of Agnew's
```

December 10, 19--/ Ms. Susan Wachtel, Manager/ The Campus Bookstore/ 395 Lupin Drive/ Miami, FL 33155/ Dear Ms. Wachtel: / SUBJECT: Damaged Shipment/ Please accept our apology for the damaged shipment of books which you received on December 4. If you find it necessary to return any of these books, we shall issue credit on Invoice No. 5976G. Just refer to this letter when returning the books to us. (¶) Our new representative in your area, Terry Munoz, tells me you will be leaving your present position soon to open your own store. I want to wish you the best of luck in this new venture and to let you know we want to continue to serve you in the future./ Very truly yours,/ Doug Simpson/ Sales Manager/ (xx)/ I'm having an examination copy of Agnew's Reference Manual mailed to you today.

Problem 2 ▪ Composing a Business Letter

Directions—1. Compose and type a letter, in answer to the letter in Problem 1, from Ms. Wachtel. Address the letter to Mr. Douglas Simpson, Sales Manager / Jan Publishing Company / 2398 Yale Avenue / Kansas City, MO 64120 / Dear Mr. Simpson: /

2. Thank Mr. Simpson for his prompt attention to the matter of the damaged shipment and for the complimentary book which he sent you. Also extend him a personal invitation to visit Ms. Wachtel's new store.

3. Use modified block style, mixed punctuation, and today's date.

4. Address a small envelope.

UNIT 2 ■ Improving Your Typewriting Techniques

General Directions ■ Lessons 14 - 20

1. Single-space (SS) sentences and drill lines. Double-space between repeated groups of lines.
2. Double-space (DS) paragraph copy. Set a tabulator stop for a 5-space paragraph indention.

Time Schedule—Beginning with this unit, practice time is given for each section of a lesson. If it seems best to vary the schedule, do so with the approval of your instructor.

Lesson 14

● *Use a 50-space line for all lessons in this unit.*

14a ■ Keyboard Review ● Each line twice   7 minutes

z   aza aza za za zeal zones doze quiz maze graze zest

?   ;?; ;?; ?; ?; Who? When? How many? Is she here?   Sit erect

ou   our four found house south though course out doubt

    Jack expects to take the very hard quiz in August.   Feet on the floor

All letters Only some boys and girls will take it before then.

```
 |  1  |  2  |  3  |  4  |  5  |  6  |  7  |  8  |  9  |  10  |
```

14b ■ Technique Builder—Typing Whole Words ● Type each line twice as your teacher dictates.   5 minutes

1   to to do do to do to do if if he he if he if he is

2   it it is is it is it is if it is if it is if it is   Think and type whole words

3   go go to go to go if it is to go if it is to go to

4   he the she to the if she if it is she if it is the

14c ■ Sentence Skill Builder   10 minutes

Directions—Type each sentence twice; then type a 1-minute writing on each. Figure your *gwam*.

Technique Goal—Try typing the short, easy words as a whole. Just think the words; type them.

1   He can do the job now all right if he is to do it.

2   She and I can do it all right if it is to be done.

3   If they are to go there, they can do all the work.   Type short words as a whole

4   To type right, she must think each word she types.

5   He can do the drill right if he types whole words.

```
 |  1  |  2  |  3  |  4  |  5  |  6  |  7  |  8  |  9  |  10  |
```

		GWAM
		1' | 5'

All letters   **DS**   A few years back it would have been tough to find someone who knew   13 \| 3   55

¶ 1
44 words
1.4 si

much about automation. This word did not exist in the dictionary. Now   28 \| 6   58

it blares at us from the daily papers. Some headlines glow. Others   42 \| 8   60

seem gloomy.   44 \| 9   61

One story may shout the good news that some new device promises   57 \| 11   63

¶ 2
48 words
1.3 si

relief for those workers who must put in long hours at boring tasks.   71 \| 14   66

Another will warn of the tragedy that comes when these automated plants   85 \| 17   69

force thousands out of their jobs.   92 \| 18   70

The electronic marvels in use these days range from simple machines   105 \| 21   73

¶ 3
52 words
1.3 si

that can furnish us with orange juice or a pint of milk to huge systems   120 \| 24   76

which run whole factories. Computers have been used to make decisions.   134 \| 27   79

Some of these machines can play chess with you.   144 \| 29   81

As machines take over and production goes up, there should be a   156 \| 31   83

rise in our standard of living. The workweek will be shorter, so many   171 \| 34   86

¶ 4
56 words
1.4 si

of us will have more free time for rest and recreation. Workers who   184 \| 37   89

have been displaced will likely now have to be retrained for different   199 \| 40   92

jobs.   200 \| 40   92

What does all this mean to those who are in school today? It means   213 \| 43   95

¶ 5
60 words
1.4 si

they must realize it will be the unskilled workers, the ones without   227 \| 45   97

adequate training, who are most likely to suffer in the world of automa-   241 \| 48   100

tion. Never before has the need for career planning been brought home   256 \| 51   103

All ¶'s
1.4 si

quite so forcefully.   260 \| 52   104

1' | 1 | 2 | 3 | 4 | 5 | 6 | 7 | 8 | 9 | 10 | 11 | 12 | 13 | 14 |
5' | 1 | 2 | 3 |

126d ■ Creative Typing • Type a paragraph, telling in your own words what the following quotation means to you.   *10 minutes*

"There are no elevators in the house of success."

Proofreading Your Work

Making typing errors cannot be avoided even if you try very hard not to make them. As you master reaches to keys and learn to type with good form, you will make fewer errors. You must learn to find and mark your errors, however. Some common errors are shown below.

1. Circle the whole word containing an error. Count only one error to a word.

2. A cut-off capital letter is an error.

3. Failure to space between words is an error.

4. A stroke that does not show is an error.

5. The wrong letter or a strikeover is an error.

6. An omitted or an added word is an error.

7. A missed or wrong punctuation mark is an error.

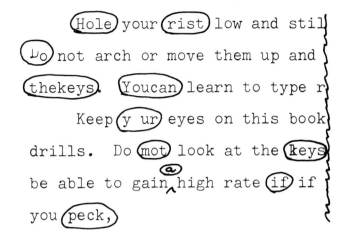

14d ▪ Continuity Practice

15 minutes

Directions—Type the copy below; circle your errors. Repeat. Try to make fewer errors.

Technique Goals—Type without pauses. Return the carriage quickly. Resume typing at once.

● *The syllable intensity, (si) is given for the paragraphs below. It is a guide to the difficulty of the material. Copy of average difficulty is said to have a si of 1.5. The material in these paragraphs is thus quite easy.*

		Words in ¶	Total Words
DS	Hold your wrists low and still as you type.	9	9
¶ 1 27 words 1.0 si	Do not arch or move them up and down as you strike	19	19
	the keys. You can learn to type right.	27	27
	Keep your eyes on this book as you type the	9	36
¶ 2 30 words 1.0 si	drills. Do not look at the keys, as you will not	19	46
	be able to gain a high rate if you must peek as	28	55
	you peck.	30	57

| 1 | 2 | 3 | 4 | 5 | 6 | 7 | 8 | 9 | 10 |

14e ▪ Paragraph Skill Builder

8 minutes

Directions—Type two 1-minute writings on each of the two paragraphs in 14d. Figure your *gwam*. Type additional 1-minute writings on the paragraph on which you made your lowest score.

125c ■ Problem Typing

30 minutes

Problem 1 ■ Business Letter with Attention Line

● *An attention line is used to direct a letter to a particular person. It is usually typed on the second line below the address, as illustrated at the right. (In addressing the envelope, type the attention line immediately below the company name.)*

```
Edgar and Pauls
3294 Belmont Drive
Cleveland, OH 44124
              ←——— Double-space
Attention Miss Alice Pauls
              ←——— Double-space
Ladies and Gentlemen:
```

60-space line	Block style	Date on line 18	Mixed punctuation	Large envelope

June 12, 19-- / Edgar and Pauls / 3294 Belmont Drive / Cleveland, OH 44124 / Attention Miss Alice Pauls / Ladies and Gentlemen: / In order for us to take appropriate action in handling the claim I mentioned on Monday, we must receive a complete accident report from you by June 20. A copy of the accident file is enclosed. (¶) I recommend that you get in touch with the Blackburn family, as well as the driver and passengers in the Blackburn car. Mr. and Mrs. Blackburn now live in or near Louisville, Kentucky. (¶) As we are not certain about injuries, we want you to give this matter priority over other files. With the assistance of your thorough service, we should be able to reach a final decision early in July. / Very truly yours, / George A. Eckenrod / Claims Department / (xx) / Enclosure

Problem 2 ■ Business Letter with Subject Line

● *When a subject line is used in a letter, it may be typed on the second line below the salutation and centered; or it may be typed at the left margin as illustrated.*

```
Miss Denise Schmidt
2094 Rolling Hills Road
Richmond, VA 23234
              ←——— Double-space
Dear Miss Schmidt
              ←——— Double-space
SUBJECT:  Homeowner's Policy No. 2038
```

50-space line	Modified block	Date on line 18	Open punctuation	Small envelope

August 23, 19-- / Miss Denise Schmidt / 2094 Rolling Hills Road / Richmond, VA 23234 / Dear Miss Schmidt / SUBJECT: Homeowner's Policy No. 2038 / We are pleased to renew your Homeowner's Policy as you requested in your letter of August 18. (¶) According to our underwriting rules, we must write coverage on a dwelling for 80 percent of its replacement value. Your home, which contains 1,800 square feet of living space, is presently valued at $85,000. Your annual premium will therefore be increased to $486. (¶) We certainly appreciate your continued confidence in our company, Miss Schmidt. If you need any further information, please call our local office. / Yours very truly / MCFERRIN INSURANCE AGENCY / Don McFerrin / Manager / (xx)

Lesson 126

● *70-space line*

126a ■ Keyboard Review ● Each line at least three times

5 minutes

All letters SS	The quickness and dexterity of this juggler amazed the viewing public.
Figure-Symbol	Mt. McKinley, the highest point in North America, is 20,320 feet high.
3rd finger	Millions of colorful followers all over the world tolled solemn bells.
Easy	It is usually better to keep your chin up than to stick your neck out.

Think as you type

| 1 | 2 | 3 | 4 | 5 | 6 | 7 | 8 | 9 | 10 | 11 | 12 | 13 | 14 |

126b ■ Skill Comparison ● Type three 1-minute writings each on 102b, page 171, and 124c, page 204. Compare rates.

10 minutes

Lesson 15

15a ■ Keyboard Review • Each line twice
7 minutes

n SS   jnj jnj nj nj no not note need nest next knew know

t   ftf ftf tf tf to tone tune tack take ton torn this   Sit erect

er   here other were where serve order there ever every

      Axel made a very quick trip to the Azores in July.   Eyes on copy

All letters   We saw a large fleet of boats in the small harbor.

    | 1 | 2 | 3 | 4 | 5 | 6 | 7 | 8 | 9 | 10 |

15b ■ Technique Builder—Typing Whole Words • Each line three times; then type a 1-minute writing on each line.

1 SS   He is to do the job all right if he can do it now.   12 minutes

2   How you type has a lot to do with how well you do.

3   She can go to the lake to see me work on the dock.   Type short words as a whole

4   Can we take a train to the game if our team plays?

    | 1 | 2 | 3 | 4 | 5 | 6 | 7 | 8 | 9 | 10 |

15c ■ Continuity Practice • Type the copy below; circle the errors. Repeat, trying to make fewer errors.
10 minutes

GWAM

	1'	2'

All letters DS   A small car may not have quite as much zip   9 | 4

¶ 1
27 words
1.0 si   as you would like, and you know that it will not   18 | 9

  have room for six or eight of your friends.   27 | 14

    It will do some good things, though. It will   9 | 18

¶ 2
31 words
1.0 si   use just half as much gas as a great big car, and   19 | 23

  you will not need to look so far to find a spot to   29 | 28

  park it.   31 | 29

  1' | 1 | 2 | 3 | 4 | 5 | 6 | 7 | 8 | 9 | 10 |
  2' | 1 | 2 | 3 | 4 | 5 |

15d ■ Sustained Skill Building
16 minutes

Directions—1. Type two 1-minute writings on each paragraph in 15c. Circle errors. Figure *gwam*.

2. Type two 2-minute writings. Circle errors. Figure *gwam*. Compare rates on short and long writings.

• *In figuring your* gwam *for the writings on the paragraphs, use the 1-minute column at the right and the 1-minute scale underneath the paragraph to figure your 1-minute rate. Use the 2-minute column and scale to figure your 2-minute rate.*

124d ■ Problem Typing
30 minutes

Problem 1 ■ Business Letter in Modified Block Style

● *An enclosure notation is used when a paper (or papers) is sent with the letter. Type the notation at the left margin a double space below the reference initials. Use the plural, **Enclosures**, if two or more items will be enclosed.*

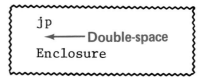

● *If necessary, see directions for addressing a large envelope which appear on page 87.*

| 60-space line | Modified block | Date on line 18 | Mixed punctuation | Large envelope |

November 10, 19-- / Dr. Joel Bluestein / 146 Thurston Street / Nashville, TN 37204 / Dear Dr. Bluestein: / Thank you for your generous contribution to Big Brothers/Big Sisters of Nashville. Your continued support will help us greatly in our efforts to maintain a quality program with reduced public funds. (¶) This program is the fastest growing youth service in the country and the most economical method of providing the individual interest a single-parent youth needs. Approximately 20% of the one-parent youths living in the area are urgently in need of adult guidance. A Big Brother or a Big Sister can help these young people over some of the rough spots encountered in growing up without mothers or fathers (¶) Please accept the enclosed membership certificate as a token of our appreciation for your assistance. / Very truly yours, / J. M. Wong / Executive Director / (xx) / Enclosure

Problem 2 ■ Business Letter in Block Style

| 50-space line | Block style | Date on line 18 | Open punctuation | Large envelope |

September 9, 19-- / Mr. Glen Blomgren / 248 Abbey Street / Milwaukee, WI 53221 / Dear Mr. Blomgren / Enclosed is the report you asked for regarding the use of passenger cars in our division during the past six months. Please keep in mind that this was not a typical period since our new models were not received until after August 1. (¶) I have also enclosed a separate sheet which shows the comparative monthly mileage figures for the past two years (¶) If you have any questions after reading these materials, please let me know. Cordially yours / Ms. Susan Liskey / Chief Accountant / (xx) / Enclosures

Problem 3 ■ Business Letter in Modified Block Style

Directions—Type the letter in Problem 2 in modified block style. Use mixed punctuation. Address a large envelope.

Lesson 125
● *70-space line*

125a ■ Keyboard Review ● Each line at least three times
5 minutes

All letters SS Howard ate five big pretzels and drank exactly two quarts of my juice.

Figure On April 11, 1965, tornadoes struck the Middle West at least 37 times.

Quick carriage return

Shift Last August, Yvette went to Atlanta to see the Braves play the Giants.

Easy They made eight field goals and six free throws to win the title game.

| 1 | 2 | 3 | 4 | 5 | 6 | 7 | 8 | 9 | 10 | 11 | 12 | 13 | 14 |

125b ■ Timed Writings ● Type a 1- and a 5-minute writing on 121c, page 198. Circle errors. Compute gwam.
10 minutes

Lesson 16

16a ■ Keyboard Review • Each line twice   *7 minutes*

b   ss bfb bfb bf bf bid bind bow bowl ban band bit built

p   ;p; ;p; p; p; par part up upon put post paid press   Elbows in

re   are care free great green press real red rest sure

         His new job in Mexico will require pluck and zeal. Eyes on book

All letters I hope that Godfrey may receive her expert advice.

| 1 | 2 | 3 | 4 | 5 | 6 | 7 | 8 | 9 | 10 |

Adjusting the Ribbon-Control Lever

1. Your typewriter has a ribbon control lever (No. 31). Find it on your machine.
2. Set the ribbon control lever to type on the upper portion of the ribbon.
3. Note the position of the ribbon control lever.
4. At the beginning of a lesson, check the ribbon control lever to see that it is in the proper position.

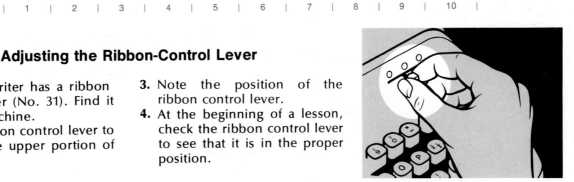

16b ■ Technique Builder—Typing Whole Words • Type each line twice as your teacher dictates

5 minutes

1   ss he | he | did | he did | he did | she did it | I did the

2   and | and I | and she | and the | and if I | and if she   Think words

3   for | for | it | it | for it | for it is | for it is the   Space quickly

4   do | go | do go | do go to | and do | and do go | and go

16c ■ Sentence Guided Writings   *15 minutes*

Directions—1. Type each line twice for practice. **2.** Type each line for one minute with the call of the guide. Try to complete each line as the guide is called. (Your teacher will tell you how the guide will be called.) **3.** Type 1-minute writings on the last sentence without the call of the guide.

			Words in Line	GWAM 20" Guide
1	ss	Type the lines with the guide.	6	18
2		Sit erect if you wish to type well.	7	21
3		Type with a keen mind and quick strokes.	8	24
4		Try to raise your rate by one word each line.	9	27
5		When work takes the place of words, we gain skill.	10	30

| 1 | 2 | 3 | 4 | 5 | 6 | 7 | 8 | 9 | 10 |

Problem 3 ■ Business Letter in Block Style

Directions—Type as shown on page 203. Type today's date on line 18; use a 50-space line. Address a small envelope.

• *The symbol (¶) in the copy below indicates the point at which a new paragraph begins.*

Mrs. Janice Arrants / 2190 Princeton Street / Portland, OR 97233 / Dear Mrs. Arrants / Thank you for your check. It pays your loan in full. I want to compliment you on the prompt manner in which you handled this account. (¶) Now that we are well acquainted, the First National Bank is the logical place to come whenever you may again be in need of extra cash. We hope, too, that you will consider opening a savings account with us in the near future. An account can be started with as little as one dollar or as much as you desire. (¶) Please stop in soon. We shall be happy to serve you. / Yours very truly / FIRST NATIONAL BANK / Lloyd Johnson / Manager / (xx)

Lesson 124

• *70-space line*

124a ■ Keyboard Review • Each line at least three times

5 minutes

All letters SS   The expensive, liquid-fueled rocket jars big windows when it zooms by.

Figure-Symbol   We could buy $28,750 worth of protection for $14.96 a month at age 32.

Quiet wrists and arms

Left hand and weak fingers   I passed the science quiz. Zelda got an extra quill for the desk set.

Easy   Both of them also spent their time working to aid others in the class.

| 1 | 2 | 3 | 4 | 5 | 6 | 7 | 8 | 9 | 10 | 11 | 12 | 13 | 14 |

124b ■ Number Expression Guides—Amounts of Money

5 minutes

Directions—Type each sentence three times. The first line gives the rule; the remaining lines apply it.

1 SS   Amounts of money, either dollars or cents, should be typed in figures.

2   If you want the books, too, the cost of the set is $17.50, not $14.39.

Reach with your fingers

3   Please buy four $4.50 tickets, four $5.50 tickets, and two $6 tickets.

| 1 | 2 | 3 | 4 | 5 | 6 | 7 | 8 | 9 | 10 | 11 | 12 | 13 | 14 |

124c ■ Skill Builder from Rough Draft • Type four 1-minute writings.

5 minutes

	Words
DS If you are looking for an *new and* unusual hoby, you ~~may~~ *might*	12
~~wish~~ *want* to consider ~~raising~~ *keeping* bees. Bee keeping maybe	22
thought of as *an* academic ~~hobby. You can even~~ *pursuit. It is easy to* think of	31
66 words 1.3 si bees as peopl. ~~since~~ they have a ~~habit of~~ storin far *madness for g*	44
more honey than they ever ~~need.~~ Like ~~people,~~ *humans* they *y could use.*	55
work hard *to* gathering wealth they ~~don't~~ need. *for which have no*	66

16d ■ Continuity Practice

10 minutes

Directions—Type the copy below; circle the errors. Repeat, trying to make fewer errors.

Technique Goal—Return the carriage quickly. Resume typing at once.

	GWAM 1'	2'

All letters

¶ 1
29 words
1.1 si

DS   It will pay you to think and type some of the | 9 | 5
words in this copy as a whole. Just read and type | 19 | 10
them as units. Do not spell them as you type. | 29 | 14

¶ 2
33 words
1.1 si

    Use quick, short, sharp strokes. Keep your | 9 | 19
wrists low and firm. Relax, but sit erect. Have | 19 | 24
a clear goal in mind; then work with zeal. You | 28 | 29
can learn to type right. | 33 | 31

```
1' |  1  |  2  |  3  |  4  |  5  |  6  |  7  |  8  |  9  |  10  |
2' |     1     |     2     |     3     |     4     |     5     |
```

16e ■ Sustained Skill Building

8 minutes

Directions—Type a 1-minute, then two 2-minute writings on the paragraphs in 16d. Try to equal your 1-minute rate on the 2-minute writings.

Technique Goals—Type without a sense of hurry. Gain speed by cutting out pauses and waste movements in your arms, elbows, and wrists.

Lesson 17

● *50-space line*

Hold the Wrists Low and Steady

Curve the fingers, not your wrists. Make the reaches to the keys with your fingers. Hold your wrists low and steady.

17a ■ Keyboard Review ● Each line twice

7 minutes

y   SS jyj jyj yj yj yet year you your yes yarn yearn eye

q   aqa aqa qa qa quart quire squire square quiet quit

nd   end send find land hand found friend second window

    Liz is quite right; I can do this wax job for Kim.

All letters   Paula will help you move their car out of the sun.

Fingers deeply curved

```
|  1  |  2  |  3  |  4  |  5  |  6  |  7  |  8  |  9  |  10  |
```

▲ ADAMS and **ASSOCIATES**
Management Consultants

8460 Wilshire Boulevard   Los Angeles, CA 90048

(213) 272-3289

18th line space

Words

April 16, 19--   3

4th line space

Address   Ms. Janet Miller   6
           1401 McKinley Avenue   11
           Houston, TX 77088   14

Salutation Dear Ms. Miller   17

Brent Whitten has just informed me that the Finance   28
Committee will hold its annual meeting in Houston on   38
June 5. Therefore, I need a motel reservation for   49
the evenings of the 4th and 5th.   55

Will you please take care of this matter for me,   65
either at the Hacienda or some comparable motel con-   76
Body   venient to the meeting site. I think the Hacienda   86
offers three different rates for single rooms. As   96
all of their facilities are excellent, the least   106
expensive rate available will be fine with me.   115

Perhaps we can get together for a short while on   125
Monday evening to discuss the agenda.   133

Complimentary close Sincerely yours   136
                                              Double-space

Company name   ADAMS AND ASSOCIATES   140
in closing

4th line space

Typed name and   Miss Kay Wiley   143
official title   Vice-President   146

Reference initials   eh   147

Business letter in block style

17b ■ Sentence Guided Writings ● As directed in 16c, page 27   *15 minutes*

		Words in Line	GWAM 20" Guide
1	SS Do the job as well as you can.	6	18
2	*Hard work is the secret of success.*	7	21
3	Plan your work right if you wish to win.	8	24
4	*Plan to make some gain in your work each day.*	9	27
5	Now is the day to do these lines in the right way.	10	30

| 1 | 2 | 3 | 4 | 5 | 6 | 7 | 8 | 9 | 10 |

17c ■ Continuity Practice   *10 minutes*

Directions—Type the copy below; circle the errors. Repeat; try to make fewer errors.

Technique Goal—Read, think, and type the short words as units, not letter by letter.

		GWAM 1'	2'
All letters DS	If you want to add some zest to what could	9	4
	well turn out to be a dull summer, here are some	18	9
	quick ideas. You can wax floors, mow lawns, make	28	14
57 words 1.1 si	and sell jewelry or other crafts, sit with kids,	38	19
	cats, dogs, and birds, or even keep watch on the	48	24
	house up the street when the owners are away.	57	29

1' | 1 | 2 | 3 | 4 | 5 | 6 | 7 | 8 | 9 | 10 |
2' | 1 | 2 | 3 | 4 | 5 |

17d ■ Sustained Skill Building   *8 minutes*

Directions—Type a 1-minute, then two 2-minute writings on the paragraph in 17c. Try to equal your 1-minute rate on the 2-minute writings.

Technique Goal — Gain speed by using quick, sharp strokes. Snap the finger toward the palm of the hand after each stroke.

17e ■ Centering Paragraph Copy   *5 minutes*

Directions—Type the paragraph in 17c on a half sheet of paper so that the space above and below the paragraph is even. Try typing the paragraph with no more than two errors.

Solution:
a. Number of lines on a half sheet. 33
b. Count lines and spaces between the lines in the paragraph. <u>11</u>
c. Subtract b from a. 22
d. Divide by 2. 11
e. From top edge of paper, space down to the 12th line. Start typing.

123b ■ Speed Stretcher • Use Speed Stretchers for 5-minute writings, or use each paragraph for 1-minute writings. *10 minutes*

All letters   1.4 si   5.3 awl   85% hfw

| | G W A M |
| | 1' | 5' |

DS Eventually, you will have to face the question about the kind of   13 | 3 49

career you will follow. You may have been advised already to choose a   27 | 5 51

career while you are still in school so that you can get ready for it.   41 | 8 55

Almost all jobs require some special training. Hopefully, you will   55 | 11 57

realize this fact before it's too late.   63 | 13 59

Just dreaming lazily about a career is not sufficient. Examine   13 | 15 61

yourself carefully. What can you do best? What do you enjoy doing?   27 | 18 64

Your parents and teachers have urged you to make a careful choice, and   41 | 21 67

then resolve to be the best in your field. This is wise advice. There   55 | 24 70

is room in any area if you are good enough.   64 | 25 72

As a general rule, you will be smart to avoid the trap that often   13 | 28 74

awaits those who know a little bit about a lot of things but not much   27 | 31 77

about anything in particular. The world has enough people like that.   40 | 34 80

Thousands of careers are available to almost anyone who wishes to   13 | 36 83

enter them. The problem is to discover the one that you can do well   27 | 39 85

and that you enjoy doing. If you cannot do it well, you'll fail. If   41 | 42 88

you dislike it, you'll miss one of the thrills life holds for us. You   55 | 45 91

certainly must select your career with care.   64 | 46 93

1' | 1 | 2 | 3 | 4 | 5 | 6 | 7 | 8 | 9 | 10 | 11 | 12 | 13 | 14 |
5' | 1   2   3 |

123c ■ Problem Typing
30 minutes

Problem 1 ■ *Business Letter in Block Style*

Directions—Type the model letter shown on page 203. Type the date on the 18th line space. (If necessary, see directions for addressing a small envelope which appear on page 84.)

• If a workbook is not available, use a small envelope or paper cut to small envelope size (6½ inches by 3⅝ inches).

Problem 2 ■ *Business Letter in Block Style*

Directions—Type the letter in Problem 1, but address it to Mrs. Marilyn Chmelka / 2000 South Rustin Street / Omaha, NE 68135. Supply an appropriate salutation. Address a small envelope.

LESSON 123 ■ PAGE 202

Lesson 18

18a ■ Keyboard Review
7 minutes

● If time permits after typing each line twice, type
1-minute writings on the last two lines. Figure your
gwam. Compare rates.

x   SS   sxs sxs xs xs lax lax mix mix fix fix box axe axle   Quick

p   ;p; ;p; p; p; play play plate plate plan plan pray   carriage return

to   to too told took top touch toward town total today   Resume

All letters   The two boys saw the young zebra near the big dam.   typing at once

          We expect Jeff Quick to take the pole vault prize.

| 1 | 2 | 3 | 4 | 5 | 6 | 7 | 8 | 9 . | 10 |

18b ■ Technique Builder—Typing Whole Words ● Each line twice
5 minutes

1   SS   he she then an and hand go got to torn he she they

2   end lend land fur for form fir firm me men man may   Type

3   go got to torn do down she held did if so also rug   whole words

4   I may pay the men to fix the torn fur rug for her.

| 1 | 2 | 3 | 4 | 5 | 6 | 7 | 8 | 9 | 10 |

18c ■ Continuity Practice
10 minutes

Directions—Type twice. Repeat if time permits.   **Technique Goal**—Return the carriage quickly. Start typing at once.

		GWAM 1'	3'
All letters DS We now know quite a lot about which jobs in		9	3 27
¶ 1 life are apt to cause the most stress. As a rule,		19	6 30
35 words 1.1 si those which require one to meet and deal with the		29	10 34
public each day head the list.		35	12 36
You need to give some extra thought as to how		44	15 39
you want to spend your working years. As you will		54	18 42
¶ 2 soon learn, the size of your paycheck each month		64	21 45
37 words 1.1 si is not the only thing to think about.		72	24 48

1' | 1 | 2 | 3 | 4 | 5 | 6 | 7 | 8 | 9 | 10 |
3' | 1   2   3   4 |

122c ■ Problem Typing

30 minutes

Problem 1 ■ Business Letter in Modified Block Style

Directions—1. Type the model letter shown on page 200. Type the date on the 18th line space.

2. Address a small envelope.

- Envelopes are printed on the back of the letterhead paper in the workbook. If a workbook is not available, use a small envelope or paper cut to small envelope size (6½ inches by 3⅝ inches).

- If necessary, see directions for addressing a small envelope which appear on page 84.

Problem 2 ■ Business Letter in Modified Block Style

50-space line
Modified block
Mixed punctuation
Small envelope

Directions—Type this letter exactly as shown in the model on page 200.

	Words
July 10, 19--	3
Mr. Robert D. Geltz	7
Public Works Director	11
296 North Alamo Street	16
Fort Worth, TX 79907	20
Dear Mr. Geltz:	23

Yesterday afternoon, during a layover at Stapleton Airport in Denver, I happened to view a film devoted to the problem of refuse collection in various cities.

33
44
55

Since the film provided a good explanation of the different methods of waste disposal, it would be excellent for our public relations program.

65
75
84

If the film is available for rent or purchase, I should very much appreciate learning how I might order a copy.

94
103
106

Sincerely yours,

109

- For this letter and for remaining letters in the book, use your own initials as reference initials.

Miss Nancy Enloe
City Manager

112
114

Lesson 123

● 70-space line

123a ■ Keyboard Review ● Each line at least three times

5 minutes

All letters SS   Pat required them to wear extra heavy fur jackets during the blizzard.

Figure-Symbol   This country has 6.5% of the world's people and 5.7% of its land area.

Eyes on copy as you return the carriage

o, i   Most older pilots violently opposed revision of admission regulations.

Easy   Half of them think they slept more than eight hours during each night.

| 1 | 2 | 3 | 4 | 5 | 6 | 7 | 8 | 9 | 10 | 11 | 12 | 13 | 14 |

18d ■ Sustained Skill Building

Directions—Type 1-, 2-, and 3-minute writings on the paragraphs in 18c. Circle errors; figure *gwam*. Try to equal your 1-minute rate on the longer writings.

• Use the 1- and 3-minute columns and scales to figure the 1- and 3-minute rates. For the 2-minute rate, use the 1-minute column and scale to get total words; then divide by 2.

18e ■ Centering Paragraph Copy

10 minutes

Directions—Type the paragraphs in 18c on a half sheet of paper so that the space above and below them is even.

Lesson 19

• 50-space line

19a ■ Keyboard Review • Each line twice

7 minutes

z   SS   aza aza za za zone zero size lazy doze dozen prize

c   dcd dcd cd cd cut ice cap cape can cancel cost cow

or   or for door floor force form more north short sort

Sharon may have paid more for this new skateboard.

All letters   Dave flew from Quebec to Danzig in just six hours.

| 1 | 2 | 3 | 4 | 5 | 6 | 7 | 8 | 9 | 10 |

Wrists and elbows still

19b ■ Technique Builder—One-Hand Words • Each line twice

5 minutes

1   SS   up as in we at my saw hip far him see upon care on

2   was ink car pop red inn bag pull read hill wet you

3   wear milk save lion star noon acre pink gave pupil

4   A brave pupil gave John See a savage lion at noon.

| 1 | 2 | 3 | 4 | 5 | 6 | 7 | 8 | 9 | 10 |

Type letter by letter

Wrists low and still

19c ■ Sentence Guided Writings • As directed in 16c, page 27

15 minutes

		Words in Line	GWAM 20″ Guide
1	SS	Most of us do far less than we can.	7	21
2		*Can you keep your fingers deeply curved?*	8	24
3		We fail to test the real power that is in us.	9	27
4		*I find that the more I know, the more I must learn.*	10	30
5		How much is it? Where do I pay? Can Joan see it?	10	30

| 1 | 2 | 3 | 4 | 5 | 6 | 7 | 8 | 9 | 10 |

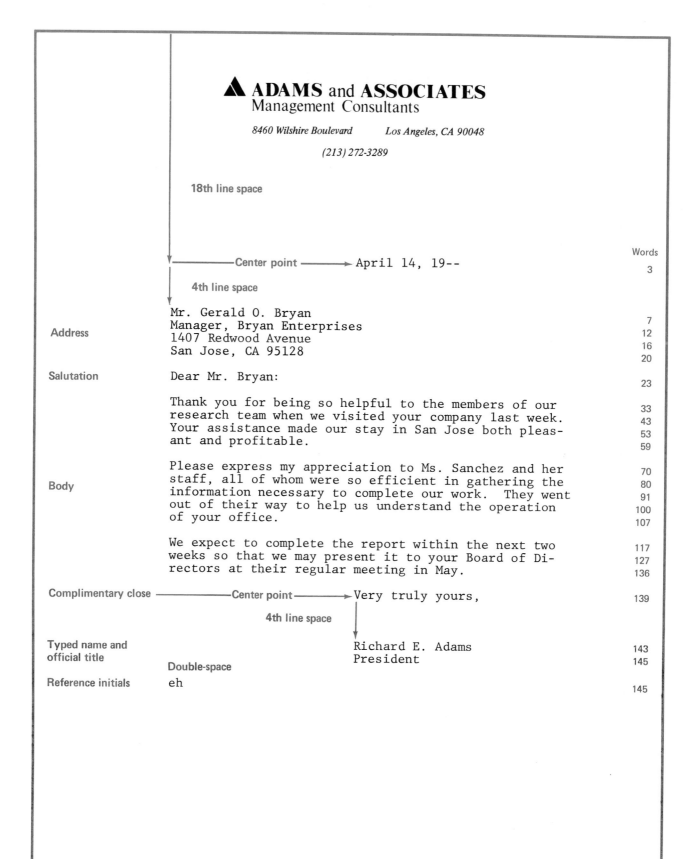

▲ ADAMS and ASSOCIATES
Management Consultants

8460 Wilshire Boulevard   Los Angeles, CA 90048

(213) 272-3289

18th line space

Words

————————Center point————→ April 14, 19--   3

4th line space

Address

Mr. Gerald O. Bryan   7
Manager, Bryan Enterprises   12
1407 Redwood Avenue   16
San Jose, CA 95128   20

Salutation

Dear Mr. Bryan: 23

Thank you for being so helpful to the members of our   33
research team when we visited your company last week.   43
Your assistance made our stay in San Jose both pleas-   53
ant and profitable.   59

Body

Please express my appreciation to Ms. Sanchez and her   70
staff, all of whom were so efficient in gathering the   80
information necessary to complete our work. They went 91
out of their way to help us understand the operation   100
of your office.   107

We expect to complete the report within the next two   117
weeks so that we may present it to your Board of Di-   127
rectors at their regular meeting in May.   136

Complimentary close ————————Center point————→ Very truly yours,   139

4th line space

Typed name and
official title   Richard E. Adams   143
                                        President   145
Double-space

Reference initials   eh   145

Business letter in modified block style

19d ■ Continuity Practice

10 minutes

Directions—Type twice. Repeat if time permits.

Technique Goals—Space quickly. Return carriage without looking from the copy.

		GWAM 1'	3'

All letters DS

¶ 1
47 words
1.1 si

Mark Twain said that nothing needs changing · 9 · 3 35

so much as the habits of others. He was thinking · 19 · 6 38

of the quirks all of us have. We spend most of · 28 · 9 41

our lives getting rid of them. No one knows just · 38 · 13 44

how much time we spend on this crazy game. · 47 · 16 47

We all know that some habits are good; some · 56 · 19 50

are bad. The bad ones can trap us as much as the · 66 · 22 53

¶ 2
48 words
1.1 si

good ones can help. We must feed well the traits · 76 · 25 57

that help. We must also put a sharp axe to those · 86 · 29 60

that can trap us before they grow into habits. · 95 · 32 63

```
1' |   1   |   2   |   3   |   4   |   5   |   6   |   7   |   8   |   9   |   10   |
3' |       1       |       2       |       3       |       4       |
```

19e ■ Sustained Skill Building

8 minutes

Directions—Type 1-, 2-, and 3-minute writings on the paragraphs in 19d. Try to equal your 1-minute rate on the longer writings.

Technique Goals—Feet on floor; body relaxed but erect. Fingers deeply curved; wrists low and still.

Lesson 20

● 50-space line

20a ■ Keyboard Review ● Each line twice

7 minutes

SS Rex found the quartz in jagged rock in New Mexico.

All letters

Easy

Easy

Burton will pay for the ticket so save it for him.

To type well, you must keep your eyes on the book.

Hold the wrists low and still as you hit the keys.

Quick, crisp, short strokes

```
|   1   |   2   |   3   |   4   |   5   |   6   |   7   |   8   |   9   |   10   |
```

20b ■ Technique Builder—Flowing Rhythm ● Each line three times from dictation

5 minutes

1   SS to my | and look | to see | to date | for her | for you

2   with you | and get | if you | it was | and be | did see

Flowing rhythm

Lesson 122

122a ■ Keyboard Review • Each line at least three times

5 minutes

All letters SS I have been lucky to exceed my first high quota and win a major prize.

Figure The Great Pyramid, 755 feet across by 481 feet high, covered 13 acres.

Type without pauses

Shift Early typewriter inventors included Pratt, Sholes, Glidden, and Soule.

Easy They tried to throw both of their keys down to us from an open window.

| 1 | 2 | 3 | 4 | 5 | 6 | 7 | 8 | 9 | 10 | 11 | 12 | 13 | 14 |

122b ■ Paragraph Guided Writings • As directed in 116b, page 188

10 minutes

DS

                           4   8   12   Words

People who repaired telephones years ago were to heed this rule: 13

                   16   .   20   .   24

"Treat others as you like to be treated, including your horse. To   27

65 words   28   .   32   .   36   .   40
1.3 si

understand the horse's side of it, merely remove your coat and hat some   41

           .   44   .   48   .   52   .

day, hitch yourself to the same post with your belt, and stand for two   55

       56   .   60   .   64

hours. In the future, don't forget the blanket."   65

| 1 | 2 | 3 | 4 | 5 | 6 | 7 | 8 | 9 | 10 | 11 | 12 | 13 | 14 |

Information About Business Letters

Letter Styles—With slight variations, the modified block style shown on page 200 is used in almost all business letters. Another style that is growing in usage is the block style illustrated on page 203.

Punctuation Styles—Two commonly used punctuations styles are open and mixed. In *open* punctuation no punctuation marks are used after the salutation or the complimentary close. In *mixed* punctuation a colon is placed after the salutation and a comma after the complimentary close.

Vertical Placement of Dateline—Vertical placement of the date varies with the length of the letter. However, in the majority of business letters the date is typed on line 18. The address is typed on the 4th line space (3 blank spaces) below the date.

Abbreviations—Excessive abbreviations should be avoided. It is acceptable, however, to abbreviate the state name in an address when using a ZIP Code. Leave one space between the state name and the ZIP Code.

Titles in Address—As a mark of courtesy, always use a personal or professional title on a letter, envelope, or card addressed to an individual: *Mr. Robert Wertz, Dr. Ann Hendricks.* When a woman's preferred title is unknown, use *Ms.* as the personal title.

Titles in Closing Lines—In the closing lines of a letter, a personal or professional title should not be used before the name of a male writer. A female may use a personal title if she wishes.

Reference Initials—Reference initials of the typist should always be typed two line spaces below the typed name of the writer of the letter.

Stationery Size—Most business letters are typed on 8½- by 11-inch stationery that is imprinted with the name and address of the company.

Envelopes—Use large or small envelopes for one-page letters and large envelopes for two-page letters or when enclosing materials within a letter.

20c ■ Sentence Guided Writings ● As directed in 16c, page 27

		Words in Line	GWAM 20" Guide

1   ss   *This drill will help you type well.*   7   21

2   We start many jobs that we never finish.   8   24

3   *A clear, sharp goal will help you type right.*   9   27

4   Start a job on time; do not stop until it is done.   10   30

5   *You will gain skill if you do a job the right way.*   10   30

| 1 | 2 | 3 | 4 | 5 | 6 | 7 | 8 | 9 | 10 |

20d ■ Continuity Practice

10 minutes

Directions—Two times. Repeat if time permits.

Technique Goal—Return the carriage quickly; resume typing at once.

	GWAM 1'	3'

All letters   **DS**   Someone with a quick wit once said that hay   9   3   33

is something we must make between the time we get   19   6   36

out of it and the time we hit it. These, I think,   29   10   40

are the exact words. The jet age, with its stress   39   13   43

on speed, moves the world along at a dizzy pace.   49   16   46

90 words   More work must be done than ever. There seems to   59   20   50
1.1 si

be much less time to do it; still we can squeeze   69   23   53

enough hours into a day to get our work done if we   79   26   56

keep in mind that the jet age makes each second   89   30   60

count.   90   30   60

| 1' | 1 | 2 | 3 | 4 | 5 | 6 | 7 | 8 | 9 | 10 |
| 3' | | 1 | | 2 | | 3 | | 4 | |

20e ■ Timed Writings

8 minutes

Directions—Type two 3-minute writings on 20d. Circle errors; figure *gwam*. Submit the better writing.

20f ■ Extra-Credit Typing

Directions—Type the paragraph in 20d on a half sheet of paper so that the space above and below it is even.

121c ■ Speed Ladder Paragraphs ● As directed in 116d, page 189   *20 minutes*

		G W A M
		1' 5'

All letters **DS**   As you have nearly completed your personal typewriting course,   13 | 3 55

¶ 1
44 words
1.4 si

it's well to take a brief glance at what you have accomplished. The   26 | 5 57

fact that you have typed this paragraph proves that some learning must   41 | 8 60

have taken place.   44 | 9 61

Your reasons for enrolling in this class likely differed. Some   57 | 11 63

¶ 2
48 words
1.3 si

wanted to learn to type because they felt it would help them in their   71 | 14 66

schoolwork. Others had an eye on the future, and they decided typing   85 | 17 69

might prove useful in getting a job.   92 | 18 70

Then, too, several students may have signed up because they felt   105 | 21 73

¶ 3
52 words
1.4 si

that learning to operate a typewriter would be fun. Chances are good   119 | 24 76

that you were not disappointed. It is fun to take a class in which   133 | 27 79

you do actually see the results of what you have learned.   144 | 29 81

No matter what your reasons for taking typing might have been, you   157 | 31 84

¶ 4
56 words
1.4 si

are sure to have gained enough basic skill to utilize this new tool to a   172 | 34 86

great extent. The personal-use typist needs to have the same command of   187 | 37 89

techniques as those students who take the class for vocational use.   200 | 40 92

It has required long hours of practice for you to reach your pres-   214 | 43 95

¶ 5
60 words
1.4 si

ent level of ability. If you neglect to maintain your speed, it will   227 | 45 98

gradually slip away from you. You have developed a skill that can be   241 | 48 100

of great assistance in the future. Make good use of it in your classes   256 | 51 103

All ¶'s
1.4 si

and in your daily life.   260 | 52 104

1' | 1 | 2 | 3 | 4 | 5 | 6 | 7 | 8 | 9 | 10 | 11 | 12 | 13 | 14 |
5' | 1   2   3 |

121d ■ Creative Typing ●   Type a paragraph, telling in your own words what the following quotation means to you.   *10 minutes*

"If it is to be, it is up to me."

UNIT 3 ■ Learning the Figure Keys

General Directions ■ Lessons 21 - 25

1. Single-space sentences and drill lines. Double-space between repeated groups of lines.

2. Double-space paragraph copy. Set a tabulator stop for a 5-space paragraph indention.

Lesson 21

● *Use a 50-space line for all lessons in this unit.*

21a ■ Keyboard Review ● Each line twice   7 minutes

● *On nearly all typewriters the figure* **1** *may be made with the letter* **l.**

SS Jacque will pick many bright flowers in the field.

All letters She gave us nearly six dozen of them to take home.

1 I saw lll deer in 11 weeks. We drove lll.1 miles.   Type **1** with the small letter **l**

Easy To type well, you must keep your eyes on the book.

Easy Keep your fingers well curved as you hit the keys.

| 1 | 2 | 3 | 4 | 5 | 6 | 7 | 8 | 9 | 10 |

21b ■ Location of 3 and 7   5 minutes

● *Reread the plan for learning the location and stroking of new keys given on page 4.*

Find **3** on the chart. Find it on your ←REACH TO 3 typewriter keyboard. Place your fingers over the home keys. Touch **d3d** lightly two or three times. Lift the first finger slightly to make the reach easily and naturally.

Type 3 with the d finger

REACH TO 7→ Find **7** on the chart. Find it on your typewriter keyboard. Place your fingers over the home keys. Touch **j7j** lightly two or three times. Make the reach without arching your wrist. Hold the other fingers in typing position.

Type 7 with the j finger

d3d d3d d3d 3d 3d 3d d3d   ● **Type twice on same line** ●   j7j j7j j7j 7j 7j 7j j7j

CYCLE 4 ■

Introduction to Business Typewriting

This cycle introduces you to some of the typewriting duties performed in the typical office.

Typing Business Letters—The two basic letter styles introduced in Cycle 2 are presented here as they are commonly used in business correspondence. You will learn how to set up letters of different lengths so that they are placed properly on the page.

Typing Business Forms—In Unit 16 you will type interoffice memorandums and invoices.

Extra-Credit Assignments—Problems are given at the end of the following Lessons for students who finish assignments: 130, 135, and 140.

Improving Your Basic Skills—By this time you have acquired considerable typewriting speed and control. Increases in speed do not come so rapidly now as they did early in the year. The skill-building material provided in this cycle will put the finishing touches on your typewriting skill.

UNIT 15 ■ Typing Business Letters

General Directions ■ Lessons 121 - 130

Machine Adjustments—Use a 70-space line for drills and timed writings in this unit. Single-space sentences and drill lines. Double-space between groups of repeated lines. Double-space paragraph copy. Much of the problem copy that you will type will be set in lines either longer or shorter than those for which your margins are set. It will be necessary for you to listen for the bell, to use the right margin release, and to divide long words coming at the ends of lines.

Correcting Errors—Your teacher will tell you whether or not you are to correct errors made on problem copy.

Special Forms—Type the problems on the special forms provided in the workbook or on plain paper.

Lesson 121

• *Use a 70-space line for all lessons in this unit.*

121a ■ Keyboard Review • Each line at least three times   *5 minutes*

All letters **SS** We made only the best quality kegs for all our expensive frozen juice.

Figure-Symbol Their bill came to $465.70, but it was not due until December 3, 1982.

Adjacent keys We were sure that her partner's voice was barely heard over the noise.

Easy Talk becomes cheap when there is a bigger supply than there is demand.

| 1 | 2 | 3 | 4 | 5 | 6 | 7 | 8 | 9 | 10 | 11 | 12 | 13 | 14 |

Begin slowly; increase speed gradually

121b ■ Speed Ladder Sentences •

Two 1-minute writings on each sentence. Your teacher may call the guide for you.

10 minutes

			GWAM		
			15"	12"	10"
1	SS	Decide what level of skill you believe you can acquire.	44	55	66
2		Be determined to attain the level you have set for yourself.	48	60	72
3		During every practice session, keep this goal fixed in your mind.	52	65	78
4		If you heed these suggestions, your typing ability is sure to improve.	56	70	84

| 1 | 2 | 3 | 4 | 5 | 6 | 7 | 8 | 9 | 10 | 11 | 12 | 13 | 14 |

21c ■ Location Drills—3 and 7

10 minutes

Directions—Each line twice.   **Technique Goal**—Think the figure as you type it.

3   SS   d3d d3d d3d 3d 3d 3d 33 days, 333 hours, 33 and 33

            Give us 333 feet.   Take 3,333 gallons.   I have 33.

Type **3** with
the **d** finger

7   j7j j7j j7j 7j 7j 7j 77 jars, 77 jolts, 77 and 777

            Send 77 sets.   Paint 777 frames.   Ship 7,777 pens.

Type **7** with
the **j** finger

Number
fluency

            I sent you 33 feet of wire and 77 pounds of nails.

            Only 37 of the 73 boys were at the game on May 13.

        | 1 | 2 | 3 | 4 | 5 | 6 | 7 | 8 | 9 | 10 |

21d ■ Technique Builder—Flowing Rhythm ● Five times from dictation   6 minutes

1   SS   and date | and look | and grade | and limp | and right

2   to regard | to jump | to show | to start | to do | to be

Flowing
rhythm

3   the date | the rest | the fee | the order | the letter

21e ■ Continuity Practice

17 minutes

Directions—1. Type the paragraph. When you complete typing it, circle any errors you may have made.

2. Type the paragraph again. Center it on a half sheet of paper. Circle your errors. Try to make no more than four errors.

| | | G W A M |
| | | 1' | 3' |

All letters DS   School trains you to do the things you should   9 | 3 34

            even though you may think they are a waste of time.   20 | 7 38

            In growing up, you will find that it is the little   30 | 10 41

            things that count.   From small deeds well done, you   40 | 13 44

93 words
1.1 si   learn how to handle jobs of large size.   You may   50 | 17 48

            not be quite ready to run your school, but you can   60 | 20 51

            do a lot of things to help.   Do those things extra   71 | 24 55

            well.   In time, they may teach you to run a school,   81 | 27 58

            solve the problems of peace, or fly a spaceship to   91 | 30 61

            the moon.   93 | 31 62

    1' | 1 | 2 | 3 | 4 | 5 | 6 | 7 | 8 | 9 | 10 |
    3' | 1 | 2 | 3 | 4 |

Cycle 4

Introduction To
Business Typewriting

Lesson 22

22a ■ Keyboard Review • Each line twice   *7 minutes*

All letters **SS**   A quiz on the constitution will be held on Friday.
                      Next week she plans to give the major examination.

3   d3d d3d 3d 3d 313 desks, 33 sets, 33 and 33 and 13   Quiet wrists
                                                                             and arms
7   j7j j7j 7j 7j 717 pints, 77 pens, 77 and 77 and 17

Easy   Hit all the keys with short, quick, sharp strokes.

                      | 1 | 2 | 3 | 4 | 5 | 6 | 7 | 8 | 9 | 10 |

22b ■ Continuity Practice • Type the paragraph as many times as you can in the time allotted.   *6 minutes*

                                                                             Words

DS   We climbed the hill until it was too dark to   9

Type   see. We climbed the hill until it was too dark to   19
without
pauses   see the road. We climbed the hill until it was too   30

         dark to see the road that led to the city.   38

         | 1 | 2 | 3 | 4 | 5 | 6 | 7 | 8 | 9 | 10 |

22c ■ Location of 5 and 9   *5 minutes*

Find **5** on the chart. Find it on your ←REACH TO 5   REACH TO 9→ Find **9** on the chart. Find it on your typewriter keyboard. Place your fingers over the home keys. Touch **f5f** lightly two or three times. Keep your left wrist low as you make the reach. Avoid moving your hand forward.

keyboard. Place your fingers over the home keys. Touch **191** lightly two or three times. Lift the first and second fingers slightly to make the reach to **9** easily.

Type 5 with the f finger

Type 9 with the l finger

f5f f5f f5f 5f 5f 5f f5f   • Type twice on same line •   191 191 191 91 91 91 191

22d ■ Location Drills—5 and 9   *6 minutes*

Directions—Each line twice.   **Technique Goal**—Think the figure as you type it.

5   **SS**   f5f f5f f5f 5f 5f 5f 55 files, 551 feet, 55 and 55   Type 5 with
                                                                  the f finger
             Sell 515 sets. Order 5,551 books. Mail 515 pins.

9   191 191 191 91 91 91 99 lakes, 919 lids, 99 and 99   Type 9 with
                                                                  the l finger
             Buy 19 dozen. Sell 191 sets. Pay for 19 and 991.

120d ■ Problem Measurement

Problem 1 ■ One-Page Report

Directions—1. Type this one-page report in regular report style.
2. Type the footnote in correct form at the bottom of the page.

- *Directions for typing a one-page report are given in the problem on page 94. Directions for typing footnotes are given on page 143. Refer to these pages if necessary.*

MAKING USE OF THE LIBRARY

When you go to the library to study or read for pleasure, you go to a room with something more than just four walls and a number of tables. No other room in your school is quite like it. It is here that you can find the key that opens the door to a whole new world for you. It is here that you can meet the wisest and wittiest people of all time.

Plato will not mind it at all if you want to turn back the pages of time to get his views on philosophy—neither will Mozart if you want to get his help in composing an opera. On the other hand, if you feel like laughing, Bennett Cerf will be glad to oblige with some of the funniest stories ever told.

Public libraries can be of great help to you, too, especially since they are generally open after school hours and on Saturdays. Some of them have separate departments which feature materials on careers, sports, travel, and other subjects of interest to teenagers. They sponsor programs geared to the interests of young adults, involving discussions of books, films, popular music, and current social issues.[1]

Books are arranged according to a system that has been worked out by librarians. Learn enough about the system to help you get the books you want quickly and easily.

---

[1] "Library," The World Book Encyclopedia (1976), XII, p. 221.

Problem 2 ■ Outline

Directions—1. Type this brief outline of a speech on a half sheet of paper.

2. Indent, space, capitalize, and punctuate the outline correctly. Place it in the exact vertical center of the page.

- *You may want to refer to 87c, page 150, for assistance in spacing your outline correctly.*

using an encyclopedia

```
  I introduction
     A importance of encyclopedia as a reference
     B rules for library use
 II body
     A how to locate information
        1 look first in the regular alphabetical place
        2 always look for last names of persons
        3 in words of two or more parts, look for the first part
     B miscellaneous hints
III conclusion
```

120e ■ Extra-Credit Typing

Problem 1

Type a note of regret to a friend who has asked you to attend a movie. Look at problem 2, page 190, for ideas, but type the message in your own words.

Problem 2

Type a postal card announcement for one of the clubs in your school. If necessary, refer to Problem 1, page 190, for help in arranging your material.

22e ■ Sentence Guided Writings

10 minutes

Directions—Type each sentence for a 1-minute writing with the call of the guide each 20 seconds. Try to complete each sentence as the guide is called.

			Words in Line	GWAM 20" Guide
1	SS	Try to type each line as time is called.	8	24
2		*Type with a keen mind and quick strokes.*	8	24
3		I must try to type with quiet hands and arms.	9	27
4		*Try to raise your rate by one word each line.*	9	27
5		If I type well, I can win the prize of high speed.	10	30
6		*When work takes the place of words, we gain skill.*	10	30

| 1 | 2 | 3 | 4 | 5 | 6 | 7 | 8 | 9 | 10 |

22f ■ Sustained Skill Building

11 minutes

Directions—Type 1-, 2-, and two 3-minute writings on the paragraph in 21e, page 35. Compute *gwam*. Try to equal your 1-minute rate on the longer writings.

• *For the 2-minute rate, use the 1-minute column and scale to get total words; then divide by 2.*

Lesson 23

• *50-space line*

23a ■ Keyboard Review • Each line twice

7 minutes

All letters	SS	Mike W. Cruz gave up his tax job and left quickly.
5, 9		f5f 191 f5f 191 5f 91 55 fans, 99 lads, 191 and 55
3, 7		He bought 173 cars. Our tour covered 3,737 miles.
Easy		Work is fun if you make it fun and do it all well.

Eyes on this copy

| 1 | 2 | 3 | 4 | 5 | 6 | 7 | 8 | 9 | 10 |

23b ■ Technique Builder—Flowing Rhythm

6 minutes

Directions—Each line five times from dictation.

Technique Goal—Blend your typing into flowing rhythm.

1	SS	if it did	if it did look	and if they were	to trade
2		it is the	it is the best	and if she reads	and pull
3		to do the	to do the best	for if they fear	they are
4		if we are	if we are free	and if they look	she sees

Flowing rhythm

119e ■ Division Sign and Degree Symbol ● Each line three times   *5 minutes*

Division sign—Type the hyphen over the colon.
Degree symbol—Pull the rachet release lever (No. 6) forward. Turn the left cylinder knob toward you slightly; type the small letter o without space between the figure and the symbol; return the rachet release lever to its original position.

1   SS   Here are my three problems: 96 ÷ 8 = 12. 96 ÷ 4 = 24. 248 ÷ 8 = 31.

2   Do you know that water boils at 212°; milk, at 215°; alcohol, at 152°?   Sit erect

| 1 | 2 | 3 | 4 | 5 | 6 | 7 | 8 | 9 | 10 | 11 | 12 | 13 | 14 |

Lesson 120
● *70-space line*

120a ■ Keyboard Review ● Each line at least three times   *5 minutes*

All letters SS   A judge watched Max very quickly analyze bad checks the forger passed.

Figure   Track and field events attracted 427,171 persons at the 1932 Olympics.   Quiet wrists and arms

4th finger   Paula, please play the part in the play. The play will open in April.

Easy   Your mind is like a good knife; it must be used often to remain sharp.

| 1 | 2 | 3 | 4 | 5 | 6 | 7 | 8 | 9 | 10 | 11 | 12 | 13 | 14 |

120b ■ Number Expression Guides ● Read the explanations. Type each example sentence three times.   *5 minutes*

Line 1—Use figures to type dates. When the day comes before the month, use a figure and follow it with *th, st,* or *d.*

Line 2—Spell a number beginning a sentence even though figures may be used later in the sentence.

Line 3—Use figures with *a.m.* and *p.m.* Use words with *o'clock.*

1   SS   We moved on May 26, 1980. I started to work on the 15th of September.

2   Fifty more were needed; only 25 applied. Eighty dollars is the price.

3   I will arrive at 9:45 p.m. I can leave at six o'clock in the morning.

| 1 | 2 | 3 | 4 | 5 | 6 | 7 | 8 | 9 | 10 | 11 | 12 | 13 | 14 |

120c ■ Speed Builder ● Type a 1-minute writing to set your goal rate; then type a 3-minute writing as your teacher calls the return at the end of each minute.   *5 minutes*

DS   If you are looking for a relaxing new hobby, one that will enable
you to remain sharp and alert, look into the art of juggling. Keeping

60 words
1.4 si   several items in the air at once is not only challenging, it is also   Flowing rhythmic stroking

good for you. Think how much exercise you will get by bending over to

retrieve your mistakes.

23c ■ Location of 4, 8, and : (colon)

5 minutes

Find **4** on the chart. Find it on your ←REACH TO 4   REACH TO 8→ Reach up with the k finger; typewriter keyboard. Place your fingers over the home keys. Touch **f4f** lightly two or three times. Keep your wrist low and quiet. Do not move your hand forward.

touch **k8k** two or three times.

LOCATION OF COLON

The : (colon) is the shift of ;. Touch ;:; two or three times. Space twice after : used as punctuation.

• Type twice on same line •

Type 4 with the f finger

f4f f4f f4f 4f 4f 4f f4f

Type 8 with the k finger

The : is the shift of ;

k8k k8k k8k 8k 8k 8k k8k

;:; ;:; ;:; :; :; :; ;:;

23d ■ Location Drills—4, 8, and :

Each line twice
Eyes on copy

8 minutes

4   SS   f4f f4f f4f 4f 4f 4f 44 firs, 414 files, 4414 feet

Pay in 44 days.   Mark 4,414 tags.   Send 14 and 44.

Type 4 with the **f** finger

8   k8k k8k k8k 8k 8k 8k 88 kits, 18 kites, 8,818 ties

Dig 818 feet.   Walk 18 miles.   Buy 8,188 new sets.

Type 8 with the **k** finger

;:; ;:; :; :; Dear Sir: Note: To: Dear Dr. Yue:

: is shift of ;

23e ■ Technique Builder—Flowing Rhythm

Each line three times; 1-minute writing on each. Compare gwam.

8 minutes

Word   SS This is her job, and she is to do it when she can.   Think words

Letter   Phyllis Aster was at ease in Red Cave in Honolulu.   Think letters

Combination   We saw Kim jump in the lake; she was in rare form.   Flowing rhythm

| 1 | 2 | 3 | 4 | 5 | 6 | 7 | 8 | 9 | 10 |

23f ■ Paragraph Guided Writings

11 minutes

Directions—1. Type for one minute. Note the *gwam*. Add four words to your *gwam* for a new goal.

2. Type three more 1-minute writings. Try to reach your new goal on each writing.

3. Type for one minute at your first rate. Your goal this time is to type without error.

Words

DS   My guide said that people are like trees.   As   9

long as they grow toward the sunlight, they fill   19

47 words
1.1 si

their places in the forest.   They fight for root   29

space in the earth and for sun and air among the   39

other trees.   When they give up, they die.   47

| 1 | 2 | 3 | 4 | 5 | 6 | 7 | 8 | 9 | 10 |

119b ▪ Punctuation Guides—Apostrophe ● Read the explanation carefully; then type each example sentence twice. *15 minutes*

Line 1—Use an apostrophe in writing contractions.
Line 2—*It's* means *it is. Its,* the possessive pronoun, does not take an apostrophe.
Line 3—Use the contraction *o'clock* (of the clock) in writing time.
Line 4—Add *'s* to form the possessive of any singular noun.
Line 5—Add *'s* to plural nouns that do not end in s.
Line 6—If a plural noun does end in s, add only an apostrophe after the s.

Line 7—The apostrophe denotes possession. Do not use it merely to form the plural of a noun.
Line 8—Use *'s,* however, to form the plural of figures, letters, signs, and words referred to as words.
Line 9—To show possession add an apostrophe and s to a proper name of one syllable which ends in s.
Line 10—To show possession add only an apostrophe to a proper name of more than one syllable which ends in s.

1	SS	It's here. She's home now. Don't go yet. I'll go, but I can't stay.
2		The sophomore class will hold its picnic soon; I hope it's a nice day.
3		If they're not here by four o'clock, we'll have to go on without them.
4		every person's rights, my son-in-law's car, Elizabeth's pin, Hal's cap
5		twelve women, twelve women's coats; eighteen men, eighteen men's ties;
6		six girls, six girls' French books; four couples, four couples' houses
7		There were only three boys in each room. There is the new boy's room.
8		My i's look just like e's; my 3's, like 5's. Take out all the that's.
9		The Jones's land is several miles down the road from the Sims's ranch.
10		Aunt Virginia enjoyed reading the story to Mrs. Roberts' son, William.

Type steadily

| 1 | 2 | 3 | 4 | 5 | 6 | 7 | 8 | 9 | 10 | 11 | 12 | 13 | 14 |

119c ▪ Paragraph Guided Writings ● As directed in 116b, page 188   *10 minutes*

DS

60 words
1.4 si

It seems that most people just can't resist trying to look into the future. As yet, though, no one has found a surefire method for predicting all aspects of it. Our hunger to learn what lies ahead is not mere curiosity. We need to possess some knowledge of the future in order to plan our actions.

Blend fast and slow stroking for flowing rhythm

119d ▪ Skill Comparison ● Two 1-minute writings on each sentence. Compare rates.   *10 minutes*

1.0 si	SS	To know how to do work well and to know that you know is a good thing.
1.2 si		We can learn to work, as there are many ways open to the right person.
1.3 si		Everyone should learn to work well with others on many kinds of tasks.
1.4 si		The people who really like their work lead much more satisfying lives.

Flowing rhythm

| 1 | 2 | 3 | 4 | 5 | 6 | 7 | 8 | 9 | 10 | 11 | 12 | 13 | 14 |

Lesson 24

24a ■ Keyboard Review • Each line twice
7 minutes

SS The people have really acquired a taste for pizza.

All letters — Many also go there to listen to their new jukebox. — Sit erect

4, 8 — f4f k8k f4f k8k 4f 8k 44 firs, 88 kits, 881 and 44

: — Use the colon with numbers: 7:45, 8:15, and 7:35. — Quiet wrists and arms

Easy — We know that tact fails the instant it is noticed.

| 1 | 2 | 3 | 4 | 5 | 6 | 7 | 8 | 9 | 10 |

24b ■ Location of 2 and 0
5 minutes

Find **2** on the chart. Find it on your ←**REACH TO 2**   **REACH TO 0**→ Find **0** on the chart. Find it on your keyboard. Place your fingers on the home keys. Touch **s2s** lightly two or three times. Lift the little finger slightly to give you freedom of action.

keyboard. Place your fingers over the home keys. Touch **;0;** lightly two or three times. Keep elbows quiet and hold the other fingers in typing position.

Type 2 with the s finger

s2s s2s s2s 2s 2s 2s s2s

● **Type twice on same line** ●

Type 0 with the ; finger

;0; ;0; ;0; 0; 0; 0; ;0;

24c ■ Location Drills—2 and 0
6 minutes

Directions—Each line twice.

Technique Goal—Keep the elbows and wrists motionless.

2 — SS s2s s2s s2s 2s 2s 2s 22 suits, 212 slides, 22 sets — Type 2 with the s finger

I am 22. I walked 212 miles in 22 days, 12 hours.

0 — ;0; ;0; ;0; 0; 0; 0; 100 pets, 110 pints, 909 tons — Type 0 with the ; finger

We may have 20, 30, 40, or 50 of these long forms.

24d ■ Script Builder
15 minutes

Directions—**1.** Type the paragraph twice for practice; then type two 1-minute writings. Figure *gwam*.

2. Type two 1-minute writings on paragraph 23f, page 38. Figure *gwam*. Compare rates on the two paragraphs.

		Words
All letters	DS	Do you realize that not all firms require one — 9
35 words 1.2 si		to go to work five days a week? Some of them will — 19
		let people put in extra hours so they can finish — 29
		their jobs in only four days. — 35

118c ■ Problem Measurement
30 minutes

Problem 1 ■ Personal/Business Letter

Full sheet
50-space line
Indented paragraphs
Mixed punctuation

Directions—1. Type the letter below as a personal/business letter in modified block style. Type the return address on the 18th line space.
2. Prepare a carbon copy. Address a small envelope. Fold the letter; insert it.

Return address—115 Orange Drive / Pekin, IL 61554 / *Current date*

Address—Miss Karen Fleming / Karen's Specialty Shop / 38 Clovis Avenue / Chicago, IL 60646

Dear Miss Fleming:

Thank you very much for sending me the special birthday candle I ordered when I was in your shop last Saturday.

I am glad to learn that in the future I shall be able to order these candles by mail. They make such unique birthday gifts.

Enclosed is the list of names I promised to send you. You will find all these people potential customers, I am sure.

Sincerely yours,
Miss Lorraine Johnson

Enclosure

Problem 2 ■ Poem

Directions—1. Type the poem in the exact vertical center on a half sheet of paper.

2. Center the copy horizontally by the second line of the first verse.

Loco-Motive

Down at the station I like to see the trains
Sticking out their chests and coming down the lanes
Dinging and a-hooing, reaching out their light--
How I wish that trains wouldn't cry at night.
Out in the country, rushing through the grass,
Trains seem happy, purring as they pass,
Or across the highway, clatter-banging by--
Why in the night time do the trains cry?

—Augusta Towner Reid

Problem 3 ■ Personal/Business Letter

Full sheet
50-space line
Open punctuation

Directions—Type the letter in Problem 1, above as a personal/business letter in block style. Type the return address on the 18th line space.

Lesson 119

● *70-space line*

119a ■ Keyboard Review ● Each line at least three times
5 minutes

All letters **SS**	Jasper waited in the quaint city of Bozeman before going to Knoxville.	
Figure	Grange, retired in 1935, carried the ball 32,820 yards in 4,000 tries.	Quick, crisp,
Double letters	A need for referring all necessary letters for approval was discussed.	short strokes
Easy	The robot shown in the movies looked as if it came from another world.	

| 1 | 2 | 3 | 4 | 5 | 6 | 7 | 8 | 9 | 10 | 11 | 12 | 13 | 14 |

24e ■ Continuity Practice

12 minutes

Directions—1. Type the two paragraphs twice. Circle any errors you may make.

2. Center the first paragraph on a half sheet of paper. Try for no more than two errors.

		GWAM
		1' 3'

All letters **DS** A good grade is the prize you get when you bet | 9 | 3 34

on yourself. You can collect the prize if you lay | 20 | 7 37

¶ 1
44 words
1.2 si

your talents and your will to learn each lesson on | 30 | 10 41

the line. Your efforts must be equal to the prize | 40 | 13 44

if you expect to win. | 44 | 15 46

Do not forget that the grade is just a symbol. | 9 | 18 49

What counts are the things you learn and the new | 19 | 21 52

¶ 2
48 words
1.2 si

skills you acquire. These are the lasting rewards | 28 | 25 55

of learning. A poor grade is the only thing you | 39 | 29 59

can get in this world without working for it. | 48 | 31 62

```
1' |  1  |  2  |  3  |  4  |  5  |  6  |  7  |  8  |  9  |  10  |
3' |     1     |     2     |     3     |     4     |
```

Lesson 25

• 50-space *line*

25a ■ Keyboard Review • Each line twice

7 minutes

SS Requiring better helmets can help reduce injuries.

All letters

Mickey Lopez won five prizes in the exciting race.

2   s2s s2s 2s 2s 22 sets, 221 slides, 22 or 222 suits   Sit erect
with elbows in

0   ;0; ;0; 0; 0; 10 pans, 101 plans, 10 or 100 plants

Easy You can judge them by the books they like to read.

```
|  1  |  2  |  3  |  4  |  5  |  6  |  7  |  8  |  9  |  10  |
```

25b ■ Technique Builder—Flowing Rhythm

5 minutes

Directions—Each line five times from dictation.

Technique Goal—Blend your typing into flowing rhythm.

1 **SS** and the set | and the sea | and the ink | and the oil

2   if they bet | if they hop | if they see | if they get Flowing rhythm

3   for the ear | for the car | for the set | for the inn

Lesson 118

• *70-space line*

118a ■ Keyboard Review • Each line at least three times   *5 minutes*

All letters   **SS**   We quickly explained most of Mr. Beltzig's peculiar views to the jury.

Figure   The population of Phoenix expanded very rapidly between 1950 and 1960.   Flowing

4th finger   Paul and Polly were appalled by the opposite views of the politicians.   rhythmic

Easy   Profit depends on whether you keep your mind or your feet on the desk.   stroking

| 1 | 2 | 3 | 4 | 5 | 6 | 7 | 8 | 9 | 10 | 11 | 12 | 13 | 14 |

118b ■ Speed Stretcher • Use Speed Stretchers for 5-minute writings, or use each paragraph for 1-minute writings.   *10 minutes*

GWAM
1' | 5'

All letters   **DS**

¶ 1
64 words
1.3 si

The renting business seems to be growing by leaps and bounds these   13 | 3 47

days. Just about everyone rents something at one time or other. It's   28 | 6 50

true that you can rent almost anything you need—even an elephant. The   42 | 8 53

price is a little high, of course, so you may want to consider a lion;   56 | 11 56

they cost only about one-third as much.   64 | 13 57

¶ 2
55 words
1.4 si

Renting is often cheaper than buying. In cities where parking   13 | 15 60

costs a lot, people rent autos so they don't have to pay for space in   27 | 18 63

a garage. It can be an inexpensive way to impress others. Some people   41 | 21 66

rent fur coats for special evenings, and some rent flashy sports cars.   55 | 24 69

¶ 3
50 words
1.4 si

Storage can be a problem for the buyer. Those who live in small   13 | 26 71

houses or apartments rent things they don't use very often, such as   27 | 29 74

tuxedos and power tools. They come out ahead because they don't have   41 | 32 77

to wonder about where to store them afterwards.   50 | 34 79

¶ 4
54 words
1.4 si

You'll probably be amazed to discover that it is possible to rent   13 | 36 81

a new lawn for an outdoor party. The lawn comes in squares of grass.   27 | 39 84

They are laid like tiles in less than an hour. After the party the   41 | 42 87

All ¶'s
1.3 si

grass is removed, and the lawn reverts to its original condition.   54 | 45 89

1' | 1 | 2 | 3 | 4 | 5 | 6 | 7 | 8 | 9 | 10 | 11 | 12 | 13 | 14 |
5' | 1 | 2 | 3 |

LESSON 118 ■ PAGE 191

25c ■ Location of 6 and 1

Find **6** on the chart. Find it on your ←REACH TO 6
typewriter keyboard.
Place your fingers over
the home keys. Touch
j6j lightly two or three
times. Make the reach
without arching your
wrist. Hold other fin-
gers in typing posi-
tion.

REACH TO 1→ Find **1** on the chart. Find it on your
typewriter keyboard.
Place your fingers over
the home keys. Touch
ala lightly two or three
times. Make the reach
without moving the
elbow in or out.

**Type 6 with
the j finger**

**Type 1 with
the a finger**

j6j j6j j6j 6j 6j 6j j6j   • Type twice on same line •   ala ala ala la la la ala

---

25d ■ Location Drills—6 and 1 • Each line twice   *8 minutes*

6   SS   j6j j6j j6j 6j 6j 6j 66 jolts, 66,666 jets, 6 or 6   Type **6** with
                                                                     the **j** finger
          I weigh 66 pounds. Send 666 now. Collect 66 now.

1   ala ala ala la la la either 11, 111, or 1,111 rods   Type **1** with
                                                                     the **a** finger
          Go north for 11 miles; then go east for 111 miles.

     | 1 | 2 | 3 | 4 | 5 | 6 | 7 | 8 | 9 | 10 |

25e ■ Sentence Guided Writings   *8 minutes*

Directions—Type each sentence for a 1-minute writing with the call of the guide each 20 seconds. Try to
complete each sentence as the guide is called.

		Words in Line	GWAM 20" Guide
1	SS	Please send them 1,600 prints.	6 / 18
2		Can Anne go there in 60 days? How?	7 / 21
3		Did Nell sell all she had? She sold 11.	8 / 24
4		They sold 66 tickets to the game on April 16.	9 / 27
5		Can the bus take the band to Portland in 16 hours?	10 / 30

     | 1 | 2 | 3 | 4 | 5 | 6 | 7 | 8 | 9 | 10 |

25f ■ Sustained Skill Building   *12 minutes*

Directions—1. Type two 1-minute writings on ¶ 1,
24e, page 40, then type two 1-minute writings on ¶ 2.
Figure your *gwam*.

2. Type two 3-minute writings on both paragraphs.
Circle errors. Figure *gwam* on the better writing.
Compare your 3-minute rate with your 1-minute
rate.

Lesson 117

117a ■ Keyboard Review • Each line at least three times

All letters **SS** Julia got very few dark boxes of any size in the shipment from Quincy.

Figure   More than 6,000 people left between June 25, 1897, and March 24, 1923.

Balanced- and one-hand   for you, for trade, for him, for war, for your, for fear, for millions

Easy   The world does not owe you a living today; it is your duty to earn it.

Wrists and elbows still

| 1 | 2 | 3 | 4 | 5 | 6 | 7 | 8 | 9 | 10 | 11 | 12 | 13 | 14 |

117b ■ Concentration Practice • Type as many times as you can in the time allowed.

10 minutes

Words

DS   Irving Berlin has written over 800 songs, including those for 26   13

60 words
1.5 si

stage shows and several movies. A few of the most famous are "God Bless   28

America," "There's No Business Like Show Business," "White Christmas,"   42

and "Easter Parade." When he was 74, Mr. Berlin was back on Broadway   56

with "Mr. President."   60

| 1 | 2 | 3 | 4 | 5 | 6 | 7 | 8 | 9 | 10 | 11 | 12 | 13 | 14 |

117c ■ Problem Measurement

30 minutes

Problem 1 ■ Postal Card Announcement

Directions—1. Use a postal card or paper cut to proper size (5½- by 3¼-inches). Insert the card, short side at the left, in your typewriter.

2. Center each line horizontally. Center the announcement vertically.

3. Address the card to your name and address. No return address.

• *Directions for finding the center of odd-size paper are on page 67.*

EDUCATION COMMITTEE MEETINGS
TO BE AT HIGH SCHOOL

Please watch bulletin for dates and times

For further information, call:

Mrs. Myra Young, Cochairperson
3982 East Gettysburg Avenue, 225-4850
or
Mr. Paul Russell, Cochairperson
5167 North Fourth Street, 435-8062

Problem 2 ■ Informal Regret to Invitation

Directions—Type the informal regret below. Use 4¼ - by 5½-inch stationery. Arrange the copy attractively.

8924 Langer Drive / Dallas, TX 75206 / *Current date*

Dear Carol
   You were so thoughtful to ask us to attend the Community Theater performance on Wednesday evening. Unfortunately, Ken has to work late that week, and we cannot accept your kind invitation. (¶) Thanks for thinking of us, Carol. I hope we can take a rain check for a future time. / Sincerely

Problem 3 ■ Postal Card Annoucement

Directions—Follow the directions given in Problem 1. Type your own name, address, and telephone number as a cochairperson. Type the same kind of information about a friend you want to designate as your cochairperson.

UNIT 4 ■ Improving Your Basic Skills

General Directions ■ Lessons 26 - 30

Spacing—Single-space lines of words and sentences; double-space between repeated groups of lines. Double-space paragraph copy, setting a tabulator stop for a 5-space paragraph indention.

Special Machine Parts—Several useful machine parts are explained in these lessons. They include the tabulator control, the margin release key, and the shift lock.

Lesson 26

● Use a 50-space line for the lessons in this unit.

26a ■ Keyboard Review ● Each line twice   7 minutes

SS Judy now plans to take her driving quiz next week.

All letters

Most kids cannot get there before the end of June.

3, 7   Please add 33 and 77. He is 37; his mother is 73.   Quiet wrists
                                                            and arms

he   he her here head help she when where neither other

Easy   He may also throw their ball down the field to me.

| 1 | 2 | 3 | 4 | 5 | 6 | 7 | 8 | 9 | 10 |

26b ■ Sentence Guided Writings   15 minutes

Directions—1. Type each sentence for a 1-minute writing with the call of the guide each 20 seconds. Try to complete each sentence as the guide is called.

2. Type the last two sentences for additional 1-minute writings, as time permits, without the call of the guide.

			Words in Line	GWAM 20" Guide
1	SS	Type with your fingers well curved.	7	21
2		We read 27 pages in our new lesson.	7	21
3		Try to strike the keys in the right way.	8	24
4		I set a new record of 38 words a minute.	8	24
5		To type right, hold the wrists low and quiet.	9	27
6		Will they need 140 tons of sand for that job?	9	27
7		Hand in all papers at the end of the class period.	10	30
8		Does Highway 956 offer a better route to the city?	10	30

| 1 | 2 | 3 | 4 | 5 | 6 | 7 | 8 | 9 | 10 |

116d ■ Speed Ladder Paragraphs *20 minutes*

● *The following paragraphs are in speed ladder form. They may be used for a variety of drills. Two practice suggestions are described here. Your teacher will tell you which one to use.*

Speed Ladder—Type the first paragraph for 1 minute. When you can type it at the rate specified, type the next paragraph. Keep climbing the ladder until you reach the top.

Control Ladder—Type a 1-minute writing on the first paragraph. Move to the second and succeeding paragraphs only when you have completed each one within the error limit specified by your teacher.

		GWAM		
		1'	5'	

All letters DS While we do not need to be experts on Emily Post to make our way `13` | `3  55`

¶ 1
44 words
1.3 si

in the world, all of us need to treat others with courtesy. We are `27` | `5  57`

simply using standard ways of showing courtesy when we practice the `40` | `8  60`

rules of etiquette. `44` | `9  61`

When you are not quite sure of the rules about good conduct in a `57` | `11  63`

¶ 2
48 words
1.4 si

certain situation, just think about the other person's feelings. Act `71` | `14  66`

in a manner that will make others comfortable. You will not go far `85` | `17  69`

wrong if you heed this bit of advice. `92` | `18  70`

Good manners are but ways of showing consideration for the other `105` | `21  73`

¶ 3
52 words
1.3 si

person. You eat with a fork because no one would want to look at you `119` | `24  76`

if you ate with your fingers. Bad manners simply indicate that you `133` | `27  79`

care more for the food than for the company at the table. `144` | `29  81`

When you use good manners, you merely put another person's comfort `157` | `31  83`

¶ 4
56 words
1.4 si

ahead of your own. That's the acid test of good manners. Do you make `172` | `34  86`

the people with whom you associate feel at ease? Do they prize your `185` | `37  89`

friendship? Let these questions guide you in your relations with others. `200` | `40  92`

In any relationship with others the use of good manners seems to `213` | `43  95`

invoke the Golden Rule. One is as likely to return kindness for kind- `227` | `45  97`

¶ 5
60 words
1.4 si

ness as to return insult for insult. It is a rogue, indeed, who will `241` | `48  100`

never respond in kind to the lure of good manners. Practice yours and `255` | `51  103`

All ¶'s
1.3 si

see if you do not agree. `260` | `52  104`

1' | 1 | 2 | 3 | 4 | 5 | 6 | 7 | 8 | 9 | 10 | 11 | 12 | 13 | 14 |
5' | 1 | | 2 | | 3 |

26c ■ Tabulator Control • Each sentence three times; single spacing   *15 minutes*

Directions—1. Clear all tab stops (see page vii).
2. Type the first sentence at the left margin.
3. Set a tab stop for the second sentence five spaces from the left margin. Set a tab stop for the third sentence ten spaces from the left margin. Set stops for the fourth and fifth sentences as indicated.

Technique Goal—On manual machines, depress the tab bar (right index finger) or tab key (right little finger) and hold down until the carriage stops. (On electrics, tap tab key with little finger.) Move quickly back to home position.

Strokes in Line		Words
50	They can learn to use the tab bar or key by touch.	10
45	5 ⟶ Just complete each line without slowing down.	9
40	10 ⟶ Move your hand to home position quickly.	8
35	15 ⟶ Indent when starting each new line.	7
30	20 ⟶ Do not look back at your keys.	6

26d ■ Paragraph Guided Writings • As directed in 23f, page 38   *8 minutes*

		Words
DS	If you cannot find the time to do a job right	9
	the first time, how in the world do you expect to	19
48 words 1.1 si	find the time to do it over? There is a lot of	29
	sense in these few words. Think about them. Save	39
	time; do a job right the first time you do it.	48

| 1 | 2 | 3 | 4 | 5 | 6 | 7 | 8 | 9 | 10 |

Lesson 27
• *50-space line*

27a ■ Keyboard Review • Each line twice   *7 minutes*

SS	The Bijou marquee lists names of six famous stars.	
All letters	Fonz was picked by one girl as her favorite actor.	
5, 9	My number is 55; hers is 99. Subtract 59 from 95.	Type steadily
at	at great water rather matter attend nation station	
Easy	They can make a big profit by working eight hours.	

| 1 | 2 | 3 | 4 | 5 | 6 | 7 | 8 | 9 | 10 |

Unit 14 ■ Improving Your Basic Skills—Measurement
General Directions ■ Lessons 116 - 120

Machine Adjustments—Follow the general directions given in earlier units of this cycle.
Measurement—Measurement of straight-copy and problem typing skills is included in this unit.

The problems are similar to those covered in Cycle 3. Very few directions are given with the problems. Apply what you have learned in earlier lessons to the typing of these problems.

Lesson 116

• *Use a 70-space line for all lessons in this unit.*

116a ■ Keyboard Review   Each line at least three times   *5 minutes*

All letters SS Benjamin expects to have twelve dozen big prints made from it quickly.

Figure-Symbol On June 30, 1899, Charles C. Murphy bicycled a mile in 57 4/5 seconds.   Quick sharp strokes

Long reach Millions of tiny ornaments have been made annually by the two artists.

Easy Some of them had questions about the amount of work done in the class.

| 1 | 2 | 3 | 4 | 5 | 6 | 7 | 8 | 9 | 10 | 11 | 12 | 13 | 14 |

116b ■ Paragraph Guided Writings   *10 minutes*

Directions—1. Set goals of 40, 50, and 60 words a minute. Type two 1-minute writings at each rate. Try to type your goal word just as time is called for writings at the various rates.

2. Your teacher may call the quarter or half minutes to guide you.
3. Type additional writings at the 50- and 60-word rates as time permits.

DS If you are planning to enter one certain trade or profession, it is important to study your fitness for such work. If you find that you are weak in certain traits, you will know where to concentrate your efforts to improve yourself. You may find that you have greater aptitude for some other work.

60 words
1.4 si

Resume typing at once

116c ■ Technique Builder—Stroking • Two 1-minute writings on each sentence   *10 minutes*

First finger SS That runner had run too far to return to first base after Beth's bunt.

Second finger Did Dick and Eddie Decker pick up all the kids' kites from their deck?   Even stroking

Third finger I saw an old notice about Lois Olson's solo in the school talent show.

Fourth finger They are puzzled, Paula; are they to write a paper and/or take a quiz?

| 1 | 2 | 3 | 4 | 5 | 6 | 7 | 8 | 9 | 10 | 11 | 12 | 13 | 14 |

27b ■ Technique Builder—Stroking ● Two 1-minute writings on each line   *15 minutes*

1   SS Our words are to our minds what keys are to doors.

2   *Time is on the side of those who will plan for it.*

3   He must think the words as he types to gain speed.   Quick, sharp strokes

4   *Give her time, and she will do the work all right.*

5   Use your head and your hands to learn how to type.

| 1 | 2 | 3 | 4 | 5 | 6 | 7 | 8 | 9 | 10 |

27c ■ Paragraph Guided Writings   *18 minutes*

Directions—1. Type a 1-minute writing on ¶ 1. Note the *gwam*. Add four words to your *gwam* for a new goal. Type two more writings, trying to reach your new goal.

2. Repeat Step 1 for ¶ 2.

3. Center the two paragraphs on a half sheet. Try to make no more than two errors per paragraph.

● *Your teacher may call the half-minute guide on the 1-minute writings to aid you in checking your rate.*

	GWAM	
	1'	3'

All letters **DS**

One of the most offbeat jobs around these   8 | 3 30
days has to be that held by a fellow out west who   18 | 6 33

44 words 1.1 si
is the head of a unique school for jumping frogs.   29 | 10 37
He says he can make them think they are the best   38 | 13 40
in the world at their trade.   44 | 15 42

He even lets them do something that you and   53 | 18 45
I might think a bit crazy or at least strange.   62 | 21 48

38 words 1.2 si
The frogs are allowed to hop into a bubble bath   72 | 24 51
to relax and then to dine on bees dipped in honey.   82 | 27 55

| 1' | 1 | 2 | 3 | 4 | 5 | 6 | 7 | 8 | 9 | 10 |
| 3' | | 1 | | 2 | | 3 | | 4 | |

27d ■ Typing in All Capital Letters ● Type twice   *5 minutes*

● *To capitalize a whole word, several words, or an entire line, depress the shift lock (No. 30) and type. To release the shift lock, depress either the right or the left shift key.*

Teachers read the WEEKLY BULLETIN to ALL students.

Lesson 115

115a ■ Keyboard Review • Each line at least three times
5 minutes

All letters SS   Banjo players who balked were required to memorize five complex songs.

Figure-Symbol   Pike's Peak, at 14,110 feet, ranks 55th among all U.S. mountain peaks.

Direct reach   My Uncle Myron brought my brother and aunt to Briton for the symphony.

Even stroking

Easy   They were to type their last names right below the title of the theme.

| 1 | 2 | 3 | 4 | 5 | 6 | 7 | 8 | 9 | 10 | 11 | 12 | 13 | 14 |

115b ■ Timed Writings
10 minutes

Directions—1. Type two 1-minute writings on paragraph 1, 101d, page 170. Compute *gwam* on the better writing.

2. Type a 5-minute writing on all the paragraphs in 101d. Circle errors. Compute *gwam*.

115c ■ Problem Typing
30 minutes

Problem 1 ■ *Notice and Agenda of a Meeting*

Directions—1. Type the notice and agenda in 97c, Problem 1, page 164, as directed in the problem.

2. Remember to use the new center point.
3. Type the page number and identifying title.

Problem 2 ■ *Minutes of Meeting*

Directions—1. Type the minutes in 98c, page 166, following the directions given with the problem.

2. Remember to use the new center point.
3. Type the page number and identifying title.

Problem 3 ■ *Report from Rough Draft*

Full sheet
60-space line
Double spacing

Directions—Type the following report, making the corrections indicated. Center an appropriate heading 2 inches from the top.

	Words
In 1869, an early explorer ~~entered~~ wrote the following descrip-	11
tion of # an amazing view form a mountain top in north eastern	23
Utah: "From this point I can look away to the north and	34
see in the dim distance the sweetwater and wind river moun-	46
tains, more # than a hundred miles away."	54
Tourists streaming through this same region today may.	65
find that the pure air and beautiful veiws ~~have vanished~~ are vanishing	76
beneath clouds of smog. Some areas in the mountain	87
states now fail to meet federal air quality standards	98
intended to protect ~~our~~ human health.	104

Lesson 28

28a ■ Keyboard Review ● Each line twice

7 minutes

SS The movie was explained in the quarterly magazine.

All letters

Jodie Foster will play the role of Becky Thatcher.

4, 8   Multiply 44 by 88. They saw 48 girls and 84 boys.   Sit erect

ha   has had hand hard have chance change happy perhaps

Easy   I believe their game is going to be action packed.

| 1 | 2 | 3 | 4 | 5 | 6 | 7 | 8 | 9 | 10 |

28b ■ Continuity Practice—Numbers ● Twice

12 minutes

Words

DS   Here are two people whose records in sports   9

have made news. Gymnast Nadia Comaneci, just 14   19

years old, was given seven perfect marks of 10.00   29

Figure Review   in the 1976 Olympics. Baseball pitcher Nolan Ryan,   39

who hurled 383 strikeouts in 1973, had his fast   49

ball clocked at a speed of 100.9 miles an hour on   59

August 20, 1974.   62

| 1 | 2 | 3 | 4 | 5 | 6 | 7 | 8 | 9 | 10 |

28c ■ Typing Outside the Right and Left Margins

8 minutes

Right Margin—To type outside the right margin after the carriage is locked, depress the margin release key (No. 32).

Left Margin—To type outside the left margin, depress the margin release key; then backspace to the desired point.

● *Depress the margin release key with the* **;** *finger. On some electric typewriters the margin release key is depressed with the* **a** *finger.*

Directions—1. Using a 50-space line, type the first line. When the carriage locks, depress the margin release key and complete the line. Repeat.

2. Now, depress the margin release key, move the carriage five spaces into the left margin, and type the second line. Repeat.

In right margin   Your typewriter has some useful gadgets. Learn to use them.

In left margin   Your typewriter has some useful gadgets. Learn to use them.

113b ▪ Timed Writings

Directions—1. Type two 1-minute writings on paragraph 1, 91c, page 156. Compute the *gwam* on the better writing.

2. Type a 5-minute writing on all the paragraphs in 91c. Circle errors. Compute *gwam*.

113c ▪ Problem Typing

30 minutes

Problem 1 ▪ *One-Page Theme*

Directions—1. Type the theme on page 94. Follow the directions given in 53c, page 93.

2. Remember to use the new center point.
3. Type the page number and identifying title.

Problem 2 ▪ *First Page of Theme with Footnotes*

Directions—1. Type the theme on page 144 in the form illustrated.
2. Remember to use the new center point.

3. Type the page number and the identifying title. Center the identifying title a double space below the last footnote.

Lesson 114

● 70-space line

114a ▪ Keyboard Review ● Each line at least three times

5 minutes

All letters **SS** Mark will need seven jars of equal size for this next biology project.

Figure   A plane speed record of 266.59 miles an hour was set November 4, 1923.

     Think as you type

Adjacent keys   Right after their retirement, other writers returned to the territory.

Easy   It is not trite, but true, that we do set goals for ourselves in life.

| 1 | 2 | 3 | 4 | 5 | 6 | 7 | 8 | 9 | 10 | 11 | 12 | 13 | 14 |

114b ▪ Timed Writings

10 minutes

Directions—1. Type two 1-minute writings on paragraph 1, 96d, page 163. Compute the *gwam* on the better writing.

2. Type a 5-minute writing on all the paragraphs in 96d. Circle errors. Compute *gwam*.

114c ▪ Problem Typing

30 minutes

Problem 1 ▪ *Sentence Outline*

Directions—1. Type the outline in 57d, Problem 1, page 100, according to the directions given.

2. Remember to use the new center point.
3. Type the page number and identifying title.

Problem 2 ▪ *Topic Outline*

Directions—1. Type the outline in 87c, Problem 1, page 150, following the directions given.

2. Remember to use the new center point.
3. Type the page number and identifying title.

28d ■ Paragraph Guided Writings • As directed in 27c, page 44   *18 minutes*

GWAM
1' 3'

All letters DS Those who pull their own weight seldom have   9 3 34

any left to throw around. While they are quick to   19 6 37

43 words do their share, they do not bother others. This   29 10 40
1.1 si fact is as true in school or on the playing fields   39 13 44

as it is on the job.   43 14 45

Look about and you will soon find that busy   52 17 48

folks just do not get into trouble. They lack the   62 21 51

time to find it. The lazy people are always the   72 24 55

49 words ones who seem to have an axe to grind. The first   82 27 58
1.2 si rule of teamwork, then, is to pull your own weight.   92 31 61

1' | 1 | 2 | 3 | 4 | 5 | 6 | 7 | 8 | 9 | 10 |
3' | 1 | 2 | 3 | 4 |

Lesson 29   • 50-space line

29a ■ Keyboard Review • Each line twice   *7 minutes*

SS Julie asked her to buy me a dozen quarts of punch.

All letters We are expecting a more exact count very soon now.

2, 0 Place 00 in column 22. I said to divide 20 by 20.   Fingers curved

is is his list miss wish visit discuss furnish island

Easy Jan says she will work with me on the paper route.

| 1 | 2 | 3 | 4 | 5 | 6 | 7 | 8 | 9 | 10 |

29b ■ Technique Builder—Flowing Ryhthm • Type from dictation   *7 minutes*

1 SS to do the | to do the work | and did it | and did the

2   if it is | if it is the | if the duty is | if they do   Think words

3   and it | and it is | and it is the | and they did the

4   in the | in the time | in the end | in the town | in it   Type rapidly

5   for the | for them | for this | for their | for them to

Lesson 112

• 70-space line

112a ■ Keyboard Review • Each line at least three times
5 minutes

All letters   SS   Rex must have delivered the wrong size pack to Fuji quite by accident.

Figure-Symbol   The 985A jet can cruise at 620 miles per hour for the 7,143-mile trip.   Instant release

eve   Have you ever realized that everyone eventually attends every evening?

Easy   To write a good report, you should learn all you can about your topic.

| 1 | 2 | 3 | 4 | 5 | 6 | 7 | 8 | 9 | 10 | 11 | 12 | 13 | 14 |

112b ■ Timed Writings
10 minutes

Directions—1. Type two 1-minute writings on paragraph 1, 86d, page 149. Follow the directions given for the problem.

2. Type a 5-minute writing on all the paragraphs in 86d. Circle errors. Compute *gwam*.

112c ■ Problem Typing
30 minutes

Problem 1 ■ *Personal Letter in Semibusiness Form*

Directions—1. Type the letter in 75c, page 129. Follow the directions given for the problem.

2. Paste this letter on an 8½- by 11-inch sheet of paper; place it so that it appears centered when bound at the left margin.

3. Type the page and identifying number.

Problem 2 ■ *Personal/Business Letter in Block Style*

Directions—1. Type the letter in 78d, Problem 1, page 135. Follow the directions given for the problem.

2. Remember that the center point should be 3 spaces to the right of the point normally used.

3. Type the page number and identifying title.

Lesson 113

• 70-space line

113a ■ Keyboard Review • Each line at least three times
5 minutes

All letters   SS   Avis was quite upset after hearing crazy music from the old jukeboxes.

Figure-Symbol   The United States grows 17.5% of the world's wheat, 41% of its cotton.   Fingers deeply curved

Shift   William A. Burt, Mount Vernon, Michigan, patented his machine in 1829.

Easy   Riding the bus to games in neighboring towns is fun for all of us now.

| 1 | 2 | 3 | 4 | 5 | 6 | 7 | 8 | 9 | 10 | 11 | 12 | 13 | 14 |

29c ▪ Skill Comparison

11 minutes

Directions—Type two 1-minute writings on each sentence. Compare *gwam* on the four lines.

Technique Goals—Type without pauses. Space quickly between words. Keep wrists quiet.

Easy   **SS**   Some things have to be believed to be seen at all.

One-hand   Dexter Lyon saw Milo pull a beaver in a red crate.

                                                  Space quickly

Figure   Nearly all 25 girls on their teams are already 16.

Script   *A pound of pluck is worth more than a ton of luck.*

| 1 | 2 | 3 | 4 | 5 | 6 | 7 | 8 | 9 | 10 |

29d ▪ Timed Writings

10 minutes

Directions—Type two 3-minute writings on 28d, page 46. Circle errors. Compute *gwam*. Submit the better writing.

29e ▪ Listening for the Bell; Right Margin Release

10 minutes

Directions—Type the paragraph with a 50-space line; then with a 60-space line (by moving your left and right margin stops out five spaces, as explained on page 45. Let the bell guide you in returning the carriage. If the carriage locks before you complete a word, depress the margin release key and complete the word.

● *Remember to set the right margin 5 to 8 spaces beyond the desired line ending. Doing this will give your copy better horizontal balance.*

                                                      Words

All letters   **DS**   While they will not set an exact day, some   9

           say the time when we will drive electric cars is   18

37 words   just around the corner. It may be quicker than   28

1.2 si   that if the present ones guzzle too much gas.   37

| 1 | 2 | 3 | 4 | 5 | 6 | 7 | 8 | 9 | 10 |

Lesson 30

● *50-space line*

30a ▪ Keyboard Review ● Each line twice

7 minutes

     SS   We all hope the speaker will tell some good jokes.

All letters

      Quite a number of citizens have to pay more taxes.

6, 1   Take Route 66, not Route 11. Next, add 61 and 16.

                                                  Wrists low and still

it   it its city permit unit profit write either little

Easy   Both of them were able to hold their balance well.

| 1 | 2 | 3 | 4 | 5 | 6 | 7 | 8 | 9 | 10 |

Student Writer's Style Guide

● *In the problems of this unit, you will prepare a booklet entitled STUDENT WRITER'S STYLE GUIDE. The following general instructions apply to all these problems.*

1. Keep the pages you prepare in this unit until the entire booklet is finished. (The booklet will contain 11 pages in all.)

2. Correct errors.

3. Number the pages as indicated in the table of contents. Type page numbers on the fourth line space from the top, 1 inch from the right edge of the paper.

4. Pages which follow the table of contents will contain the identifying title shown in the table of contents. Except as otherwise directed, center this title in capital letters on the sixth line space from the bottom of the page.

5. The booklet will be stapled at the left side. Thus, for all pages in the booklet, except the title page, the center point is 3 spaces to the right of the point normally used. Use this center point in centering titles and in setting margins when the directions call for setting a certain space line, such as a 50-space line.

111c ■ Problem Typing

30 minutes

Problem 1 ■ *Title Page of Style Guide*

Directions—Prepare a title page similar to the one shown on page 147. Type the title, STUDENT WRITER'S STYLE GUIDE, your name, and the current date on the page.

Problem 2 ■ *Table of Contents*

Directions—1. Type the table of contents below for your style guide.

2. Set your margins for a 60-space line. (Remember that the center point should be 3 spaces to the right of the point normally used.)

3. Allow a 2-inch top margin. Triple-space between the title and the heading for the page numbers. Double-space between items.

TABLE OF CONTENTS

	Page
Personal Business Letter in Modified Block Style	1
Personal Business Letter in Block Style	2
Personal Letter in Semibusiness Form	3
One-Page Theme	4
First Page of Theme with Footnotes	5
Sentence Outline	6
Topic Outline	7
Notice and Agenda of a Meeting	8
Minutes of Meeting	9

Problem 3 ■ *Personal/Business Letter in Modified Block Style*

Directions—1. Type the letter in 47d, Problem 1, page 82. Use the directions given for the problem.

2. In setting margins for a 50-space line, remember to use the new center point.

3. Ref to the style guide general directions given above for the placement of the page number and the identifying title.

30b ■ Timed Writings

Directions—Type two 3-minute writings on this paragraph.
Circle errors. Compute *gwam*. Submit the better writing.

GWAM
1' 3'

All letters DS Morley said that there is one rule for being   9 | 3 28

a good talker; learn to listen. It is a good   18 | 6 31

quotation to keep in mind. To talk well, give   28 | 9 35

others a chance to express their views. Learn   37 | 12 38

76 words   what they know. Try their views on for size.   46 | 15 41
1.2 si

Talk only when you have something worth saying.   56 | 19 44

Just keep in mind that the star of the show is the   66 | 22 48

one who sings one song too few, not one too many.   76 | 25 51

1' | 1 | 2 | 3 | 4 | 5 | 6 | 7 | 8 | 9 | 10 |
3' | 1 | 2 | 3 | 4 |

30c ■ Tabulator Control   *18 minutes*

Directions—1. Clear all tab stops as directed on page vii.
2. Check to see that margin stops are set for a 50-space line.
3. Type the first column at the left margin.

4. Set the tab stop for the second column 21 spaces from the left margin. Set the stop for the third column 21 spaces from the second.
5. Type the list of words pertaining to athletics once. Type across the page. Repeat if time permits.

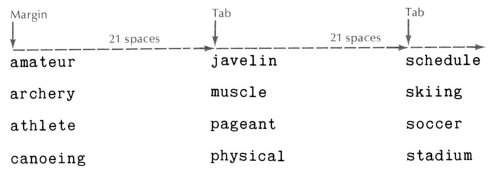

Margin   Tab   Tab

→   21 spaces   →   21 spaces   →

amateur   javelin   schedule

archery   muscle   skiing

athlete   pageant   soccer

canoeing   physical   stadium

30d ■ Listening for the Bell   *10 minutes*

Directions—Type the paragraph with a 50-space line; then with a 60-space line. Let the bell guide you in returning the carriage. Use the margin-release key to allow you to type beyond your margin stop.

Words

DS Before you take a timed writing, get ready   9

for it. Be sure to have enough clean paper in your   19

46 words   machine. Have the margin stops set for the right   29
1.2 si

length of line. Place your copy so it is easy to   39

read. Clear your desk for action.   46

Problem 2 ▪ *Article with Justified Right Margin* • As directed in Problem 1, page 182

SKI CLUB HEADS FOR SLOPES

Badger Pass will be the destination of at least 30 enthusiastic Tioga skiers on Saturday, February 5. The bus will leave from the school at 7:15 a.m.

Betty Steinmetz, club president, has announced that any additional students who want to make the trip must sign up before January 20.

Beginners are welcome. Lessons on a dry ski slope are available each evening during the week at Metry's Sporting Goods on the corner of Ashlan and Blackstone Avenues. Anyone who does not have equipment may rent it from the store for $5.

Mr. Stevenson, club sponsor, says the bus will be back by 8:00 p.m. Saturday evening. Travel permits are required.

110d ▪ Extra-Credit Typing

Problem 1

Directions—Type 94c, page 160, in a form suitable for a school newspaper. Justify the right margin. Provide a suitable title.

Problem 2

Directions—Compose an article about a coming school activity. Follow the directions in 108c, page 180.

Problem 3

Directions—Type a horizontal bar graph, similar to the one on page 172, showing your own speed growth in the typing class.

Unit 13 ▪ Preparing a Student-Writer's Style Guide

General Directions ▪ Lessons 111 - 115

Machine Adjustments—Follow the general directions given in earlier units of this cycle.

Lesson 111

• *Use a 70-space line for all lessons in this unit.*

111a ▪ Keyboard Review • Each line at least three times   *5 minutes*

All letters SS	The project was quickly moved by citizens anxious to avoid any fights.	
Figure-Symbol	A total of 2,819,246 immigrants entered the country between 1955-1964.	Eyes on this copy
Adjacent keys	Roberta tried to remove their tire as we drew near on the return trip.	
Easy	The one who uses few words does not have to take so many of them back.	

| 1 | 2 | 3 | 4 | 5 | 6 | 7 | 8 | 9 | 10 | 11 | 12 | 13 | 14 |

111b ▪ Timed Writings   *10 minutes*

Directions—1. Type two 1-minute writings on paragraph 1, 81d, page 140. Compute the *gwam* on the better writing.

2. Type a 5-minute writing on all the paragraphs in 81d. Circle errors. Compute *gwam*.

UNIT 5 ■ Learning the Basic Symbol Keys

General Directions ■ Lessons 31 - 35

Line Length—Beginning with this lesson, set margin stops for a 60-space line. Make this adjustment at the start of each lesson.

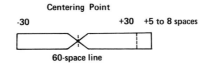

Centering Point
-30   +30   +5 to 8 spaces

60-space line

Spacing—Single-space lines of words and sentences; double-space between repeated groups of lines. Double-space paragraph copy.

Lesson 31

● *Use a 60-space line for all lessons in this unit.*

31a ■ Keyboard Review ● Each line twice   *5 minutes*

All letters   **SS**   Her big objective was to set a complex zone defense quickly.

Figure   Set one margin at 12, the other at 90, and a tab stop at 35.

Easy   Kate tossed the ball right to him as she ran down the court.

| 1 | 2 | 3 | 4 | 5 | 6 | 7 | 8 | 9 | 10 | 11 | 12 |

Quick
sharp
strokes

31b ■ Location of $ (dollar sign) and / (diagonal)

$
Shift, then reach up to $ with the **f** finger. Do not space between the $ sign and the number which follows it.

/
The **/** is the lower case of **?**. To type **/**, reach down with the **;** finger. Do not space before or after the diagonal.

Type $ with the f finger

Type / with the ; finger

f4f f$f f4f f$f $f $f $4 $44   ● **Type twice on same line** ●   ;/; ;/; ;?; 1/3 2/5 3/8 3/16

31c ■ Location Drills—$ and / ● Each line twice   *10 minutes*

● *Space once between a whole number and a fraction.*

$ **SS**   They paid $4.40, $4.50, $4.80, and $4.90 for the four books.

                  Luis may earn $48.75 this week. Last week he earned $44.30.

/   Use the / to type fractions, as 1/3, 1/5, 1/6, 11/16, 15/16.

                  Space once between a whole number and a fraction, as 15 1/2.

$ shift of 4

/ lower case of ?

Lesson 110

110a ■ Keyboard Review • Each line at least three times   *5 minutes*

All letters SS   All six kids are crazy about having peanut butter with jam frequently.

Figure   Going 90 miles per hour, a skier jumped 281 feet on February 26, 1933.

Long reach   This is an unpopular policy. We hunted quail near the munitions dump.

Easy   It is not right to talk when your mouth is full or your head is empty.

| 1 | 2 | 3 | 4 | 5 | 6 | 7 | 8 | 9 | 10 | 11 | 12 | 13 | 14 |

110b ■ Timed Writings   *15 minutes*

Directions—Type two 5-minute writings on 106c, page 177. Compute your *gwam*. Submit the better of the two writings.

Justifying the Right Margin

School newspapers prepared on a duplicating machine are sometimes typed so that all the lines, except the last one in a paragraph, are even at the right margin. This practice is known as justifying the right margin. The copy then has the appearance of a printed page.

To get an even right margin, extra spaces are added between words to fill out short lines. The copy is first typed as illustrated below. It is then retyped with the extra spaces.

First, type a line of diagonals (/) to indicate the maximum length line: 30 spaces, pica; 36 spaces elite.

Second, type the article. Add diagonals to the short lines to make them even with the line of diagonals at the top.

Third, retype the article. Add extra space between words for each diagonal in that line. Try to avoid putting extra spaces in one line under extra spaces in the line above.

110c ■ Problem Typing   *25 minutes*

Problem 1 ■ Article with Justified Right Margin

Directions—1. Type the short article at the right on one of your 4½- by 11-inch pieces of paper. Type the first draft with diagonals for the short lines; then the final draft with the justified lines.

2. Follow the same directions you have been using in preparing copy for the school newspaper in Lessons 108 and 109, but justify the right margin.

3. Use this title for the article: WHAT'S YOUR TITLE?

///

First draft

No matter what kind of job you/// have these days, you can be sure//// someone will give it a title that/// sounds important. A janitor is an// engineer of sanitation; an usher is/ an audience guide; and a dog catcher is a supervisor of missing canines.

Justified draft

No matter what kind of job you have these days, you can be sure someone will give it a title that sounds important.   A janitor is an engineer of sanitation, an usher is an audience guide; and a dog catcher is a supervisor of missing canines.

31d ■ Comparison Sentence Skill Builder ● Two 1-minute writings on each line. Compare rates. *10 minutes*

Easy **SS** She did say that some things have to be believed to be seen.

Figure-Symbol The men may have sold 57 1/3 acres of land for $425 an acre. Type steadily

Shift Here are the winners: Ramon Hamai, Tanya Dart, and Ann Cyr.

| 1 | 2 | 3 | 4 | 5 | 6 | 7 | 8 | 9 | 10 | 11 | 12 |

31e ■ Speed Ladder Paragraphs *15 minutes*

Directions—1-minute writings. When you can complete the first paragraph in one minute, type the second; then the third, fourth, and fifth. Your teacher may call the half-minutes to guide you.

● *The rate increases 5 words a minute with each succeeding paragraph.*

		GWAM 1'	3'

¶ 1
20 words
1.2 si

DS It is common knowledge that your mind is the key to ½ ... 10 | 3
your actions, so just think right to type right.¹ ... 20 | 7

¶ 2
25 words
1.2 si

Use your mind and save your fingers. Let this be your ... 11 | 10
motto ½ in your typing class. It will pay you to think before ... 23 | 14
you type. ... 25 | 15

¶ 3
30 words
1.2 si

You will have to live with yourself. You must thus see ... 11 | 19
that you ½ are in good company. Try to develop the traits which ... 24 | 23
you enjoy most in your friends.¹ ... 30 | 25

¶ 4
35 words
1.2 si

It is often said that temper is such a good thing that ... 11 | 29
we should do our best never to lose ½ it. We are at our very ... 23 | 33
best when we are pleasant. We fail when we lose our temper.¹ ... 35 | 37

¶ 5
40 words
1.1 si

You cannot keep your eyes on the ball and a clock at ... 11 | 40
the same time. If you try this feat, you will ½ surely strike ... 23 | 44
out. You must measure each day by the jobs you finish, not ... 35 | 48

All ¶ s
1.2 si

by the hands on the clock.¹ ... 40 | 50

| 1' | 1 | 2 | 3 | 4 | 5 | 6 | 7 | 8 | 9 | 10 | 11 | 12 |
| 3' | | 1 | | 2 | | 3 | | 4 | |

31f ■ Extra-Credit Typing

Directions—Type as many of the paragraphs as you can without error. You will type without timing. Move from one paragraph to the next when you type errorless copy.

Lesson 109

70-space line

109a ■ Keyboard Review • Each line at lease three times

5 minutes

All letters SS They were required to save the jigsaw puzzles in the black box for me.

Figure-Symbol The 1964 Civil Rights Act filibuster lasted 75 days, March 26–June 10.

Flowing rhythm

exa I wasn't exactly exalted, but exasperated, at the exaggerated example.

Easy Change the shape of the figure and you can have it placed right there.

| 1 | 2 | 3 | 4 | 5 | 6 | 7 | 8 | 9 | 10 | 11 | 12 | 13 | 14 |

109b ■ Sentence Skill Builder from Rough Draft • Two 1-minute writings on each sentence

10 minutes

Words

1 SS we *k* now that we can see *in* others some of ~~of~~ our own traits--good or bad.   14

2 ☐ The quick *est* way *to* gain your *own* goals is to help ~~another~~ *others* gain ~~his~~ *theirs*.   14

3 Always *try to* choose those words ~~which~~ *that will* give li *f* e to your thoughts.   14

4 *most people can* ~~All of us must~~ listen about *four* times ~~a~~ a person ~~talks~~ *as fast as will talk*.   14

109c ■ Problem Typing

30 minutes

• *You will continue typing items for the school newspaper in this lesson. Follow the directions given under 108c, page 180.*

Problem 1 ■ *Items of Special Interest*

Directions—In an article entitled _____ SAYS—, include the following items. Use an appropriate subheading for each item. Type your name in the blank space.

81e	Continuity Practice from Script	page 140
87b	Paragraph Skill Builder	page 150
102b	Paragraph Skill Builder	page 171

Problem 2 ■ *Feature Story*

Directions—**1.** Compose and type a feature story on one of the following topics. The references following each topic are to similar articles in this textbook. You may get ideas from these articles, but do not copy them. Compose your own story.

2. Type your final copy in the same form that you used in typing the other items for the school newspaper.

3. Type your name as the author. Give your story an appropriate title.

The Energy Crisis	61e	Paragraph Guided Writing	page 107
Is College for Me?	73b	Speed Stretcher	page 126
How Many People?	98b	Speed Stretcher	page 165

LESSON 109 ■ PAGE 181

Lesson 32

32a ■ Keyboard Review • Each line twice
5 minutes

All letters SS Max delivered the wrong size pack to Jeff quite by accident.

Figure On June 15, Flight 59 left at 7:35 with 17 men and 39 women.

Easy All work that is well done has a way of speaking for itself.

| 1 | 2 | 3 | 4 | 5 | 6 | 7 | 8 | 9 | 10 | 11 | 12 |

Keep
eyes on
this copy

32b ■ Location of % (percent) and - (hyphen)
5 minutes

%
Shift, then reach up to
% with the f finger.
Do not space between
a number and a fol-
lowing % sign.

**Type % with
the f finger**

-
To type -, reach up
with the ; finger. Type
two hyphens to make
a dash.

**Type - with
the ; finger**

f5f f%f f5f f%f %f %f %f 55%   • Type twice on same line •   ;-; ;-; ;-; -; -; -- 48-foot

32c ■ Location Drills—% and - • Each line twice
10 minutes

% SS They may deduct discounts of 20%, 15%, and 5% on all orders.

% shift of 5

Rate increases were as follows: 17%, 15%, 9%, 23%, and 17%.

- Hyphenate these words: re-use, send-off, know-how, mid-May.

Type - with
the ; finger

My son-in-law had a clear-cut view of the well-known museum.

-- The cabin--the one near the lake--will be sold in mid-March.

Type two
hyphens

The dates set for these concerts are correct--and desirable.

32d ■ Script Skill Builder
10 minutes

Directions—Type the paragraph twice for practice;
then type two 1-minute writings. Figure *gwam*.

Technique Goal—Read the copy carefully. Type
without pauses.

Words

DS Time is one thing we all have in equal amount. We do   11

not all show the same amount of wisdom in the way we use   22

our time, though, and the difference underlies the level of   34

54 words
1.2 si

success we achieve in the things we do. It takes time and   46

the way we use it to be a high achiever.   54

Preparing Newspaper Copy

Many schools, clubs, and other organizations prepare and issue newspapers and newsletters of the type you will prepare in the next three lessons. Items of interest are composed and typed in accordance with set rules and given to an editor. The editor checks the items and arranges the copy on plan sheets. The copy is typed from the plan sheets on master sheets for spirit duplication or on stencils for mimeographing. The paper is duplicated, stapled, and distributed.

- *In the next three lessons you will prepare copy for the editor. This copy is for a two-column newspaper duplicated on 8½- by 11-inch paper.*

108c ■ Problem Typing

30 minutes

1. Cut several sheets of 8½- by 11-inch paper in half lengthwise. Each piece should be 4¼- by 11-inches.

2. Type each article or item on a separate piece of paper.

3. Type main headings in all capitals, centered. Type subheadings, if used, in capital and lower case, with triple spacing before and double spacing after.

4. Set margins for a 3-inch line—30 spaces, pica; 36 spaces, elite. (When justifying the right margin, the maximum line length is 30 or 36.)

5. Single-space the final copy; double-space between paragraphs. Indent paragraphs 3 spaces.

6. You need not center the copy vertically. Start typing each article about one inch from the top.

- *Directions for centering lines on odd-size paper are on page 67.*

Problem 1 ■ Feature Article

Directions—1. Type 101d, page 170, as a feature story for the school newspaper. Use the following heading: THE PERFECT GIFT.

2. In typing your copy, follow the general directions given above.

3. Your copy should look like the copy in the partial illustration at the right.

THE PERFECT GIFT

The next time you are faced with the problem of what to buy the person who has everything, why not consider buying a mule? While this idea might sound odd at first, you should realize the many advantages of such a gift.

Here are just a couple of them. First of all, a mule requires much less upkeep than

---

Problem 2 ■ Special Items

Directions—1. The second sentence in many Keyboard Reviews in Cycle 3 is a factual statement of general interest. Select six or more of these sentences for an article. Use the following heading: FACTS OF LIFE.

2. Use your own name as the author.

3. Your copy should look like the copy in the partial illustration at the right.

FACTS OF LIFE

Your name

Our nation ranked fourth in production in 1860; we were first by 1894.

During that day--May 29, 1962, the market average rose over 27 points.

Problem 3 ■ Short Item

Directions—Type the paragraph in 77b, page 132, as an item for the paper. Provide a suitable title for it. Use your own name as the author.

Articles typed on 4¼- by 11-inch paper

32e ■ Timed Writings

Directions—Type two 3-minute writings on 31e, page 50. Compute *gwam*. Submit the better of the two writings.

32f ■ Technique Builder—Repeated Letters • Each line twice

Technique Goal—Strike repeated letters with the same force used on the other letters.

1 SS three happy agree room bill week inn message sleep mood well

2 issue guess look good less smooth apply proof speed too free

  Even stroking

3 will allow apply feel fall soon floor offer matter add dress

4 full assign buzz funny little rubber spill muzzle poor bluff

Lesson 33

• *60-space line*

33a ■ Keyboard Review • Each line twice

All letters SS Jerry Diamond packed the fine quartz in twelve larger boxes.

Figure Mt. Whitney ranks among the highest of peaks at 14,495 feet.

  Type without pauses

Easy Give equal force to the strokes so your typing will be even.

| 1 | 2 | 3 | 4 | 5 | 6 | 7 | 8 | 9 | 10 | 11 | 12 |

33b ■ Location of (and) (parentheses)

(
Shift, then reach up to (with the l finger. Do not space between the (and the material it encloses.

Type (with the l finger

)
Shift, then reach up to) with the ; finger. Do not space between the) and the material it encloses.

Type) with the ; finger

191 1(1 191 1(1 (1 (1 (1 (1 • **Type twice on same line** • 0;0):) 0:0);0););););

33c ■ Location Drills—(and) • Each line twice

(SS To type (, shift and strike the 9. Type 9; then (9 and (99. (shift of 9

) To type), shift and strike the 0. Type 0; then 0) and 00).) shift of 0

Most of the students (190 to be exact) passed all the test.

The report (handwritten) is quoted in full. (See page 124.)

The record (206.9 miles per hour) was held by Brown (Paris).

Type attractively
on a half sheet

Problem 2 ■ Bulletin Board Notice

─────────────── PHYSICAL FITNESS PERFORMANCE AWARDS ───────────────

Grand Slammer Award   :   Seventh Grade Winner: CHRIS BARKER

PATTY BRYAN   :

     :   Eighth Grade Winner: LOWELL REYNOLDS

─────────────── PHYSICAL FITNESS PERFORMANCE AWARDS ───────────────

Lesson 108

● *70-space line*

108a ■ Keyboard Review ● Each line at least three times

5 minutes

All letters   **SS** The explosive magazine articles were rejected only by a quirk of fate.

Figure-Symbol   New subscriptions cost $4.87 for 39 weeks and only $6.10 for 52 weeks.

Long words   A correspondent should study the environment and location of the firm.

Easy   The pitch that I missed was thrown right down the middle of the plate.

Quick, crisp
short strokes

| 1 | 2 | 3 | 4 | 5 | 6 | 7 | 8 | 9 | 10 | 11 | 12 | 13 | 14 |

108b ■ Speed Stretcher ● As directed in 98b, page 165

10 minutes

	GWAM
	1' 5'

All letters   **DS**   The problem of too much noise is drawing quite a bit of attention   13 | 3 35

from people who are concerned with quality of life these days. While   27 | 5 38

¶ 1
64 words
1.3 si   we have known for a long time that prolonged exposure to high noise   41 | 8 41

levels can cause deafness, doctors now tell us noise is bad because it   55 | 11 43

affects nearly all the functions of the body.   64 | 13 45

As crazy as it may sound, some experts suggest that we add more   13 | 16 48

¶ 2
46 words
1.3 si   noises to drown out the racket around us. One firm even sells a gadget   27 | 18 51

which makes a constant hum, like a breeze blowing in the trees, to mask   42 | 21 54

other unwanted sounds.   46 | 22 55

Such an idea may have some merit, but not all authorities think   13 | 25 57

¶ 3
52 words
1.3 si   this solution is a sensible one. They say adding more noise may just   27 | 27 60

make a bad problem worse. In their view, the only real answer is to   41 | 30 63

All ¶'s
1.3 si   find the source of the noise and take steps to reduce it.   52 | 32 65

| 1' | 1 | 2 | 3 | 4 | 5 | 6 | 7 | 8 | 9 | 10 | 11 | 12 | 13 | 14 |
| 5' | | | 1 | | | | 2 | | | | 3 | | |

33d ■ Continuity Practice

8 minutes

Directions—After typing the paragraph, circle any errors you may have made. Type correctly three times the words in which you made an error along with the word preceding and the word following the error. See how many times you can type the paragraph without any errors in the time allowed.

			Words
All letters	**DS**	Since wages can rise only so fast, firms try quite	10
		hard to keep workers pleased in other ways. Some let them	22
44 words		take extra time off; or they may offer low cost loans or	33
1.2 si		even prizes to help make sure people like their jobs.	44

| 1 | 2 | 3 | 4 | 5 | 6 | 7 | 8 | 9 | 10 | 11 | 12 |

33e ■ Timed Writings

17 minutes

Directions—**1.** Type a 3-minute writing. Compute *gwam*.
2. Type two 1-minute writings on each paragraph.
3. Type another 3-minute writing. Compute *gwam*. Compare this rate with the rate on the first 3-minute writing.

GWAM

			1'	3'
	DS	Mistakes might be a sign of progress. They are made when	12	4 33
¶ 1		we try out new or better ways of doing a job. The people who	24	8 37
39 words		succeed do not make the same mistake twice; they try to make	36	12 41
1.2 si		some new ones.	39	13 42
		The world is full of willing people; some are willing to	11	17 45
¶ 2		work; the rest are willing to let them. You must know that	23	21 49
47 words		there is no such thing in this world as something for nothing.	36	25 54
1.1 si		We must all be willing to work for the things we want.	47	29 57

1' | 1 | 2 | 3 | 4 | 5 | 6 | 7 | 8 | 9 | 10 | 11 | 12 |
3' | | 1 | | 2 | | 3 | | 4 |

Lesson 34

• *60-space line*

34a ■ Keyboard Review • Each line twice

5 minutes

All letters	**SS**	Nick and Paula gave them exquisite old jewelry for a bazaar.	
Figure		Type these numbers with your eyes on the copy: 236 347 590.	Quiet wrists and arms
Easy		She kept her body at the right angle and thus won the title.	

| 1 | 2 | 3 | 4 | 5 | 6 | 7 | 8 | 9 | 10 | 11 | 12 |

Lesson 107

107a ■ Keyboard Review • Each line at least three times 5 minutes

All letters SS Seven plucky ushers quenched a major fire blazing about the west exit.

Figure-Symbol Ancient card packs had 78 cards--56 ordinary, 21 "tarots" and a "fou."

Even stroking

Shift Steven, Janet, Scott, and Ted all liked Mrs. Severson's English class.

Easy People should realize there is nothing much busier than an idle rumor.

| 1 | 2 | 3 | 4 | 5 | 6 | 7 | 8 | 9 | 10 | 11 | 12 | 13 | 14 |

107b ■ Punctuation Guides—Quotation Marks 10 minutes

Directions—Read the explanation carefully; then type each example sentence twice.

Line 1—Place quotation marks around the exact words of a speaker.

Line 2—When the quotation is broken to identify the speaker, put quotation marks around each part.

Line 3—If the second part of the quotation is a new sentence, use a capital letter.

Line 4—Use no quotation marks with an indirect quotation.

Line 5—Use quotation marks around the titles of articles, songs, poems, themes, short stories, and the like.

Line 6—Always place the period or comma inside the quotation mark.

1 SS Professor Cole said, "Only 29 percent of the earth's surface is land."

2 "The deepest mine in the world," they continued, "is 9,811 feet deep."

3 "We are going to Hawaii," she replied softly. "Here are our tickets."

Quick, firm reach to the shift key

4 David said he thinks that the Grand Coulee is the world's biggest dam.

5 Gayle Sobolik wrote the report entitled, "Automation Isn't Automatic."

6 "Sweden," the first speaker insisted, "has the highest literacy rate."

| 1 | 2 | 3 | 4 | 5 | 6 | 7 | 8 | 9 | 10 | 11 | 12 | 13 | 14 |

107c ■ Problem Typing 30 minutes

Problem 1 ■ Bulletin Board Notice

Directions—Type the bulletin board notice at the right on a half sheet of paper. Arrange your copy attractively.

```
                          0
                       0    0
        ANNUAL  CITY-WIDE  GEOGRAPHY  BEE
                       0    0
                          0

              Notice to All Contestants

         BUS LEAVES FOR IRWIN JUNIOR HIGH SCHOOL
    Faculty Parking Lot                    Wednesday, May 18
                 8:30 a.m.
```

Bulletin board notice

34b ■ Location of ' (apostrophe) and ! (exclamation point) *5 minutes*

MANUAL (UNIVERSAL KEYBOARD)

'

Shift, then reach up to ' with the **k** finger. The apostrophe does not have a space before or after it.

Type ' with the k finger

!

On some manuals, to type **!**, type the ', backspace, and type the period. Space twice after **!** at the end of a sentence, which may be a single exclamatory word.

Type ', backspace, type the period

k8k k'k k8k k'k 'k 'k 'k k'k   ● Type twice on same line ●   k8k k!k k8k k!k !k !k !k k!k

ELECTRIC

The ' is to the right of ; and is controlled by the ; finger.

Type ' with the ; finger

On electrics and some manual typewriters, the **!** is on a special key, often the shift of Figure **1**. Type it with the **a** finger.

Type ! with the a finger

;'; ;'; ;'; '; '; '; ;'; ;';   ● Type twice on same line ●   ala a!a ala a!a !a !a !a a!a

34c ■ Location Drills— ' and ! ● Each line twice   *10 minutes*

'   **SS**   don't, I'll, '89, We can't work. Nancy isn't at Eva's home.

Mr. and Mrs. O'Neill can't pay the bill for their son's car.

!   Stop! Danger ahead! The river has damaged the long bridge!

Get ready! Begin! Run faster! Try harder! Hurry! Great!

34d ■ Continuity Practice—Numbers and Symbols ● Twice

	Words
DS Things and people holding records make news. Did you	11
know that Mickey Mantle's 565-foot home run is the longest?	23
Joe Nuxhall, at 15 years 10 months 11 days, was the youngest	35
major league player of all time. The people living in Alaska	48
lead all others in incomes ($10,178 per person). The average	60
for the country is $6,441. Honolulu leads all our cities	71
with the highest median family income, $12,539.	81

| 1 | 2 | 3 | 4 | 5 | 6 | 7 | 8 | 9 | 10 | 11 | 12 |

106c ■ Speed Ladder Paragraphs ● As directed in 96d, page 163 · *20 minutes*

<table>
<tr><td></td><td colspan="3" style="text-align:right">GWAM</td></tr>
<tr><td></td><td>1'</td><td colspan="2">5'</td></tr>
</table>

		1'	5'
All letters **DS** For thousands of years now, ever since the beginning of history		13	3 55
¶ 1 44 words 1.3 si in fact, people have searched far and wide for gold. To locate this		27	5 57
most precious metal, they have moved and crushed enough rock to build		41	8 60
a mountain range.		44	9 61
While gold was first discovered on or near the ground, today the		57	11 63
¶ 2 48 words 1.3 si majority of it is mined far beneath the surface. It is found buried in		71	14 66
quartz veins often more than two miles deep. We dig deeper for gold		85	17 69
than for any other mineral we use.		92	18 70
Despite this constant searching, however, we have been able to		105	21 73
¶ 3 52 words 1.3 si accumulate only a modest supply. Hard as it may be to believe, all the		119	24 76
gold in the world could be placed in a cube about fifty feet high. It		133	27 78
could be stored on the first floor of the White House.		144	29 81
Gold has been used in many different ways throughout the years.		157	31 83
It serves quite well for money because it lasts a long time and can be		171	34 86
¶ 4 56 words 1.3 si shaped easily into coins. Since it is much desired for its beauty,		185	37 89
it is often made into jewelry. Much gold also goes into fillings for		199	40 92
teeth.		200	40 92
Although no one knows for certain exactly how much more gold is		213	43 94
left to be discovered, experts say there is not a lot. It now appears		227	45 97
¶ 5 60 words 1.3 si that gold may well be in short supply before the end of this century.		241	48 100
If these predictions are accurate, gold will become even more precious		255	51 103
All ¶'s 1.3 si to us than it is today.		260	52 104

```
1'| 1 | 2 | 3 | 4 | 5 | 6 | 7 | 8 | 9 | 10 | 11 | 12 | 13 | 14 |
5'|       1       |       2       |       3       |
```

106d ■ Creative Typing ● Type a paragraph, telling in your own words what the following quotation means to you.   *10 minutes*

"The best place," Banks said, "to find a helping hand is at the end of your arm."

34e ■ Speed Ladder Paragraphs

15 minutes

Directions—Type 1-minute writings on the following paragraphs. When you can complete the first paragraph in one minute, type the second; then the third, fourth, and fifth. Your teacher may call the half minutes to guide you.

		GWAM 1'	GWAM 3'

¶ 1
20 words
1.2 si

DS   This is a lesson on keeping your machine in top shape. | 11 | 4

A cloth, a stiff brush, and oil are needed. | 20 | 7

¶ 2
25 words
1.2 si

Your typewriter must be ready to use at all times. The | 11 | 10

three steps that follow will help you take good care of your | 23 | 14

machine. | 25 | 15

¶ 3
30 words
1.2 si

First, wipe the dust from all parts of your machine | 10 | 18

after each use. If you do not do this, the keys may be | 22 | 22

sticky, and the carriage will move slowly. | 30 | 25

¶ 4
35 words
1.2 si

Next, using a stiff brush, remove the ink and dirt from | 11 | 29

the face of the keys. This simple step consumes only a few | 23 | 33

seconds; yet it will make your copy clean and easy to read. | 35 | 37

¶ 5
40 words
1.2 si

Lastly, with a cloth, clean the grooved bars on which | 11 | 40

the carriage moves. Apply a little oil on the bars about | 22 | 44

once a week. If you take good care of your machine, it will | 35 | 48

All ¶'s
1.2 si

help you produce good work. | 40 | 50

| 1' | 1 | 2 | 3 | 4 | 5 | 6 | 7 | 8 | 9 | 10 | 11 | 12 |
| 3' | | 1 | | | 2 | | | 3 | | | 4 | |

Lesson 35

● *60-space line*

35a ■ Keyboard Review ● Each line twice

5 minutes

All letters   **SS**   Oakmont citizens have explored ways of quieting the big jet.

Symbol   Type right! In fact, that is how simple it is to typewrite!

Think as you type

Easy   The way to fail is to do only as much as you must to get by.

| 1 | 2 | 3 | 4 | 5 | 6 | 7 | 8 | 9 | 10 | 11 | 12 |

105c ■ Problem Typing
25 minutes

Problem ■ Luncheon Program and Menu

Directions—Follow the directions given in 104d, page 174. Space and arrange the copy attractively on both pages of the fold-over sheet.

Cover Page

LUNCHEON MEETING

JUNIOR ACHIEVEMENT ASSOCIATION

```
        XX
      X    X
    X        X
   X   JA   X
    X        X
      X    X
        XX
```

Crystal Dining Room

Ramada Inn

May 17, 19--

Inside Page

Presiding	Terry McDonald, President
Introductions	Dennis Clark, Vice-President
Keynote Address	R. A. Flam, Chairperson Industry-Education Council

Partners in Progress

Awards	Sandra Pietrowski, Manager Garabedian Enterprises

LUNCHEON MENU

Tossed Salad	Green Bean Casserole
Veal Cordon Bleu	Rolls, Butter, and Jelly
Baked Potato	Bavarian Cream Pie
	Coffee, Tea, Milk

Lesson 106

• *70-space line*

106a ■ Keyboard Review • Each line at least three times
5 minutes

All letters   **SS**   Five or six quarters, won as prize money, jingled in the boy's pocket.

Figure-Symbol   Nearly 20% of the students were making $2.90 an hour in January, 1979.   Wrists low and still

u, i   They required us to build a building suitable for a public sanitarium.

Easy   Sign your name and also type it on the right–hand side of your papers.

| 1 | 2 | 3 | 4 | 5 | 6 | 7 | 8 | 9 | 10 | 11 | 12 | 13 | 14 |

106b • Skill Comparison • Type two 1-minute writings on each sentence. Compare gwam.
10 minutes

Easy   **SS**   Do not rest your fingers on the keys if you wish to reach a high rate.

Figure-Symbol   Each person's share (according to the 1980 figures) was less than $15.   Type steadily

Rough draft   the poeple who work hard always seem to gain the most fun out of the life.

Shift   Madge saw June and Mildred Avery at the Georgia State Fair in Atlanta.

| 1 | 2 | 3 | 4 | 5 | 6 | 7 | 8 | 9 | 10 | 11 | 12 | 13 | 14 |

35b ■ Location of " (quotation marks) and ___ (underline)

MANUAL (UNIVERSAL KEYBOARD)

The " is the shift of **2**. Reach with the **s** finger. Type the " without a space between it and the word it encloses.

Type " with the s finger

The __ is the shift of **6**. Reach with the **j** finger. Do not space up to type the underline directly below the copy.

Type __ with the j finger

s2s s"s s2s s"s "s "s "s s"s • Type twice on same line • j6j j_j j6j j_j _j _j _j j_j

ELECTRIC

The " is the shift of ' on electrics. Type it with the ; finger.

Type " with the ; finger

The __ is the shift of the hyphen key on electrics. Type the __ with the ; finger.

Type __ with the ; finger

;'; ;"; ;'; ;"; "; "; "; ;'; • Type twice on same line • ;—; ;_; ;—; ;_; _; _; _; ;_;

35c ■ Location Drills—" and __ • Each line twice   *10 minutes*

- *In underlining words, type the material to be underlined, then backspace to the first letter of the word (or move the carriage by hand) and strike the underline. If several words are to be underlined,* *use the shift lock. The underline is not broken between words, unless each word is to be considered separately.*

"	SS	Type "forty," not "fourty." Ken typed "ninty" for "ninety."
		Hannah typed "advice" for "advise" and "libel" for "liable."
—		Type <u>slowly</u>. Work for <u>control</u>. Keep your <u>eyes</u> on the <u>copy</u>.
		Did they all read "The Sun Starts to Rise on Solar" in <u>Time</u>?
'		June's work isn't right, and Ian's problems aren't finished.
-		An out-of-town speaker--a 37-year-old man--gave a fine talk.
--		Change--like it, hate it, or prize it, but get ready for it.

Quiet wrists and arms

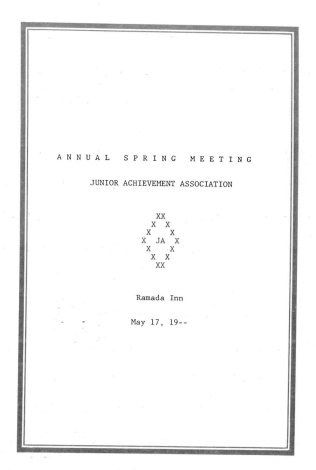

ANNUAL SPRING MEETING

JUNIOR ACHIEVEMENT ASSOCIATION

```
        XX
       X  X
      X    X
     X  JA  X
      X  .X
       X  X
        XX
```

Ramada Inn

May 17, 19--

Cover page

PROGRAM

9:00	Registration	Lobby, Ramada Inn
	Refreshments	Roundup Room
10:00	General Session	Grand Ballroom
	Greetings	Terry McDonald President
	Welcome	Joseph Brucia, President Wiley and Company
	Response	Dennis Clark Vice-President
	Address	"Looking Ahead to 1990" Mary Hagen, President Drummond Corporation
11:30	Introduction of Delegates	Ronald Hays Chapter 38
	Special Awards	Terry McDonald President
12:30	Luncheon	Crystal Dining Room

Inside page

One-fold program

Lesson 105

• *70-space line*

105a ■ Keyboard Review • Each line at least three times

5 minutes

All letters **SS** Jason knew exactly why he received a bad grade on that final map quiz.

Figure-Symbol Joan sent Check 6932 (dated September 15) for $178 to The Stereo Shop.

Sit erect

Double letters All smaller book committees will still meet three weeks in succession.

Easy If you get some bumps, it is a sign you are traveling out of your rut.

```
| 1 | 2 | 3 | 4 | 5 | 6 | 7 | 8 | 9 | 10 | 11 | 12 | 13 | 14 |
```

105b ■ Timed Writings

15 minutes

Directions—Type two 5-minute writings. on 101d, page 170. Compute your *gwam*. Submit the better of the two writings.

35d ■ Technique Builder—Flowing Rhythm

5 minutes

Directions—Each line three times.

Technique Goal—Blend stroking into flowing rhythm.

1 SS if she gets | if he sees | if she reads | if he cares | if they were

2   he did see | she did look | he did get | she did pull | they did set

3   if they join | if they trade | if they jump | to my | if it only did

4   she may set | he may oil | he may rest | she may draw | she may wear

35e ■ Timed Writings

10 minutes

Directions—Type two 3-minute writings on 34e, page 55. Compute *gwam*. Submit the better of the two writings.

35f ■ Spacing After Punctuation Marks—Review

10 minutes

Directions—Each line once. Read the explanation for a line before you type it.

EXPLANATIONS

Lines 1, 2, and 3—Space twice after end-of-sentence punctuation.

Line 4—Do not space after a period within an abbreviation. Space once after a period that ends an abbreviation; twice if that period ends a sentence.

Line 5—Space once after a comma.

Line 6—Space twice after a colon. Exception: Do not space before or after a colon in stating time.

Line 7—Type the dash with two hyphens, without spacing before or after.

Line 8—Do not space before or after the hyphen in a hyphenated word.

SENTENCES

1 SS Joan heard the bell. It rang at night. Al did not hear it.

2   Will they go? Can he drive? Where does he live? Who's it?

3   Dash to the nearest exit! Hurry! Beware! This is madness!

4   I saw him at 11 a.m. They will leave on the 10 p.m. flight.

Eyes and mind on copy as you type

5   She bought statues, jewelry, and other gifts in Rome, Italy.

6   I used these figures: 39, 58, and 20. He left at 4:16 p.m.

7   Ridicule is thus the first--and the last--argument of fools.

8   The well-known skin diver could not find the life preserver.

| 1 | 2 | 3 | 4 | 5 | 6 | 7 | 8 | 9 | 10 | 11 | 12 |

Lesson 104

104a ■ Keyboard Review • Each line at least three times

5 minutes

All letters SS Karla expected me to realize that use of jargon was very questionable.

Figure-Symbol Johnson, our 36th President, received 61.1% of the votes cast in 1964.

Fingers
deeply
curved

4th finger Pamela saw that Pat wasn't able to adapt adequately to that apparatus.

Easy The right mind set will help you make the typewriter do its work well.

| 1 | 2 | 3 | 4 | 5 | 6 | 7 | 8 | 9 | 10 | 11 | 12 | 13 | 14 |

104b ■ Punctuation Guides—Dash and Parentheses

5 minutes

Directions—Read the explanation carefully; then type each example sentence twice.

Line 1—Use a dash to show a sudden break in thought.

Line 3—Use parentheses to enclose an explanation.

Line 2—Use a dash before the name of an author when it follows a direct quotation.

• *A dash is made by typing two hyphens without space before or after.*

1 SS Time may be what all of us want most--but what we often use the worst.

2 "We have nothing to fear but fear itself."--Franklin Delano Roosevelt.

Reach with
your fingers

3 They will start typing on the 13th line space (2 inches) from the top.

| 1 | 2 | 3 | 4 | 5 | 6 | 7 | 8 | 9 | 10 | 11 | 12 | 13 | 14 |

104c ■ Paragraph Skill Builder from Rough Draft • Type four 1-minute writings

5 minutes

Words

DS Being ab̲l̲e̲ to type we sill for one minute is one thing; 11

being able to do well on a longer writings is quite 21

54 words
1.3 si

another. You must, of course, learn to be a steady/study 32

learner and worker. In a way, this is writing is a 41

text of your staying power. how well are you meeting 52

the this test? 54

104d ■ Problem Typing

30 minutes

Problem ■ *Program of Meeting*

Directions—1. Fold an 8½- by 11-inch sheet of paper to a fold-over program of 5½ by 8½ inches.

2. Insert the folded sheet with the fold at the left.

3. Arrange the copy for the cover page, shown on page 175, in an attractive form.

• *To align items at the right margin, set the carriage at the margin, backspace for the letters and spaces in the item, type.*

4. Before typing the inside page, reverse the fold, and reinsert the folded sheet with the fold at the left.

5. Arrange the copy for the inside page as illustrated on page 175. The copy is to be centered vertically with ½-inch side margins.

• *For directions on how to center lines on paper of odd size, refer to page 67, if necessary.*

Cycle 2

Basic Personal
Typewriting Operations

Problem ■ *School Organization Budget*

Directions—Standard 2-inch top margin. Space the report vertically as shown below. Leave 10 spaces between the columns.

● *Leaders are made by alternating a period and a space. They are aligned vertically as shown.*

● *Place the $ before the first amount and the total, typed so the $ will be 1 space to the left of the longest amount in the column.*

● *Double lines are made by using the ratchet release to move the carriage forward slightly prior to typing the second line.*

ASSOCIATED STUDENT BODY BUDGET

19-- to 19--

Triple-space ──────────→

Anticipated Income

←──────────── Double-space

Security Bank, Interest . . . . $ 40.00

Student Body Card Sales 1,500.00

Vending Machines 350.00

Total $1,890.00

←──────────── Triple-space

Anticipated Expenditures

Activities . . . . $ 625.00

Awards 140.00

Yearbook 250.00

Newspaper 400.00

Student Body Cards 50.00

Equipment and Supplies 125.00

Total $1,590.00

Triple-space ──────→

Total Budgeted Income $1,890.00

Total Budgeted Expense 1,590.00

Total Budgeted Balance . . . . $ 300.00

Budget

CYCLE 2 ■

Basic Personal Typewriting Operations

You are now ready to start using the typewriter to prepare some of your school and personal papers. This is a quick preview of some of the kinds of problems you will type in Cycle 2.

Notices, Personal Notes, and Letters—You will type announcements, personal notes, and personal business letters in acceptable form. These papers will be typical of those typed by students.

Themes, Outlines, and Tables—These papers are an important part of school work. The guides that you will be given are those generally used in typing themes, outlines, and tables.

Composing Personal Papers—One of your goals in this course is to be able to compose personal and school papers on the typewriter. The composing drills, spelling aids, and capitalization guides included in this cycle will help you to achieve this goal.

Extra-Credit Assignments—Problems are given at the end of each unit for students who finish assignments ahead of schedule. Type these problems as time permits. Extra credit will be given for them.

Building Basic Skill—The higher your skill becomes on the typewriter, the easier it will be for you to use it for your written work. The ideal is to be able to type so well that you can forget the typewriter and concentrate on the papers you are preparing. That is why you will continue to work on speed and control in Cycle 2.

How You Can Help—Much of what you get out of the lessons in Cycle 2 will depend upon you. Here are some points to keep in mind as you prepare your lessons:

1. Have the desire to improve. You learn best when you really want to learn.

2. Have a clear goal in mind for each practice. You can't learn if you don't know what you should be learning. Keep this goal in mind as you type the drills and problems.

3. Learn to plan your work. Part of this job requires you to read and hear directions correctly. You will get some practice in working with directions every day. Make the most of this practice.

UNIT 6 ■ Centering Notices and Announcements

General Directions ■ Lessons 36 - 40

Machine Adjustments—For the lessons in this unit, use a 60-space line. Single-space lines of words and sentences; double-space between repeated groups of lines. Double-space paragraph copy.

Correcting Errors—Instructions for making corrections are given in Lesson 39 of this unit. Your teacher will tell you whether or not you are to correct errors on problems in Lessons 39 and 40.

Lesson 36

• *Use a 60-space line for all lessons in this unit.*

36a ■ Keyboard Review • Each line three times   5 minutes

All letters   SS   Their expert jumpers dazzled Billy Wycoff with quick diving.

Figure-Symbol   Even sums like $580 or $476 don't require decimals or zeros.

Easy   The folks to get even with are the ones who have helped you.

| 1 | 2 | 3 | 4 | 5 | 6 | 7 | 8 | 9 | 10 | 11 | 12 |

Quick sharp strokes

Problem 2 ■ Horizontal Bar Graph

Directions—Center the graph on a half sheet; space as directed in Problem 1.

FIRST-SEMESTER TYPING SPEED GROWTH FOR KRISTIE ROYAL

September	xxx
October	xxxxxx
November	xxxxxxxxxxxxx
December	xxxxxxxxxxxxxxxxxxxxx
January	xxxxxxxxxxxxxxxxxxxxxxxxx
GWAM	10 20 30

Lesson 103

103a ■ Keyboard Review ● Each line at least three times   5 minutes

All letters SS Mr. Brown just received six dozen packages of quilts from the factory.

Figure-Symbol   The first electric vacuum cleaner (made about 1905) weighed 92 pounds.   Instant

e, i   Neither of their neighbors knew of vacancies in the secretarial field.   key

Easy   Four of their friends had to pay more than usual for items they found.   release

| 1 | 2 | 3 | 4 | 5 | 6 | 7 | 8 | 9 | 10 | 11 | 12 | 13 | 14 |

103b ■ Speed Stretcher ● As indicated in 98b, page 165   10 minutes

		GWAM
		1' 5'

All letters DS Although they spend many years in school, most students do not know   14 | 3 39

¶ 1   how to study. Even worse, they don't know what to study. As you read   28 | 6 42
56 words
1.3 si   a lesson, therefore, search for the needle in the haystack--find the   42 | 8 44

main idea. Look at the headings; study the visual aids in the textbook.   56 | 11 47

When you finish a lesson, try summarizing it in a few words. This   13 | 14 50

¶ 2   is the real test of learning--putting in your own words the meat of a   27 | 17 53
55 words
1.3 si   lesson. Many students often discover that they learn better if they   41 | 19 55

recite to themselves. They list the chief points in their own words.   55 | 22 58

It will pay you to overlearn anything you need to learn well.   13 | 25 61

Reading a lesson through quickly only once is like getting a fish   26 | 27 63

¶ 3   on your hook and not bothering to land it. Most of us forget about half   40 | 30 66
69 words
1.3 si   of anything we learn the first hour or so after learning it. We need to   55 | 33 69

All ¶'s
1.3 si   go over the major points any number of times to fix them in our minds.   69 | 36 72

| 1' | 1 | 2 | 3 | 4 | 5 | 6 | 7 | 8 | 9 | 10 | 11 | 12 | 13 | 14 |
| 5' | | | 1 | | | | 2 | | | | 3 | | |

36b ■ Technique Builder—Stroking • Each line three times

Upper row	**SS**	Will you try to keep up my treatment as so many others have?
Double letters		The school cannot accept the small books that Lee possesses.
Figure-Symbol		Type amounts as follows: $740 (not $740.00), but $1,935.64.
Difficult reaches		They are doubtful I will be able to collect many place mats.
Bottom row		We know that the girl held the big soap box when she met us.
Fourth finger		We were asked to apply a quick answer to that quaint puzzle.

Fingers deeply curved

Quiet wrists and arms

| 1 | 2 | 3 | 4 | 5 | 6 | 7 | 8 | 9 | 10 | 11 | 12 |

36c ■ Spelling and Proofreading Aid • Each line three times

5 minutes

● *Accurate spelling is basic to accurate typing and proofreading. Teach your fingers to spell the following words correctly.*

1 **SS** attempt coming fourth library prior finally until using paid

2 quantity excellent privilege particular substantial mortgage   Even stroking

3 efficient continuing guarantee superintendent accommodations

36d ■ Paragraph Guided Writings

15 minutes

Directions—1. Type a 1-minute writing on the first paragraph. Note your *gwam*. Add four words to your *gwam* for a new goal.
2. Type two more 1-minute writings on the paragraph. Try to reach your goal.

3. Now type a 1-minute writing on the paragraph at your first rate. Your goal this time is to type without error.
4. Repeat Steps 1, 2, and 3 for the second and third paragraphs.

		GWAM 1'	3'
DS	You have heard it said that if you save your pennies,	11	4 36
¶ 1 30 words 1.2 si	your dollars will take care of themselves. You will find that	23	8 40
	this is also true in typewriting.	30	10 42
	Watch the little things in typing, and speed will take	41	14 46
¶ 2 32 words 1.2 si	care of itself. Note the position of your fingers. Be sure	53	18 50
	that they are curved and close to your keys.	62	21 53
¶ 3 34 words 1.2 si	Keep your eyes on the copy. Do not waste time glancing	73	24 58
	from the copy to the paper in your machine. When you come	85	28 60
All ¶'s 1.2 si	to the end of a line, just return the carriage quickly.	96	32 64

| 1' | 1 | 2 | 3 | 4 | 5 | 6 | 7 | 8 | 9 | 10 | 11 | 12 |
| 3' | | 1 | | | 2 | | | 3 | | | 4 | |

Lesson 102

102a ■ Keyboard Review ● Each line at least three times

5 minutes

All letters **SS** Excited crowds enjoy big trapeze events and frequently clap them back.

Figure-Symbol A crowd of 49,936 witnessed the 1966 All-Star game in 100-degree heat.

Long reach I brought the pink linoleum and lumber with me. I broke the monument.

Easy Fine typists have learned to keep their eyes on the copy as they type.

| 1 | 2 | 3 | 4 | 5 | 6 | 7 | 8 | 9 | 10 | 11 | 12 | 13 | 14 |

Quick
carriage
return

102b ■ Paragraph Skill Builder from Script ● Type four 1-minute writings.

5 minutes

Words

60 words
1.3 si

DS *Very often the little things in life will turn out to be the most
important. The art of printing was suggested by one who cut letters
in the bark of a tree. An accident with a red-hot skillet led to the
making of vulcanized rubber. It seems that a thing can't be too small
to demand our attention.*

13
27
41
55
60

102c ■ Building Skill on Figures and Symbols ● Each line three times

5 minutes

1 **SS** I read "The Magic Label" by Jack Hankins. It's a very timely article.

2 Their bank pays 6% interest on savings accounts. Pam received $12.96.

3 Check 529 (dated June 14) will cover this 25-cent charge, will it not?

| 1 | 2 | 3 | 4 | 5 | 6 | 7 | 8 | 9 | 10 | 11 | 12 | 13 | 14 |

Fix key
locations
in mind

102d ■ Problem Typing

30 minutes

Problem 1 ■ *Horizontal Bar Graph*

Directions—1. Center the graph on a half sheet.
2. To determine the left margin stop, center the carriage and backspace once for each 2 spaces in the longest name, the space between the names and the bars, and the longest bar. Set a tab stop where the bars begin.

3. Each *x* represents one word a minute. Place an apostrophe under the first *x* in each group of ten as shown. Center the GWAM figures under the apostrophe by depressing the backspace key half way.

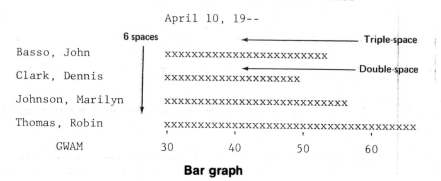

Bar graph

36e ■ Composing at the Typewriter

10 minutes

Directions—1. Type an answer to each question. Use complete sentences.

2. If time permits, retype any sentences in which you made typing errors.

● *An answer is given for the first question as an illustration.*

Questions:
1. What is your favorite sport?
2. What is your favorite subject?
3. What is the name of your school?
4. What is your typewriting teacher's name?
5. Name the state in which you live.
6. Name the city in which you were born.

Sample Answer:

```
1. My favorite sport is basketball.
```

Lesson 37

● *60-space line*

37a ■ Keyboard Review ● Each line three times

5 minutes

All letters **SS** Bob Jade was given extra maps quickly as he was in a frenzy.

Figure-Symbol Mary claimed that 80.6% of all car trips are under 10 miles.

Quiet wrists and arms

Easy They then have to make out both forms for their entire team.

| 1 | 2 | 3 | 4 | 5 | 6 | 7 | 8 | 9 | 10 | 11 | 12 |

37b ■ Typing from Dictation and Spelling Checkup

5 minutes

Directions—Your teacher will dictate the words in 36c, page 60. Type the words from dictation. Check your work for correct spelling. Retype the words in which you made an error.

37c ■ Timed Writings

10 minutes

Directions—Type two 3-minute writings on 36d, page 60. Compute *gwam*. Submit the better of the two writings.

Vertical Centering Steps

● *Centering material so that it will have uniform top and bottom margins is called vertical centering.*

Step 1—Count the lines in the copy to be centered. If your copy is to be double spaced, remember to count the spaces between the lines. There is only one line space following each line of copy when material is double spaced.

Step 2—Subtract the total lines from the lines available on the paper you are using. (There are 33 lines on a half sheet, 66 on a full sheet.)

Step 3—Divide the number of lines that remain by 2. The answer gives you the number of lines in the top and bottom margins. If the result contains a fraction, disregard it.

Step 4—Insert your paper so that the top edge is exactly even with the aligning scale (No. 21). Bring the paper up the proper number of line spaces. Start typing on the next line space.

101d ▪ Speed Ladder Paragraphs • As directed in 96d, page 163.   *20 minutes*

All letters   **DS**   The next time you are faced with the problem of what to buy the   `13 | 3 55`

¶ 1
44 words
1.3 si   person who has everything, why not consider buying a mule? While this   `27 | 5 57`

idea might sound odd at first, you should realize the many advantages   `41 | 8 60`

of such a gift.   `44 | 9 61`

Here are just a couple of them. First of all, a mule requires   `57 | 11 63`

¶ 2
48 words
1.3 si   much less upkeep than a nifty sports car and has fewer moving parts   `70 | 14 66`

than a wristwatch. To be perfectly frank, I must admit that sometimes   `84 | 17 69`

a mule has absolutely no moving parts.   `92 | 18 70`

Mules are smart, stubborn, and not the least bit choosy when it   `105 | 21 73`

¶ 3
52 words
1.4 si   comes to eating. They will eat whatever is in sight, including wooden   `119 | 24 76`

fences. Mule lovers claim their favorite animals have good sense since   `133 | 27 79`

they won't do anything that will end up hurting them.   `144 | 29 81`

Mules, which often live to be about thirty years old, work until   `157 | 31 83`

the day they die. They are used in national parks, in the movies, in   `171 | 34 86`

¶ 4
56 words
1.3 si   fishing camps, and down on the farm. Armies have used mules to carry   `185 | 37 89`

ammunition. West Point football games would never be the same without   `199 | 40 92`

one.   `200 | 40 92`

Surely you are interested by now. Therefore, it is only fair to   `213 | 43 95`

warn you of one minor problem. A mule's stubborn streak can sometimes   `227 | 45 97`

¶ 5
60 words
1.3 si   be troublesome. If the ears go down, you had better watch out. You   `241 | 48 100`

can always take comfort in the fact, however, that a mule won't kick   `255 | 51 103`

All ¶'s
1.3 si   you unless you deserve it.   `260 | 52 104`

1' | 1 | 2 | 3 | 4 | 5 | 6 | 7 | 8 | 9 | 10 | 11 | 12 | 13 | 14 |
5' | 1 | 2 | 3 |

101e ▪ Continuity Practice •   Type the last paragraph of 101d without timing. Type it as many times as you can in the time that remains.   *5 minutes*

37d ■ Problem Typing

25 minutes

Problem 1 ■ Report on Half Sheet

Half sheet
60-space line
Double spacing

Directions—Center the short report below. Your teacher will tell you where you are to type your name and the problem numbers for the problems you type.

		Words
7		
8	**Start on**	
9	**Line 9** A half sheet of paper contains 33 lines; a full sheet	11
10		
11	has 66 lines. It does not make any difference what kind of	23
12		
13	typewriter you are using. All are the same on this point.	35
14		
15	To center copy vertically, up and down, count the lines in	46
16		
17	the copy. Subtract this total from 33 if you are using a	58
18		
19	half sheet or 66 if you are using a full sheet. Divide the	70
20		
21	difference by 2 to get top and bottom margins for exact cen-	82
22		
23	tering. If the result contains a fraction, just disregard	94
24		
25	it. Type the copy. You will find that it is neatly placed.	106
26		
27		
28	*Lines in half sheet 33*	
29	*Lines and line spaces in copy 17*	
30	*Line spaces in top and bottom margins . . . 16*	
31	*Divide by 2. Top margin . . . . 8 **	
32	*Bottom margin . . . . 8 **	
33	** Start typing on the 9th line space from the top.*	

Report centered on half sheet of paper

Problem 2 ■ Report on Full Sheet

Full sheet
60-space line
Double spacing

Directions—Type the short report in Problem 1 again. This time type it on a full sheet. Center it neatly.

Lesson 38

●*60-space line*

38a ■ Keyboard Review • Each line three times

5 minutes

All letters **ss** The quiz show Jack Palm entered had six girls and five boys.

Symbol   Place added information (such as a date) within parentheses.

*Feet on
the floor*

Easy   You win when you get your mind to stick to a job to the end.

| 1 | 2 | 3 | 4 | 5 | 6 | 7 | 8 | 9 | 10 | 11 | 12 |

LESSON 38 ■ PAGE 62

Problem 3 ■ *Typing Postal Card from Script*

Directions—1. Type another postal card containing the message given in Problem 1, page 168.

2. Address the card to Chris Van Elswyk, 2947 Herndon Avenue, Ellensburg, WA 98926.

Lesson 101

• 70-space line

101a ■ Keyboard Review • Each line at least three times

5 minutes

All letters SS   Joe believed that my trip from Arizona to New York was quite exciting.

Figure-Symbol   The price has been reduced from $45,750 to $38,500, effective April 8.

Weak fingers   Patti and/or Paul will acquaint us with techniques of raising azaleas.

Easy   Very few are too busy to take the time to tell just how busy they are.

| 1 | 2 | 3 | 4 | 5 | 6 | 7 | 8 | 9 | 10 | 11 | 12 | 13 | 14 |

Fix key locations in mind

101b ■ Punctuation Guides—Colon

5 minutes

Directions—Read the explanation carefully; then type each example sentence twice.

Line 1—Use a colon to introduce a list of items or expressions.

Line 2—Use a colon to separate the hours and minutes when they are expressed in figures.

Line 3—Use a colon to introduce a question or long quotation.

1   SS   They will ship these items: uniforms, shoes, gloves, bats, and balls.

2   Lori left from Seattle at 7:15 p.m.; she arrived in Butte at 9:20 p.m.

3   The question before us is this: Can we complete the projects in time?

| 1 | 2 | 3 | 4 | 5 | 6 | 7 | 8 | 9 | 10 | 11 | 12 | 13 | 14 |

Feet on the floor

101c ■ Sentence Control Builder

10 minutes

Directions—Type two 1-minute writings on each sentence. Try typing each without error.

1   SS   We will not expect to lead others farther than we have gone ourselves.

2   Folks who think too much of themselves usually aren't thinking enough.

3   If they get half their wishes, they will likely double their troubles.

4   You have the right to risk those things if no one else will be harmed.

| 1 | 2 | 3 | 4 | 5 | 6 | 7 | 8 | 9 | 10 | 11 | 12 | 13 | 14 |

Space quickly

● All letters are used in these paragraphs

	GWAM
	1' │ 3'

DS   Do relax your shoulders as you type. Do not sit in a   11 │ 4 38

¶ 1
32 words
1.2 si   tight, cramped position. It will make you tense and tired,   23 │ 8 42

and you will make more errors than you should.   32 │ 11 45

       Do sit erect; have your feet flat on the floor, with   43 │ 14 48

¶ 2
34 words
1.2 si   one foot just ahead of the other. Don't slump in your seat   55 │ 18 52

or wrap your feet around the chair legs in a lazy manner.   66 │ 22 56

       Do set the margin stops, and listen for the bell to tell   77 │ 26 60

¶ 3
36 words
1.2 si   you when the lines end. Do not look up for line endings.   89 │ 30 64

Looking up breaks your rhythm and is a frequent cause of   101 │ 34 68

All ¶'s
1.2 si   errors.   102 │ 34 68

```
1' | 1 | 2 | 3 | 4 | 5 | 6 | 7 | 8 | 9 | 10 | 11 | 12 |
3' |     1     |       2       |       3       |       4       |
```

Horizontal Centering Steps

● *Centering headings and paragraph material so that there will be equal left and right margins is called horizontal centering.*

Step 1—Check the placement of the paper guide. Turn to page vi, and read the directions for adjusting the paper guide.
Step 2—Move the carriage to the center point.

Step 3—Backspace once for each 2 spaces in the line to be centered. If there is one letter left, do not backspace for it. Begin to type at the point where the backspacing is completed.

38c ▪ Problem Typing   *25 minutes*

Practice Problem ▪ *Centering Lines Horizontally*

Directions—Using practice paper, center each line horizontally as explained above.

FINAL GAME OF THE SEASON

See the Blue and Gold Warriors in Action!

Saturday, November 10, 2 p.m.

Surprise Stunts at Halftime

Lesson 100

100a ▪ Keyboard Review • Each line at least three times
5 minutes

All letters   SS   Frank soon realized how very much Peg enjoyed excellent Baroque music.

Figure-Symbol   Arabic numbers like 1, 2, and 3 are sometimes typed (1), (2), and (3).
Think as

Adjacent keys   We said the captain was astonished to see several sailors fast asleep.   you type

Easy   Neither of the two had enough chairs to handle such a tough situation.

| 1 | 2 | 3 | 4 | 5 | 6 | 7 | 8 | 9 | 10 | 11 | 12 | 13 | 14 |

100b ▪ Timed Writings • Type two 5-minute writings on 96d, page 163. Compute your gwam. Submit the better of the two.
15 minutes

100c ▪ Problem Typing
25 minutes

Problem 1 ▪ *Postal Card from Script*

Directions—1. Type the following message on a postal card or on paper cut to proper size (5½- by 3¼-inches). Use modified block style.

2. Insert the card, short side at the left. Determine the horizontal center; set margin stops 4 spaces in from each side of the card.

3. Address the card to Ms. Joy Palmquist, 129 Chestnut Drive, Ellensburg, WA 98926.

4. Type the following return address in the upper left hand corner of the address side of the postal card: Doug Calhoun, 15 Poe Street, Seattle, WA 98101.

July 1, 19-- / Dear Service Club Member / We are making plans for Orientation Day in the fall. We need the help of as many of our returning members as we can get. (¶) Please let me know if you can serve as a new student guide during Orientation Day, September 5. / Doug Calhoun / Secretary

Problem 2 ▪ *Composing Postal Card Message*

Directions—1. Assume the message in Problem 1 had been mailed to you. Compose an answer and type it in proper form on a postal card.

2. Explain that you can work as a guide during the morning of September 5 but that you have to work in the testing office in the afternoon.

Problem 1 ■ Centered Announcement

Half sheet
Double-space

Directions—Using clean paper, center the practice problem, page 63, vertically. Center each line horizontally. In double-spaced copy, one line space appears between lines.

Problem 2 ■ Centered Announcement

Directions—Center the following problem vertically. Center each line horizontally. In triple-spaced copy, two line spaces appear between the typed lines.

CAMERA CLUB MEETING

Tuesday, November 13, 2:30 p.m.

Half sheet
Triple-space

Room 242

Prizes for Outstanding Photographs

Refreshments

Lesson 39

● *60-space line*

39a ■ Keyboard Review ● Each line three times

10 minutes

All letters	SS	Peg and Mark will quickly adjust five bird boxes at the zoo.
Symbol		I quoted three sources: <u>Time</u>, <u>Newsweek</u>, and <u>The New Yorker</u>.
Easy		The right angle to use in solving problems is the try angle.

Instant
release

| 1 | 2 | 3 | 4 | 5 | 6 | 7 | 8 | 9 | 10 | 11 | 12 |

39b ■ Speed Ladder Sentences

5 minutes

Directions—Type 1-minute writings on each sentence. Try typing each four times in the minute. Your teacher will call the return of the carriage each 15 seconds to guide you.

● *The rate increases 5 words a minute with each succeeding line.*

GWAM
15"
Guide

1	SS	To type right, sit erect.	20
2		Type the lines with the guides.	25
3		Try typing with the call of the guide.	30
4		The aim is to type this line with the guide.	35
5		Few of us know what a big job a little job can be.	40

| 1 | 2 | 3 | 4 | 5 | 6 | 7 | 8 | 9 | 10 |

Lesson 99

99a ■ Keyboard Review • Each line at least three times

5 minutes

All letters SS   The next evening Jack quickly scanned the horizon from Briarwood Peak.

Figure   Mt. Everest, India, at 29,018 feet, is the highest point on the earth.

Quick, sharp strokes

Shift   Edmund Hillary and Tenzing Norkey scaled Mt. Everest in the Himalayas.

Easy   The biggest mistake we can make is to believe that we cannot make one.

| 1 | 2 | 3 | 4 | 5 | 6 | 7 | 8 | 9 | 10 | 11 | 12 | 13 | 14 |

99b ■ Concentration Practice • Type twice for control—more if time permits. Think the letters and figures as you type.

10 minutes

Words

DS   On May 20, 1927, a 25-year-old airmail pilot, Captain Charles A.   13

Lindbergh, flew his single-engine plane, The Spirit of St. Louis, from New   32

73 words
1.4 si

York to Paris, completing the first nonstop flight, in 33 hours,   46

29 minutes, 30 seconds. On May 26, 1961, Air Force Major W. R. Payne,   60

piloting a B-58, cut the time to 3 hours, 19 minutes, 45 seconds.   73

| 1 | 2 | 3 | 4 | 5 | 6 | 7 | 8 | 9 | 10 | 11 | 12 | 13 | 14 |

99c ■ Problem Typing • Directions for centering lines on odd-size paper are on page 67.

30 minutes

Problem 1 ■ *Typed Admission Tickets*

Directions—1. Type three tickets of the kind illustrated below. Use 5- by 3-inch cards or paper cut to that size. Arrange the copy neatly on the card.

2. Note that some of the lines are centered; some are typed at the left and right margins.

3. Number the cards in sequence, beginning with No. 150.

Problem 2 ■ *Typed Membership Cards*

Directions—1. Type three membership cards, using the copy below. Use 5- by 3-inch cards or paper cut to that size. Arrange the copy neatly on the card.

2. Number the cards in sequence, beginning with No. 75.

3. Membership is to June 1 of the next year. Type in the correct year date.

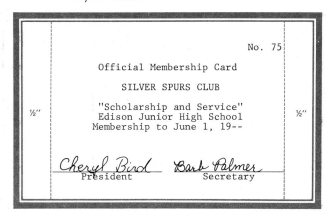

Admission ticket

Membership card

			Words
All letters	DS	*A late quote from the College Board states that the*	10
44 words		*broad major field of health ranks first choice of many*	21
1.2 si		*high school students who plan to go to college. Business*	39
		now receives a fair-sized interest from both sexes too.	44

Correcting Errors

Errors made in themes, personal notes, and other papers often need to be corrected. Therefore, you should learn to use the basic methods for correcting typing errors. Three of them are explained in Problem 1, below.

● *Your teacher will tell you whether you are to erase and correct errors made in typing the problems that follow.*

39d ■ Problem Typing

25 minutes

Problem 1 ■ Short Report

Full sheet
60-space line
Double spacing

Directions—Center the report vertically on a full sheet. Center the heading horizontally.

	Words
CORRECTING ERRORS	4

Triple-space ⟶

Unless the typewriter has a special correcting ribbon,	15
you may correct errors with a typing eraser, with correction	27
fluid, or with correction tape.	33
When using a typing eraser, move the carriage to one	44
side to keep the crumbs from falling into the machine. Roll	56
your paper up two or three spaces, then hold the paper firmly	68
against the platen while making the erasure.	77
To correct an error with correction fluid, just paint	88
over the incorrect letter. Make sure the fluid is dry before	101
typing the correct letter.	106
Correction tape should be placed between the ribbon and	117
your error. Simply retype your error, allowing powder from	129
the tape to cover the incorrect letter.	137

Minutes of Meetings

The minutes of a meeting are an exact record of what happened at a meeting. There is no set form which is used by all clubs and organizations for recording minutes. The form recommended in this lesson is acceptable and widely used.

98c ■ Problem Typing

30 minutes

Directions—Type a copy of the minutes that follow in the form illustrated at the right below. A 1½-inch left margin and a 1-inch right margin are used as minutes are usually placed in a binder.

● *The center point will be 3 spaces to the right of the point normally used. Keep this point in mind in centering headings.*

AHWAHNEE SCHOOL SERVICE CLUB

Minutes of Meeting

    Date: September 24, 19--
    Time: 12:10 p.m.
    Place: Room 119, Ahwahnee School
Present: About 35 students in addition to the advisers, Mr. Holmes and Miss Code

1. Dennis Kerns, President, presided. He introduced the officers and our two advisers.

2. The president outlined the goals of the club and the requirements for membership. Dues are 50 cents per member.

3. Mr. Holmes explained that the principal would like the Service Club to sponsor after-school movies once a month. The cost to students will range from 25 cents to 50 cents depending upon the rental cost of the film.

4. Miss Code asked for volunteers to help paint trash cans after school on September 26.

5. Pat Anderson reported that the Halloween Costume Party would be held Friday evening, October 31.

6. The president asked members to list their free periods when they would be available to act as guides.

7. A decision was made to hold meetings on the first Wednesday of each month at 12:10 p.m.

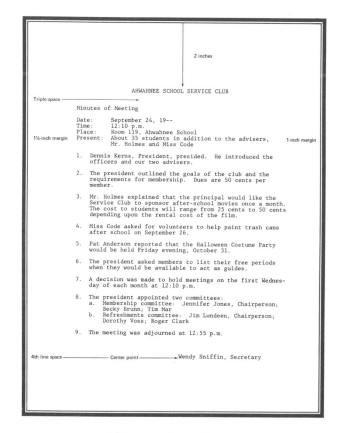

Minutes of meeting

8. The president appointed two committees:
    a. Membership committee: Jennifer Jones, Chairperson; Becky Brunn; Tim Mar
    b. Refreshments committee: Jim Lundeen, Chairperson; Dorothy Voss; Roger Clark

9. The meeting was adjourned at 12:55 p.m.

Wendy Sniffin, Secretary

Common Proofreaders' Marks

∧	Insert	⊐	Move right	∿	Transpose
◡	Close up	⊏	Move left	#	Space
⸔	Delete	≡	Capitalize	¶	Paragraph

Problem 2 ■ Short Report from Rough Draft

Half sheet
60-space line
Double spacing

Directions—Center the report vertically. Center the heading. Make the corrections as you type. If necessary, refer to the proofreaders' marks above.

- When rough draft copy must be centered, you can count the lines in the draft and add or deduct lines from the total, depending upon the kind of corrections made; or you can type it, with corrections made, on practice paper first. The lines can then be counted, and the second typing can be centered as directed. Your teacher will tell you which practice you are to follow for this problem.

```
                                                              Words
Triple →        SELLING  YOURSELF                               3
Space
             good
    ¶ Finding a summer job, or any other jobs for that          14

    matter, usually boils down to selling yourself. In dealing  26

    with people who can hire you, remember to project the image 38

    that you are more interested in what you can do for them than 59

    In what they can do for you. ¶ Since employers are only     61

    human, they are more interested in their needs than in yours. 74

    understanding this psychology will help you sell your skills, 86
                                      interests.
    experience, and talents.                                   91
```

Lesson 40

40a ■ Keyboard Review • Each line three times   5 minutes

All letters SS Please pack my boxes with five dozen jugs of liquid varnish.

Figure-Symbol Use a diagonal for "made" fractions such as 2 7/8 or 15 3/4.   Quick, crisp, short strokes

Easy He tried to learn to keep his eyes on the ball at all times.

| 1 | 2 | 3 | 4 | 5 | 6 | 7 | 8 | 9 | 10 | 11 | 12 |

Problem 2 ■ *Notice and Agenda of a Meeting*

Directions—Follow the directions given in Problem 1.

AHWAHNEE SCHOOL "A" CLUB

Regular Meeting, October 15, 19--

Room 126   3:30 p.m.

AGENDA

1. Approval of September 12 minutes

2. Report by Treasurer, Chris Combs

3. Discussion of new business
   a. Need to raise money for club activities
   b. Volunteers to work at October 25 PTA meeting

Lesson 98

● *70-space line*

98a ■ Keyboard Review ● Each line at least three times

5 minutes

All letters **SS**	I was quite lucky that my jams won five prizes at today's big exhibit.
Figure-Symbol	Our address is 932 West 15th Street; our new phone number is 468-7038.
Long words	Andromeda is also the remotest heavenly body visible to the naked eye.
Easy	The problem they have right now is caused by the slant of their hands.

Flowing rhythm

| 1 | 2 | 3 | 4 | 5 | 6 | 7 | 8 | 9 | 10 | 11 | 12 | 13 | 14 |

98b ■ Speed Stretcher ● Use Speed Stretchers for 5-minute writings, or use each paragraph for 1-minute writings.

10 minutes

GWAM
1' | 5'

All letters **DS**   A subject receiving a good bit of thought these days is something   13 | 3 34

¶ 1
54 words
1.3 si   we might refer to as the people explosion. The number of us who now   27 | 5 37

inhabit the globe has passed the four billion mark. At present growth   41 | 8 40

rates, it will climb two billion more by the end of the century.   54 | 11 43

In all of our millions of years on earth, this number was not half   13 | 13 45

¶ 2
53 words
1.3 si   that size until about sixty years ago. That is within the lifetimes   27 | 16 48

of many who are still living. Experts say that a quarter of all the   41 | 19 51

persons who ever lived on this planet are still alive today.   53 | 21 53

¶ 3
52 words   While estimates vary, of course, we know that a great many of these   14 | 24 56

people do not receive enough of the right kinds of food to function at   28 | 27 59

their best. Because of this fact, a great debate now rages as to how   42 | 30 62

All ¶'s
1.3 si   many people the resources of the earth can support.   52 | 32 64

| 1' | 1 | 2 | 3 | 4 | 5 | 6 | 7 | 8 | 9 | 10 | 11 | 12 | 13 | 14 |
| 5' | | | 1 | | | | 2 | | | | 3 | | | |

40b ■ Timed Writings

Directions—Type two 3-minute writings on 38b, page 63. Compute *gwam*. Submit the better of the two writings.

Finding the Horizontal Center Point of Odd-Size Paper or Cards

● *In order to center headings on paper or cards of different sizes, you must learn how to find the center point of these papers or cards.*

Step 1—Insert paper or card into the machine.
Step 2—Add the numbers on the cylinder scale at the left and right edges of the paper or card.

Step 3—Divide the sum obtained in Step 2 by 2. The resulting figure gives you the center point of the paper or card.

40c ■ Problem Typing

Problem 1 ■ Practice Problem

Directions—**1.** Insert a half sheet of practice paper (5½- by 8½ inches) with the long edge at the left.

2. From the top edge, space down to the 17th line space. Set your machine for triple spacing.

3. Determine the center of the half sheet. Set a tab stop at this point.

4. Center horizontally each line of the problem over the center point of the half sheet.

● *There are six vertical line spaces to an inch. An 8½-inch sheet contains 51 vertical line spaces: 8½ × 6 = 51.*

```
                THE COMPUTER CLUB

                   Announces

              a Free Demonstration

                    of the

            Universal Language System

         Thursday, March 10, 2:30 p.m.

                  Room 382
```

Problem 2 ■ Announcement on Odd-Size Paper

Directions—Using clean paper, type the practice problem again as directed.

LESSON 40 ■ **PAGE 67**

Lesson 97

97a ■ Keyboard Review • Each line at least three times

5 minutes

All letters **SS** The judge will request several dozen back copies of my deluxe edition.

Figure-Symbol Pat actually delivered all 104 newspapers before 6:30 a.m. on July 24!

Balanced and one-hand and the date, and the case, and the only, and the rest, and the faster

Easy Rains which fell in the city during the night helped to clean the air.

| 1 | 2 | 3 | 4 | 5 | 6 | 7 | 8 | 9 | 10 | 11 | 12 | 13 | 14 |

Eyes on copy as you return the carriage

97b ■ Control Ladder Paragraphs

10 minutes

Directions—Type 1-minute writings on the paragraphs in 96d, page 163. When you can type a paragraph within the specified error limit, move to the next one.

97c ■ Problem Typing

30 minutes

Problem 1 ■ *Notice and Agenda of a Meeting*

Full sheet
50-space line
2-inch top margin

Directions—1. Type the notice and agenda of a meeting from the copy below. Follow the form used in the illustration.

2. Items in the third line are to be typed at the left and right margins of the 50-space line.

AHWAHNEE SCHOOL SERVICE CLUB

Notice of the First Meeting

September 24, 19--   12:10 p.m.

Room 119

AGENDA

1. Introduction of officers and advisers
2. Discussion of Service Club organization
   a. Aims
   b. Membership requirements
3. Discussion of major projects for the year
   a. Sponsoring of monthly movies
   b. Club's role in the "Beautify Your School" campaign
   c. Halloween Costume Party
   d. Guide service for school visitors
4. Decision on meeting dates and time
5. Appointment of program committee
6. Appointment of refreshments committee
7. Adjournment by 12:55 p.m.

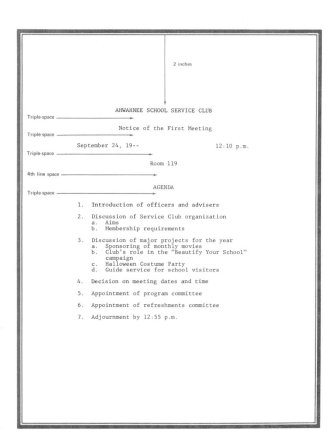

Notice and agenda of meeting

Problem 3 ■ Announcement on Odd-Size Paper

Directions—1. Insert a half sheet of paper with the long edge at the left.

2. Center each line horizontally. Center the problem vertically, triple-spaced.

GLEE CLUB CANDY SALE

at Main Entrance

Friday, October 20

Bring Your Nickels and Dimes

Delicious Candy

Send Glee Club to the District Contest

● You must know the number of line spaces in the sheet of paper.

Problem 4 ■ Announcement on Odd-Size Paper ● As directed in Problem 3

● *Do not type the diagonal lines. They indicate carriage-return points.*

JOIN THE EXPLORERS' CLUB / Meetings on Fridays, 2 to 3 p.m. / Dues Only $1 a Semester / Tours, Exhibits, Demonstrations / First Meeting, Friday, September 28 / Movie: "Undersea Secrets"

40d ■ Extra-Credit Typing

Problem ■ Report from Rough Draft

Full sheet
60-space line
Double spacing

Directions—Provide a heading for the report. Center it on a full sheet. Make the corrections as you type.

	Words
(Provide appropriate heading)	4
While, ~~people~~ folks generally take the university of Okoboji	15
seriously, this "College for Every one" is all in fun. Located	28
in the lakes region of Northwest Iowa, it considers all the	40
residents and those who vacation there as its student body.	52
¶ Although you ~~might~~ may not know anyone who played football at	63
this particular institution, your might have seen one of the	75
University T-shirts. its insignia includes the school motto	87
and small representations of sports the area is noted for.	99

96d ■ Speed Ladder Paragraphs

20 minutes

Directions—Type as many 1-minute writings as time permits. When you can type the first paragraph at the rate specified, type the next one.

Alternate Procedure—Start with the first paragraph moving to the succeeding one when you have completed each within the error limit specified by your teacher.

		GWAM	
		1'	5'

All letters   DS

¶ 1
40 words
1.4 si

Can you imagine wearing a size 38 shoe or buying a dress shirt 13 | 3 51
that has a size 39 collar? Such items aren't for giants but are for 26 | 5 53
normal people who use the metric system of weights and measurements. 40 | 8 56

¶ 2
44 words
1.3 si

In the days before most of the world went metric, chaos reigned. 53 | 11 59
In fact, if you had crossed Europe a century or two ago, you would have 68 | 14 62
found that a different system was used in almost every country, town, 82 | 16 64
or province. 84 | 17 65

¶ 3
48 words
1.3 si

Systems used throughout the world at one time or other have been 97 | 19 67
quite varied. Often, common objects such as kernels of grain were used 111 | 22 70
as weights. According to legend, a yard was the distance from the tip 126 | 25 73
of a person's thumb to the nose. 132 | 26 74

¶ 4
52 words
1.3 si

By the close of the middle ages, such odd ways of measuring were 145 | 29 77
a hindrance to trade. There was a boom in trade because of the finding 159 | 32 80
of new lands and new routes for travel. At the same time scientists 173 | 35 83
began to want to measure things with greater accuracy. 184 | 37 85

¶ 5
56 words
1.3 si

The metric system is not hard to grasp once you have learned a 197 | 39 87
few basic prefixes. At the end of the last century, people in many 210 | 42 90
countries the world over were using meters and grams. They say that 224 | 45 93
it will be only a matter of time before you will have to be thinking 238 | 48 96

All ¶
1.3 si

metric too. 240 | 48 96

```
1' |  1  |  2  |  3  |  4  |  5  |  6  |  7  |  8  |  9  | 10  | 11  | 12  | 13  | 14  |
5' |        1        |        2        |        3        |
```

96e ■ Continuity Practice

5 minutes

Directions—Type the last paragraph of 96d as many times as you can without timing.

Technique Goals—Work for continuous stroking, with eyes on copy, with quiet wrists and arms.

UNIT 7 ■ Typing Personal Notes and Letters

General Directions ■ Lessons 41 - 50

Except as otherwise directed, use a 60-space line. Single-space lines of words and sentences, but double-space between repeated groups of lines. Double-space paragraph copy.

● *Your teacher will tell you whether or not to correct errors on problem typing.*

Lesson 41

● *60-space line*

41a ■ Keyboard Review • Each line three times

5 minutes

All letters   SS   Fay quoted six or seven major zoning laws checked by police.

Figure-Symbol   Hank is almost 5'8", Mary is 5'10", and Jose is nearly 6'2".

Easy   Use well the gift of learning to add to the things you know.

| 1 | 2 | 3 | 4 | 5 | 6 | 7 | 8 | 9 | 10 | 11 | 12 |

Feet on the floor

41b ■ Technique Builder—Flowing Rhythm • Each line three times from dictation

10 minutes

1   SS   for him | if the cases | they were | and the date | for the text

2   and the set | to do my | for the only | to see | and read | to act

3   to save | and look | for you | and see | if you | they saw | to join

4   and they join | and she sees | she did care | go after | for him

Flowing, rhythmic stroking

41c ■ Sentence Skill Builder from Script

Directions—Type a 1-minute writing on each sentence. Compute *gwam*.

5 minutes

Words

1   SS   *Our school newspaper is now being published every two weeks.*   12

2   *All news items have to be submitted to the advisor's office.*   12

3   *The editor was chosen because of her ability and experience.*   12

4   *One or two important jobs on the staff have not been filled.*   12

41d ■ Spelling and Proofreading Aid • Each line three times

5 minutes

1   SS   toward similar practice valuable salary acknowledge hesitate

2   dollar financial procedure situation separate volume session

3   convenient responsibility circular calendar specific license

Type letter by letter

Unit 12 ▪ Typing for Club and Community Activities

General Directions ▪ Lessons 96 - 110

Machine Adjustments—Follow the general directions given earlier units of this cycle.

Lesson 96

• *Use a 70-space line for all lessons in this unit.*

96a ▪ Keyboard Review • Each line at least three times   5 minutes

All letters SS Vickie Morgan did an excellent job of sewing the skirt zipper quickly.

Figure   Over 45,780 attended the fair during the weeks of April 9, 16, and 23.

br   bright bray bring brought brace braid bread brain bran break brilliant

Easy   You have to use the right touch if you want to do good work in typing.

| 1 | 2 | 3 | 4 | 5 | 6 | 7 | 8 | 9 | 10 | 11 | 12 | 13 | 14 |

Wrists and elbows still

96b ▪ Times and Equal Signs • Each line three times   5 minutes

Times sign—Use a small letter *x* with a space before and after it.

Equal sign—If your typewriter does not have an equal key, type hyphens, one below the other. In typing the second hyphen, turn the left cylinder knob away from you, or depress the left shift key slightly.

1 SS Here is the way I figured the discount on this sale: $150 $\times$ .06 = $9.

2   The clerk said that the tax was figured as follows: $650 $\times$ .04 = $26.

Feet on the floor

96c ▪ Punctuation Guides—Semicolon   10 minutes

Directions—Read the explanation carefully; then type each example sentence twice.

Lines 1 and 2—Use a semicolon between the clauses of a compound sentence when no conjunction is used.

Line 3—If a conjunction is used to join the clauses, use a comma between them.

Lines 4 and 5—Use a semicolon betweeen the clauses of a compound sentence that are joined by such words as *also, however, therefore,* and *consequently.*

Line 6—Use a semicolon between a series of phrases or clauses that are dependent upon a main clause.

1 SS Kathy Denin arrives in Chicago today; she will be in Detroit tomorrow.

2   Our fine softball team won easily; they will play again next Thursday.

3   Dave plans to be in Memphis today, but he will go to Atlanta tomorrow.

4   This is the current plan; however, it is subject to Martha's approval.

5   Laura and Don plan to go; consequently, they will need the automobile.

6   We saw Linda Bell, Ogden; Henry Abels, Reno; and Renee Freeman, Provo.

| 1 | 2 | 3 | 4 | 5 | 6 | 7 | 8 | 9 | 10 | 11 | 12 | 13 | 14 |

Think as you type

41e ■ Paragraph Guided Writings ● As directed in 36d, page 60   *15 minutes*

● All letters are used in these paragraphs

		GWAM	
¶ 1 34 words 1.2 si	DS Before you start to look for your first job, you will be	11	4 42
	wise to consider some techniques of job seeking that have been	24	8 46
	helpful to others. They can also pay off for you.	34	11 50
¶ 2 40 words 1.2 si	For example, show that you are not lazy by listing the	45	15 53
	kinds of work you have done. You might have delivered papers	57	19 57
	or taken care of children. Be sure to include work for which	70	23 62
	you did not get paid.	74	25 64
¶ 3 41 words 1.1 si	The strong points of your school record should be noted,	85	28 67
	of course. It will help if you can say you missed only two	97	32 71
	days of school in three years or that your typing rate was	109	36 75
All ¶'s 1.2 si	one of the best in the class.	115	38 77

1' | 1 | 2 | 3 | 4 | 5 | 6 | 7 | 8 | 9 | 10 | 11 | 12 |
3' | 1 | | 2 | | 3 | | 4 |

41f ■ Composing at the Typewriter   *5 minutes*

Directions—Type answers to as many of these questions as time permits. Use complete sentences.

1. How many vertical line spaces are there on a full sheet of paper?

2. How many vertical line spaces are there on a half sheet of paper?

3. How many vertical line spaces are there on a sheet of paper 6 inches in length?

4. Why should you move the carriage to one side or the other before erasing an error?

Lesson 42   ● *60-space line*

42a ■ Keyboard Review ● Each line three times   *5 minutes*

All letters	SS	The quiz kept Jim and Dick Law busy for six very long hours.	
Figure-Symbol		Namath once completed 15 consecutive passes--12 in one game!	Sit erect
Easy		If you wish to think well of yourself, think well of others.	

| 1 | 2 | 3 | 4 | 5 | 6 | 7 | 8 | 9 | 10 | 11 | 12 |

Lesson 95

95a ■ Keyboard Review • Each line at least three times

All letters SS   Judge Roby was quick to penalize all sixteen for moving the green car.

Figure-Symbol   Jan lives at 5767 North Bond Street; the telephone number is 432-1980.   Reach with

e, i   Their retired neighbors tried hard to remain silent on certain issues.   your fingers

Easy   There is going to be a good market for their product in foreign lands.

| 1 | 2 | 3 | 4 | 5 | 6 | 7 | 8 | 9 | 10 | 11 | 12 | 13 | 14 |

95b ■ Timed Writings • Type a 1- and a 5-minute writing on 91c, page 156. Circle errors. Compute gwam.

10 minutes

95c ■ Problem Typing

30 minutes

Problem 1 ■ *Title Page for Formal Library Report*

Directions—1. Type the title page; use the data given at the right. It is a title page for the report that you have just typed.

2. Follow the directions given in the illustration on page 147, or use any attractive arrangement that is acceptable to your teacher.

WRITING A FORMAL LIBRARY REPORT

By

Your name
Typewriting II

Current date

Problem 2 ■ *Bibliography for Formal Library Report*

Directions—1. Type the bibliography for your formal report on a separate sheet of paper. List the references given below.

2. Assemble your report as follows: title page, body of the report, bibliography. Bind the report at the left.

• *See page 148 for an illustration of a bibliography.*

BIBLIOGRAPHY

Burken, Judith L. Introduction to Reporting. Dubuque: William C. Brown Company, Publishers, 1976.

Crump, Spencer. Fundamentals of Journalism. New York: McGraw-Hill Book Company, 1974.

Donelson, K. "Forward to Five Basics in Composition." Clearing House, October, 1977, pp. 60-3.

James, T. F. "Hemingway at Work." Cosmopolitan, August, 1957, p. 54.

Warriner, John E., and Sheila Y. Laws. English Grammar and Composition, Second Course. New York: Harcourt Brace Jovanovich, Inc., 1973.

Williamson, Daniel R. Feature Writing for Newspapers. New York: Hastings House, Publishers, Inc., 1975.

95d ■ Extra Credit Typing

Problem 1

Directions—Type a short report based on the outline in 87c, Problem 1, page 150. Type it in regular report form.

Problem 2

Directions—Type a short report based on the outline in 87c, Problem 2, page 151. Type it in regular report form.

Problem 3

Directions—Type the option you did not type in 91e, page 157. Follow the directions given with the problem you select.

42b ■ Typing from Dictation and Spelling Checkup

5 minutes

Directions—Your teacher will dictate the words in 41d, page 69. Type the words from dictation. Check for correct spelling. Retype any words in which you made an error.

42c ■ Timed Writings

10 minutes

Directions—Type two 3-minute writings on 41e, page 70. Circle errors. Compute *gwam*. Submit the better writing.

42d ■ Problem Typing

25 minutes

Problem 1 ■ *Personal Note in Block Style*

Half sheet
50-space line
Open punctuation

Directions—Type a copy of the personal note that follows. Type the date on the 7th line space from the top of the paper. (*The date is always typed on the 7th line space in all half-page personal notes.*) Type the salutation on the 5th line space from the date.

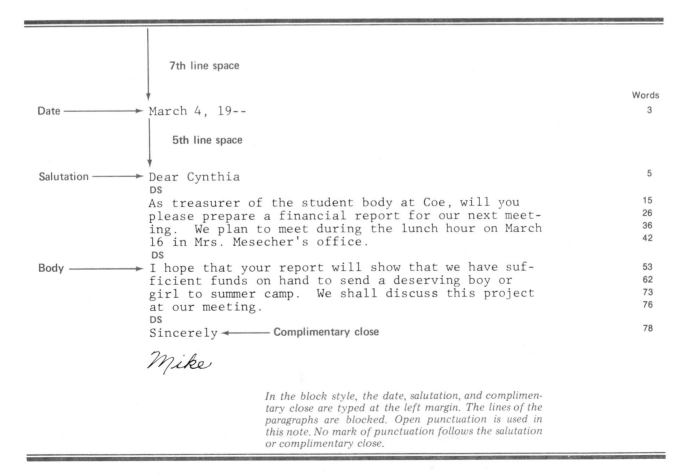

		Words
7th line space		
Date → March 4, 19--		3
5th line space		
Salutation → Dear Cynthia		5
DS		
As treasurer of the student body at Coe, will you		15
please prepare a financial report for our next meet-		26
ing. We plan to meet during the lunch hour on March		36
16 in Mrs. Mesecher's office.		42
DS		
Body → I hope that your report will show that we have suf-		53
ficient funds on hand to send a deserving boy or		62
girl to summer camp. We shall discuss this project		73
at our meeting.		76
DS		
Sincerely ← Complimentary close		78
Mike		

In the block style, the date, salutation, and complimentary close are typed at the left margin. The lines of the paragraphs are blocked. Open punctuation is used in this note. No mark of punctuation follows the salutation or complimentary close.

Personal note in block style

Lesson 94

94a ■ Keyboard Review • Each line at least three times
5 minutes

All letters SS Mark will require five dozen big boxes for the apricots early in July.

Figure Kennedy was our President from January 20, 1961, to November 22, 1963.

Quiet wrists and arms

Long reach The mayor announced the results of the voting. An unknown doctor won.

Easy Now is the time for more of them to make a few plans for their future.

| 1 | 2 | 3 | 4 | 5 | 6 | 7 | 8 | 9 | 10 | 11 | 12 | 13 | 14 |

94b ■ Punctuation Guides—Comma
10 minutes

Directions—Read the explanation carefully; then type each example sentence twice.

Line 1—Use commas to set off parenthetic expressions that break the flow of a sentence.

Line 2—If the parenthetic expression begins or ends a sentence, use one comma.

Line 3—Use a comma to set off *yes, no, well, now.*

Line 4—Use commas to set off the name of the person addressed.

Line 5—Use commas to set off appositives that give additional information about the same person or object and that can be omitted without changing the meaning of the sentence.

Line 6—Do not use a comma to separate two nouns, one of which identifies the other.

Line 7—Use commas to separate the date from the year and the name of a city from the name of the state.

1 SS Bob Aldrich, however, cannot hit well enough to make the regular team.

2 Moreover, Tina plans to stop at Yosemite Lodge for three or four days.

3 Well, Patsy Anderson saved the game for us by hitting those home runs.

4 Scott, did you really see us there? The first day, Ted, is Wednesday.

Wrists low and still

5 Ms. Jill Coffey, our new math teacher, wrote a book on wise investing.

6 My husband's sister Sue lives in Chicago. My sister Joyce is in Rome.

7 I think the drumming record was set on May 2, 1956, in Columbus, Ohio.

| 1 | 2 | 3 | 4 | 5 | 6 | 7 | 8 | 9 | 10 | 11 | 12 | 13 | 14 |

94c ■ Paragraph Skill Builder • Type four 1-minute writings.
5 minutes

DS It has been estimated that a person spends somewhat more than half of the day listening. Listening means more than just hearing sounds. Hearing requires only two ears; but if you listen, you must use your mind as well. Don't merely hear a speaker with your ears turned on and your mind turned off.

60 words
1.3 si

Resume typing at once

94d ■ Problem Typing
25 minutes

Directions—Continue typing the manuscript of the formal library report started in Lesson 92. Keep the margins and spacing uniform throughout the manuscript.

Problem 2 ■ Personal Note in Block Style

Directions—Type the personal note below. Type to-day's date in the proper place. Type the salutation on the 5th line space from the date.

• Three words are counted for today's date, although the date may have more or fewer than 15 strokes.

		Words
Half sheet	*Today's date*	3
60-space line		
Open punctuation	**5th line space**	

Dear Tami — 5

I must write a short paper for my English class on one of — 17
our national parks. Since I have never been to any of our — 28
parks, this is quite an order. I would like to write a good — 41
paper. — 42

I recall your telling me that you camped in Yosemite last — 54
summer. Do you have any booklets on Yosemite that you could — 66
lend me? I shall be sure to return them to you. — 76

Sincerely — 78

Sign your name

Lesson 43

• *60-space line*

43a ■ Keyboard Review • Each line three times

5 minutes

All letters SS Max Cady just loves a big frozen pie after he quits working.

Figure-Symbol Raul said, "To get the answer, add 9 1/3, 6 5/8, and 7 3/4."

Quick, sharp strokes

Easy Those who were in good shape ran down the field at halftime.

| 1 | 2 | 3 | 4 | 5 | 6 | 7 | 8 | 9 | 10 | 11 | 12 |

43b ■ Sentence Skill Builder from Script

10 minutes

Directions—Type two 1-minute writings on each sentence. First writing: push for speed. Second writing: drop speed; work for control.

Words

1 SS *Many fields require some sort of training after high school.* — 12

2 *We all hope to find out where our talents and interests lie.* — 12

3 *Quite a few of our class members now plan to attend college.* — 12

4 *They have just begun to study the various careers available.* — 12

Prepare the Title Page and Bibliography. Long, formal reports usually have a title page and bibliography. The title page contains the name of the report and its writer. The bibliography contains titles of references that have been consulted.

It will pay you to learn how to write clear, interest-holding papers. It's not an easy job, but with a plan to guide you and some practice, you can turn out good work on your typewriter.

[1] T. F. James, "Hemingway at Work," Cosmopolitan, August, 1957, p. 54.

[2] John E. Warriner and Sheila Y. Laws, English Grammar and Composition, Second Course (New York: Harcourt Brace Jovanovich, Inc., 1973), p. 416.

[3] Ibid., p. 418

Lesson 93

● *70-space line*

93a ■ Keyboard Review ● Each line at least three times

5 minutes

All letters **SS**
Figure-Symbol
Long reach
Easy

Janice and David must take that final geography quiz before next week.
Though 1,493 students took the 20 tests, only 76 scored more than 85%.
The humble drummer stumbled, then jumped to avoid the other musicians.
If you want to get rid of your enemies, change them into your friends.

Eyes on copy

| 1 | 2 | 3 | 4 | 5 | 6 | 7 | 8 | 9 | 10 | 11 | 12 | 13 | 14 |

93b ■ Speed Stretcher ● As directed in 78b, page 134

10 minutes

	G W A M
	1′ 5′

All letters **DS**

One of the biggest counting jobs in the world occurs every ten | 13 | 3 36

¶ 1
67 words
1.3 si

years when the nation's census is taken. While the practice is as old | 27 | 5 39

as collecting taxes and building an army, this country was the first | 41 | 8 42

large one to plan such a count of its people. Since early times, the | 55 | 11 45

census has been conducted in those years that ended in a zero. | 67 | 13 47

¶ 2
62 words
1.3 si

Today, the task is much more than just a head count and is used | 13 | 16 50

for a lot of things other than finding out who will pay taxes or fight. | 27 | 19 53

The data serve as the basis for the distribution of federal money to | 41 | 22 55

states and cities. They are also used to help determine social trends | 55 | 24 58

and the need for public services. | 62 | 26 60

¶ 3
41 words
1.3 si
All ¶'s
1.3 si

Most households, all except one in six, are given a form which | 13 | 28 62

contains a series of questions to be answered. Census officials say an | 27 | 31 65

eighth grader should be able to fill it out in much less than an hour. | 41 | 34 68

| 1′ | 1 | 2 | 3 | 4 | 5 | 6 | 7 | 8 | 9 | 10 | 11 | 12 | 13 | 14 |
| 5′ | | 1 | | 2 | | 3 | |

93c ■ Problem Typing

30 minutes

Directions—Continue typing the manuscript of the formal library report started in Lesson 92. Keep the margins and spacing uniform throughout the manuscript.

Problem 1 ■ *Personal Note in Modified Block Style*

Half sheet
60-space line
Open punctuation

Directions—Type the personal note that follows. The dateline and complimentary close start at the center point of the paper. Type the salutation on the 4th line space from the date.

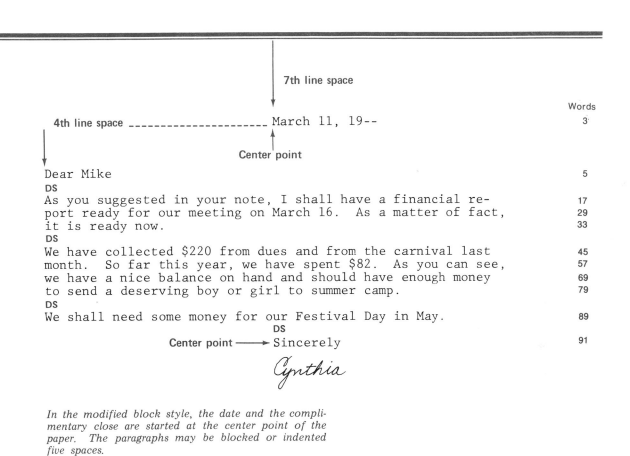

Words

7th line space

4th line space _____ March 11, 19--   3

Center point

Dear Mike   5
DS
As you suggested in your note, I shall have a financial re-   17
port ready for our meeting on March 16. As a matter of fact,   29
it is ready now.   33
DS
We have collected $220 from dues and from the carnival last   45
month. So far this year, we have spent $82. As you can see,   57
we have a nice balance on hand and should have enough money   69
to send a deserving boy or girl to summer camp.   79
DS
We shall need some money for our Festival Day in May.   89
                                              DS
Center point ——→ Sincerely   91

Cynthia

In the modified block style, the date and the complimentary close are started at the center point of the paper. The paragraphs may be blocked or indented five spaces.

Personal note in modified block style

Problem 2 ■ *Personal Note in Modified Block Style*

Half sheet
60-space line
Open punctuation

Directions—Type the personal note on the next page in modified block style, with indented paragraphs. Type the salutation on the 5th line space from the date.

WRITING A FORMAL LIBRARY REPORT

"The test of a book," said Ernest Hemingway, "is how much good stuff you can throw away."[1] He added that anything that does not have the ring of hard truth, that seems the least bit overdone, must go into the wastebasket. Deep feelings about something written in words that stick--these are the things a writer must get.

We can't all gain the fame that Hemingway gained as a writer. He worked hard and long at perfecting his skill. We can all learn how to write a short paper, however, long before we get into Hemingway's class. Almost all of us can learn to write a clear, interesting account about something we have read, heard, or seen. Let's see how you might go about this job.

Choose the Right Subject. To begin with, you need to select a subject you know something about. One authority says such a choice may be the most important decision you make in planning and writing your composition.[2] You can't write about the growing of figs unless you know how figs are grown. You can get information from books, from talks with fig growers, or from growing figs yourself.

Limit Your Subject. Don't try to cover too much ground in your paper. Young writers often butt their heads against this wall without getting anything more than a sore head for their trouble. As Warriner says, "Probably more student compositions turn out badly because their subjects are too broad than for any other reason."[3]

Narrow your subject down. Write about the kind of soil fig trees like or how figs are prepared for the market. You can't cover the whole life of a fig, from seedling to fig sauce, in two hundred words, no matter how skilled you become as a writer.

Prepare a Preliminary Outline. Jot down the major topics you expect to cover. This is the preliminary outline. It consists only of a number of topic headings. No subpoints need to be included.

Prepare Bibliography Cards. After you select a subject and prepare your preliminary outline, you must find out where you can obtain the information you need. For most students, books and articles will furnish the needed help.

As you find books and articles that appear to be helpful, write their titles on cards. On each card, write complete information about a single reference so the card can be used later to prepare the footnotes and bibliography for your paper.

Read; Take Notes. Start your reading. As you read, take notes. Record important facts, ideas, and quotations on note cards so that you can refer to them as you write your paper.

Each note card should be given a heading which describes the notes. Use one of the main headings of your preliminary outline, if you can, to identify each card. Write each note on a separate card. In every case, indicate the page number and reference from which the note was taken.

Prepare the Final Outline. When you have taken notes on all your readings, organize your cards in some order. This will usually be determined by the order of the points in the preliminary outline. You may find that some of the main points should now be changed. Try to group the cards under each major point into two or more subgroups. These will make up the subpoints of your outline.

Remember that an outline shows clearly what points are the most important as well as those that are less important. The Roman numerals show the chief ideas. The capital letters and Arabic numerals give details under the main points.

Write the First Draft. The first writing of a paper will usually not be the final one. Present the material you have collected. Don't worry too much about words, spelling, and typing mistakes.

Revise the First Draft. When the first draft has been completed, check it for wording and mistakes. Mark your corrections with a pen or pencil. Careful writers read and correct their copy two or three times to make sure that their papers read well. It is recommended that you do this too.

Prepare the Final Copy. Good appearance in papers is important. Follow accepted rules for typing the final copy. Pay close attention to margins, placement of footnotes, and other similar details.

December 3, 19--

Dear Pam   5

Indent ¶'s   I'm really looking forward to spending the holidays with   17
you and your family this year. If the weather forecasts are   29
correct, we should be able to give our skis a good workout.   41

      Dad made reservations for me yesterday. I will arrive   52
December 18 on Flight 84 at 5:15 p.m.   59

      Thanks a million for inviting me. I'll see you Sunday.   71

Sincerely   72

Kathy

Problem 3 ▪ *Personal Note Typed Lengthwise on 5½- by 8½-inch Paper*

Directions—1. Type the note in Problem 2 on 5½- by 8½-inch paper inserted lengthwise. This note is shown at the right.

2. Start typing the name and address of the writer one-half inch (4th line space) from the top. Set off the return address by typing a line of hyphens from the left to the right edge of the paper, a line space or two below the return address.

3. Use a 40-space line. This will give you left and right margins of about one inch on both pica and elite machines.

4. Type the date at the center point of the paper on the 3d line space below the hyphens under the return address.

- *To find the center point, refer to page 67; or fold your paper to bring left and right edges together. Crease lightly at the top.*

5. Type the salutation on the 6th or 7th line space from the date.

6. Start the complimentary close at the center point of the paper.

KATHY MORENO
375 Almendra Avenue
Topeka

December 3, 19--

Dear Pam

    I'm really looking forward to spending
the holidays with you and your family this
year. If the weather forecasts are correct,
we should be able to give our skis a good
workout.

    Dad made reservations for me yesterday.
I will arrive December 18 on Flight 84 at
5:15 p.m.

    Thanks a million for inviting me. I'll
see you Sunday.

       Sincerely

       Kathy

Note typed on personal stationery

Half sheet
Double spacing
60-space line

Directions—Type the following quotation; then, add a few sentences telling what the quotation means to you. Correct your copy; retype. Give your short report a title. Center it on the half sheet. Use a 60-space line.

Alternate suggestion—With your teacher's approval, type a summary of the article in 91c, page 156. Use the directions given at the left.

> Mark Twain said, "Nothing so needs reforming as other people's habits."

Lesson 92

● *70-space line*

92a ■ Keyboard Review ● Each line at least three times   *5 minutes*

All letters   **SS** Very few sixth graders in the math class ever joked about pop quizzes.

Figure   On December 17, 1903, Orville Wright made the very first plane flight.

Long words   The study of a file of correspondence will yield valuable information.

Easy   One of the big problems she had was to think of a title for her theme.

| 1 | 2 | 3 | 4 | 5 | 6 | 7 | 8 | 9 | 10 | 11 | 12 | 13 | 14 |

Wrists low
and still

92b ■ Paragraph Skill Builder   *10 minutes*

Directions—Type a 1-minute writing to determine your goal word. Then type a 5-minute writing. The return will be called at the end of each minute. Try to reach your goal word.

60 words
1.3 si

DS   You may be the type of person who likes to sit along the sidelines rather than play in the game. You should weigh quite carefully the ideas of others. However, you must also reserve the right to do your own thinking. Your mind can be most effective when it is active. Keep your mind in the game.

Blend fast
and slow
stroking for
flowing
rhythm

92c ■ Problem Typing   *30 minutes*

Problem ■ *Formal Library Report with Footnotes*

Directions—**1.** Prepare a manuscript of the report on pages 158 and 159. Follow the directions for typing bound manuscripts given on page 145.

2. In the problem which follows, the footnotes are placed at the end of the report. Type them at the bottom of pages on which reference is made to them.

● *You will not be able to type the entire report in this lesson. Type as far as you can. You will be given time to complete the manuscript in Lessons 93 and 94. In Lesson 95, you will type a title page and bibliography for this report; then bind it at the left.*

Lesson 44

• 60-space line

44a ■ Keyboard Review • Each line three times

7 minutes

All letters **SS** Mavis Grable will quickly explain what John made for prizes.

Figure-Symbol That company was in business there for 96 years (1882-1978).

br Debra Bray may bring her bright brother Brad to play bridge. *Elbows in*

Hyphen Sixty-two people heard the one-hour lecture on self-defense.

Easy It will pay you to learn what you are to do before you type.

| 1 | 2 | 3 | 4 | 5 | 6 | 7 | 8 | 9 | 10 | 11 | 12 |

44b ■ Paragraph Guided Writings • As directed in 36d, page 60

15 minutes

• All letters are used in these paragraphs

	GWAM
	1' 3'

DS

¶ 1
42 words
1.2 si
The half hour news broadcast which you watch each night | 11 | 4 42
involves a lot more than the few people that you see on the | 23 | 8 46
screen. Nearly a hundred staff workers may be required to | 35 | 12 50
plan just one network news program. | 42 | 14 53

¶ 2
38 words
1.2 si
They have to decide which of the dozens of stories of | 53 | 18 56
the day are the best ones for us to see. Some writers work | 65 | 22 60
on foreign news, some work on local news, and some work on | 77 | 26 64
special features. | 80 | 27 65

¶ 3
36 words
1.2 si
You will find that working with the news can be most | 91 | 30 69
exciting. It is not like most desk jobs because the hours | 102 | 34 73
are often long, and you may have to work weekends and late | 114 | 38 77

All ¶'s
1.2 si
at night. | 116 | 39 77

| 1' | 1 | 2 | 3 | 4 | 5 | 6 | 7 | 8 | 9 | 10 | 11 | 12 |
| 3' | | 1 | | 2 | | 3 | | 4 | |

44c ■ Problem Typing

23 minutes

• Cut two sheets of 8½- by 11-inch paper in two so that each of the four pieces measures 5½- by 8½-inches. Type your name and address at the top. Use clever wording or arrangement if you wish. Set off the return address by a line of hyphens as shown on page 74. You will use these sheets in typing the following problems.

• The lines in the problems are not set line-for-line the way you will type them. Set margin stops properly; return your carriage with the bell.

LESSON 44 ■ PAGE 75

G W A M

	1'	5'

All letters **DS**

·   4   ·   8   ·   12   ·

Soccer, the world's most popular sport, may soon become one of our   13 | 3 51

¶ 1
40 words
1.3 si

·   16   ·   20   ·   24   ·

nation's newest pastimes. Players on each team bat a medium-sized ball   28 | 6 54

28   ·   32   ·   36   ·   40

around with their heads and feet rather than with their hands.   40 | 8 56

·   4   ·   8   ·   12

Views on soccer's spectator appeal differ. A few sports fans say   53 | 11 59

¶ 2
44 words
1.4 si

·   16   ·   20   ·   24   ·

there is too much frantic running around without enough scoring. Those   68 | 14 62

28   ·   32   ·   36   ·   40

who enjoy the game are quick to point out the fact that it is a most   82 | 16 64

44

exciting one.   84 | 17 65

·   4   ·   8   ·   12

In some countries to the south of the U.S., soccer arouses such   97 | 19 67

¶ 3
48 words
1.4 si

·   16   ·   20   ·   24   ·

passions that the halftime entertainment is often a riot. In a stadium   112 | 22 70

28   ·   32   ·   36   ·   40

in Brazil the playing field has a moat on both sides to keep fans and   126 | 25 73

44   ·   48

players from each other's throats.   132 | 26 74

·   4   ·   8   ·   12

So far, the sport has not really caught on big in this country.   145 | 29 77

¶ 4
52 words
1.4 si

·   16   ·   20   ·   24   ·

Here, the old standbys like baseball, football, and hockey can keep   159 | 32 80

28   ·   32   ·   36   ·   40

the fans pretty well occupied. Lack of star players is a problem too.   173 | 35 83

44   ·   48   ·   52

Soccer backers now say, however, that America is ready.   184 | 37 85

·   4   ·   8   ·   12

To prove it, they can tell you how soccer already has made its   197 | 39 87

·   16   ·   20   ·   24   ·

mark on the city of San Francisco. Without a doubt, some fans have   210 | 42 90

¶ 5
56 words
1.3 si

28   ·   52   ·   36   ·   40

been caught up in the real spirit of the game. At one amateur match   224 | 45 93

·   44   ·   48   ·   52

played there, the referee's call sent hundreds of spectators into a   238 | 48 96

All ¶'s
1.3 si

·   56

brief melee.   240 | 48 96

1' | 1 | 2 | 3 | 4 | 5 | 6 | 7 | 8 | 9 | 10 | 11 | 12 | 13 | 14 |
5' | 1 | 2 | 3 |

91d ■ Correcting Errors—Spreading Letters   *5 minutes*

Directions—1. Type the sentence below just as it appears; then erase the *tra* in *exttra*.

2. Move carriage to the second space following *ext*. Depress the backspace key half way. Type *r*.

3. Release the backspace key. Depress the back space key half way; type *a*.

Error: Correct the exttra letter.

Correction: Correct the extra letter.

Problem 1 ■ *Personal Note in Modified Block Style*

Directions—Modified block style; blocked paragraphs; today's date. Type the salutation on the 6th line space from the date.

Dear Ying

Will your school be sending any students to the District Fair next month?

Mrs. Mendes, who is our club advisor, asked me to find out how many schools in our area will be sending students this year.

We thought it would be fun to have a picnic lunch together Friday at noon so we can get better acquainted before the activities begin.

Please let me know if any members from Sierra will be able to attend.

Sincerely

Problem 2 ■ *Personal Note in Block Style*

Directions—Block style; today's date. Decide for yourself where to type the salutation.

Dear Andy

Thanks very much for sending me the information about stereo equipment. It was pretty easy to understand, even for a beginner like me.

I'll have to admit that the explanations about such things as watts per channel and total harmonic distortion were a little confusing,

but I did learn a lot. I didn't realize how many different kinds of receivers and speakers there were to choose from.

With luck, I should have enough money saved to buy a pretty good system after Christmas. Get ready to share your record collection.

Sincerely

Problem 3 ■ *Creative Typing*

Directions—Compose and type a reply to the personal note in Problem 1. Use the modified block style with indented paragraphs. Arrange the note neatly on your personal stationery. Date your letter three days from today.

Alternate Suggestion
Type the note in Problem 1 in modified block style, indented paragraphs.

44d ■ Extra-Credit Typing

Directions—Use the choice you did not select in typing Problem 3. Use a sheet of personal stationery of the same size used in typing the three problems in this lesson.

Lesson 45

● *60-space line*

45a ■ Keyboard Review ● Each line three times

5 minutes

All letters   **SS**   Rex Fuji positively warned us smoking can be quite a hazard.

Figure-Symbol   Mr. Lang's 28 students collected $46.90 in their fund drive.

Eyes on this copy

Easy   Remember that the kind words we use are seldom used in vain.

| 1 | 2 | 3 | 4 | 5 | 6 | 7 | 8 | 9 | 10 | 11 | 12 |

SECOND CARD

Heading—Introduction

Notes—"The test of a book is how much good stuff you can throw away." Anything that does not have the ring of hard truth, that seems the least bit overdone, must go into the wastebasket. Deep feelings about something written in words that stick—these are the things a writer must get.

Reference and page number—James, p. 54.

THIRD CARD

Heading—Writing effectively

Notes—Descriptive paragraphs:
1. Concentrate upon words that make appeals to our senses.
2. Describe how things appear to us.
3. Put us in touch with the physical world.
4. Let us sense (experience) what is being related.

Reference and page number—Conlin, p. 304.

FOURTH CARD

Heading—Prepare the final outline

Notes—An outline shows what points are most important as well as those that are less important. It is a plan of relationships. The Roman numerals in your outline show the chief ideas. The capital letters and Arabic numerals give details under the main points.

Reference and page number—Green, p. 251.

Lesson 91

• *70-space line*

91a ■ Keyboard Review • Each line at least three times

5 minutes

All letters   SS   We explorers made several quick journeys throughout Venezuela by fall.

Figure-Symbol   Check 3904 (dated June 7) for $68 was sent to Brown and Company today.

Adjacent keys   Their newer engineers were prepared there before November or December.

Hold wrists steady

Easy   Do not tell others of their faults until you have no more of your own.

| 1 | 2 | 3 | 4 | 5 | 6 | 7 | 8 | 9 | 10 | 11 | 12 | 13 | 14 |

91b ■ Number Expression Guides—Typing Fractions

5 minutes

Directions—Read the explanation; then type each line twice.

Line 1—Use the figure keys and the diagonal for typing fractions not on the keyboard ("made" fractions).

Line 2—Space between whole numbers and "made" fractions.

1   SS   "Made" fractions should be made in this way: 2/3, 3/5, 5/6.

2   They will need 5 2/3 yards of red nylon cloth to do the job.

Wrists and elbows still

3   Try to give him 7 2/3 yards of wool for 6 1/2 yards of silk.

| 1 | 2 | 3 | 4 | 5 | 6 | 7 | 8 | 9 | 10 | 11 | 12 |

45b ■ Timed Writings

10 minutes

Directions—Type two 3-minute writings on 44b, page 75. Compute *gwam*. Submit the better of the two writings.

45c ■ Problem Typing

30 minutes

Problem 1 ■ *Message Typed on Postal Card*

Directions—**1.** Insert card; determine horizontal center; set margin stops 4 spaces in from each edge of card.

2. Type the date on Line 3; then type the remaining lines as illustrated on the card.

● *Use paper cut to postal card size (5½- by 3¼-inches) if cards are not available.*

Card holders

● *When you insert the card into your typewriter, adjust the card holders, as shown above, and use the paper bail to keep the card from slipping.*

Problem 2 ■ *Addressing a Postal Card*

Directions—**1.** Type the return address and address on the card typed in Problem 1.

2. Type the return address on Line 2 from the top and 3 spaces from the left edge.

3. Type the address about 2 inches from the top and 2 inches from the left edge.

4. The 2-letter state abbreviations (typed in capital letters without a period or space between) may be used, the standard abbreviation may be used, or the state name may be typed in full. The 2-letter state abbreviations are shown on page 116.

● *ZIP Code numbers are typed one space after the state name.*

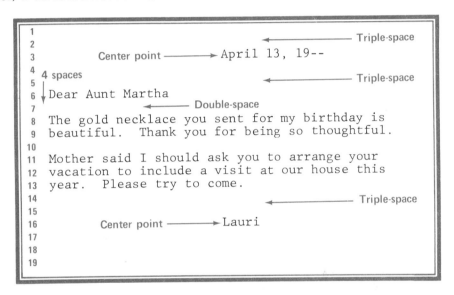

1	
2	←──── Triple-space
3	Center point ──→ April 13, 19--
4	4 spaces
5	↓ ←──── Triple-space
6	Dear Aunt Martha
7	←── Double-space
8	The gold necklace you sent for my birthday is
9	beautiful. Thank you for being so thoughtful.
10	
11	Mother said I should ask you to arrange your
12	vacation to include a visit at our house this
13	year. Please try to come.
14	←──── Triple-space
15	
16	Center point ──→ Lauri
17	
18	
19	

Postal card in modified block style

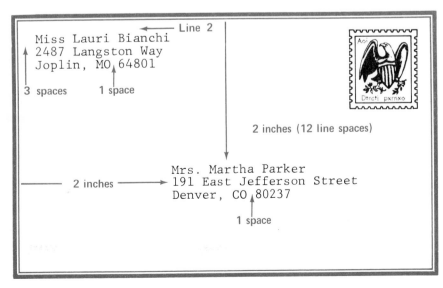

Miss Lauri Bianchi
2487 Langston Way
Joplin, MO 64801

3 spaces   1 space

2 inches (12 line spaces)

2 inches ──→ Mrs. Martha Parker
191 East Jefferson Street
Denver, CO 80237

1 space

Postal card address

SECOND CARD

Author—Williamson, Daniel R.

Title—<u>Feature Writing for Newspapers</u>

Publication information—New York: Hastings House Publishers, Inc., 1975

Short description—All essentials in feature writing are presented. Various techniques are explained within the context of actual newspaper experiences.

Library call number—PN
4778

THIRD CARD

Author—Burken, Judith L.

Title—<u>Introduction to Reporting</u>

Publication information—William C. Brown Company, Publishers, 1976

Short description—A text that concisely states the principles of writing necessary in beginning reporting. It provides a practical application of what it preaches, including examples in simple language and logical sequence.

Library call number—PN
245
B86

Lesson 90

● *70-space line*

90a ■ Keyboard Review ● Each line at least three times

5 minutes

All letters **SS** We made expensive jacks of high quality, but they were the wrong size.

Figure Mariner 4 flew a total distance of 325 million miles in only 228 days.

Shift Jennifer and Carl Nelson, Dr. R. Norton, and M. Diaz live in New York.

Feet on the floor

Easy Place all eight chairs on the field where they will be handy for them.

| 1 | 2 | 3 | 4 | 5 | 6 | 7 | 8 | 9 | 10 | 11 | 12 | 13 | 14 |

90b ■ Timed Writings

10 minutes

Directions—Type a 1- and a 5-minute writing on 86d, page 149. Circle errors. Compute *gwam*.

90c ■ Problem Typing

30 minutes

● *Note cards contain ideas, facts, and quotations to be used in preparing the body of a formal report or speech. A note card is illustrated below. Study it carefully.*

Problem ■ Note Cards

Directions—1. Prepare four note cards on 5- by 3-inch card stock. Prepare the first card from the illustration at the right. Prepare the other cards from the information that follows.

2. Type the heading on each card about three spaces from the top and three spaces from the left edge.

Heading

Notes

Reference and page numbers

```
Rules for making note cards

     A note card should carry only one idea.

     The topic heading for each card should
appear in the upper left-hand corner.

     Topic headings are usually taken from the
tentative outline.

     Make reference to the source in the lower
left-hand portion of the card.

Sigband, pp. 39-40.
```

Note card

Problem 3 ■ *Message Typed on a Postal Card*

Directions—Type the following message on a postal card in modified block style. The return address is Jerry Bryan / 814 North Tamera / your city, state, and ZIP Code. Address the card to Miss Karen Nelson / 527 East Palm / your city, state, and ZIP Code.

Single spacing
Open punctuation
Modified block

Current date

Dear Karen

Our annual barbecue will be held in O'Neal Park next Friday, *(give the date)* at 6 p.m.

Please remind all the students to bring their own dishes and silverware. All the food and soft drinks will be furnished.

Jerry Bryan
Student Body President

Problem 4 ■ *Message Typed on a Postal Card*

Directions—Type this message on a postal card in block style. Correct as indicated. The return address is David Santana / 28 College Drive / your city, state, and ZIP Code. Address the card to your name / street address / city, state, and ZIP Code.

Single spacing
Open punctuation
Block style

Current date

Dear (*Your name*)

I was able to get five tickets to the rock concert for next saturday. At least two new groups will be on the program, including the Seventh Dimension and the Vagabonds.

Several other people have told me they would like to go, so I need to know your plans right away. I hope you can make it.

David Santana

45d ■ Extra-Credit Typing

Directions—Compose and type a reply to the message in Problem 4. Arrange the message neatly on a postal card. Address the card to David Santana / 28 College Drive / your city, state, and ZIP Code. Type your name and address in the upper left corner of the address side of the card.

Lesson 89

89a ■ Keyboard Review • Each line at least three times

5 minutes

All letters SS Everybody expected a big kid my size to qualify for the javelin throw.

Figure One giant Sequoia is 272 feet 4 inches tall with a girth of 79.1 feet.

Sit erect

Long reach This was a challenging message, representing another appeal to thrift.

Easy Most of our team members do hard work to keep their body weights down.

| 1 | 2 | 3 | 4 | 5 | 6 | 7 | 8 | 9 | 10 | 11 | 12 | 13 | 14 |

89b ■ Correcting Errors—Squeezing Letters

5 minutes

Directions—1. Type the line just as it appears below.
2. Erase the *ed* in *omited*. The correct spelling is *omitted*.
3. Move the carriage to the space immediately following *omit*.

4. Depress the backspace key half way. Hold it. Type the second *t*.
5. Release the backspace key; depress it half way. Hold it. Type *e*.
6. Release the backspace key; depress it half way. Hold it. Type *d*.

Error: A letter has been omitted in the middle of a word.

Correction: A letter has been omitted in the middle of a word.

89c ■ Speed Ladder Sentences • Type each sentence for 1 minute. The guide will be called at 15-, 12-, or 10-second intervals.

5 minutes

			G W A M		
			15″	12″	10″
1	SS	Always use a quick, sharp stroke as you type.	36	45	54
2		Curve the fingers and hold them close to the keys.	40	50	60
3		Keep your wrists and elbows steady as you hit the keys.	44	55	66
4		Just try to think and type the short, easy words as a whole.	48	60	72

| 1 | 2 | 3 | 4 | 5 | 6 | 7 | 8 | 9 | 10 | 11 | 12 |

89d ■ Problem Typing

30 minutes

• *Bibliographical cards contain information about references you expect to use in preparing formal reports. Note the information that is included by referring to the illustration that follows.*

Problem ■ Bibliographical Cards

Directions—1. Prepare three bibliographical cards on 5- by 3-inch card stock. Prepare the first card from the illustration at the right. Prepare the second and third cards from the information that follows on page 154.

2. Type the first entry on the card about three spaces from the top and three spaces from the left edge. To keep the card from slipping, adjust the card holders to hold the card firmly against the cylinder.

Author Crump, Spencer

Title Fundamentals of Journalism

Publication information New York: McGraw-Hill Book Company, 1974

Short description   Emphasizes the "how-to-do-it" techniques of professional journalism. Newspapers are the primary subject of the book. It includes chapters on news gathering, writing, and editing.

Library call number PN 4874

Bibliographical card

Lesson 46

46a ■ Keyboard Review • Each line three times

5 minutes

All letters	SS	Gary Wells put five dozen quarts of jam in the box for Jack.
Figure-Symbol		Barbara's score was 84%, Tim's was 89%, and Nancy's was 91%.
Easy		Their problem was to enter the figures right the first time.

Wrists low
and still

| 1 | 2 | 3 | 4 | 5 | 6 | 7 | 8 | 9 | 10 | 11 | 12 |

46b ■ Spelling and Proofreading Aid • Each line three times

5 minutes

• *Study carefully the spelling of each word as you type it.*

1   SS   remittance laboratory signature proposal eligible sufficient

2   via cooperate analysis definite capacity develop commitments

3   tremendous beautiful essential consequently survey recommend

Fingers
deeply
curved

46c ■ Timed Writings

15 minutes

Directions—1. Type a 3-minute writing. Compute your *gwam*.
2. Type two 1-minute writings on each paragraph; the first for speed, the second for control.

3. Finally, type another 3-minute writing on all paragraphs. Compute your *gwam*. Compare the *gwam* and number of errors for the 3-minute writings.

			GWAM	
			1'	3'
All letters	DS	The first rule of getting along with others is so simple	11	4 43
¶ 1 36 words 1.2 si		that it is amazing more of us do not observe it. People will	24	8 47
		pay you back. They will treat you as well as you treat them.	36	12 51
		If you like people, they will like you. If you respect	47	16 55
¶ 2 38 words 1.2 si		them, they will respect you. If you are courteous to them,	59	20 59
		they will be courteous to you. The rule works. People will	71	24 63
		pay you back.	74	25 64
		Experts say that courtesy pays off. It makes work more	85	28 68
¶ 3 44 words 1.2 si		fun. You can get things done with less effort, and you can	97	32 72
		get them done more quickly. Give praise to those who de-	109	36 76
All ¶'s 1.2 si		serve it. Just praise usually works both ways.	118	39 79

| 1' | 1 | 2 | 3 | 4 | 5 | 6 | 7 | 8 | 9 | 10 | 11 | 12 |
| 3' | | 1 | | 2 | | 3 | | 4 | | | |

88c ■ Problem Typing

30 minutes

● *In this lesson, you will start preparing some of the materials used in writing the formal library report that you will type in Lessons 92-95. A preliminary outline, bibliography cards, note cards, and a final outline are usually prepared before a report is writ-* ten. These, then, are the items you will type in Lessons 88, 89, and 90. With your teacher's approval, keep these items until you finish typing the formal report so that you can refer to them.

Problem 1 ■ Preliminary Outline for Formal Library Report

● *A preliminary outline is a mere listing of the topics you expect to treat in a report.*

Directions—Use a 40-space line. Center the entire outline vertically on a full sheet. The outline below is set in problem form. Double-space the items in the outline. Arrange it correctly.

WRITING A FORMAL LIBRARY REPORT

1. Prepare introduction.
2. Choose subject.
3. Prepare preliminary outline.
4. Collect reading references.
5. Read; take notes.
6. Prepare final outline.
7. Prepare first draft.
8. Correct and revise first draft.
9. Prepare final copy.
10. Prepare title page and bibliography.

Problem 2 ■ Final Outline for Formal Library Report

Directions—Use a 60-space line and the standard 2-inch margin at the top of a full sheet.

WRITING A FORMAL LIBRARY REPORT

I. STEPS TO TAKE BEFORE WRITING STARTS.

   A. Choose the right subject.
      1. Choose a topic that intrigues you.
      2. Choose a topic about which you know something.
   B. Limit your subject.
   C. Prepare a preliminary outline.
      1. Jot down the major points only.
      2. This outline acts as a guide in your search for information.
   D. Prepare bibliography cards.
      1. The cards should contain information on your readings.
      2. The data recorded should be complete and accurate.
   E. Read; take notes.
      1. Use note cards.
      2. Record important facts, opinions, and quotations.
   F. Prepare the final outline.
      1. Organize the information collected.
      2. Group note cards under topics used in the preliminary outline.

II. STEPS TO TAKE IN WRITING THE PAPER.

   A. Write the first draft.
      1. The explanations should be clear, complete, to the point, and accurate.
      2. The sentences should be in logical order.
      3. Illustrate points by references to personal experiences.
      4. Compare your topic with one that is more familiar to the reader.
   B. Revise the first draft.
      1. Check the first draft for wording, spelling, and typographical errors.
      2. Make pencil or pen corrections.
   C. Prepare the final copy.
      1. Good appearance is important.
      2. Use standard rules on arrangement of reports.
   D. Prepare the title page and bibliography.
      1. A title page contains the name of the report, the writer's name, and the date.
      2. The bibliography names the references consulted.

46d ■ Technique Builder—Carriage Return

10 minutes

Directions—1. Type the first line of the paragraph three times as your teacher gives the signal each 20 seconds. Return quickly; resume typing at once.

2. Repeat for lines 2, 3, and 4.
3. Finally, type a 1-minute writing without the call of the guide. Determine your *gwam*.

		GWAM	
		1'	20" Guide

All letters   DS

44 words
1.2 si

One type of job you may wish to inquire about when — 10 | 30
you get out of school is working for a temporary help firm. — 22 | 35
Most towns of any size have such firms which hire both men — 34 | 35
and women if they need extra help at certain times. — 44 | 30

46e ■ Capitalization Guides

10 minutes

Directions—The following are the capitalization guides that you are to study *prior* to typing the lines.

Line 1—Capitalize the first word of a complete sentence.
Line 2—Capitalize the first word of a quoted sentence. (A period or comma is typed before the ending quotation mark.)
Line 3—The names of school subjects, except languages and numbered courses, are not capitalized.

Study the guide; then type the line applying the guide. Type each line twice.

Line 4—Do not capitalize a quotation resumed within a sentence.

Line 5—Capitalize the pronoun *I*, both alone and in contractions.

Line 6—Capitalize titles of organizations, institutions, and buildings.

1   SS   Electronics is a growing field with many rich opportunities.

2   An old proverb says, "Kind words don't wear out the tongue."

3   Sheila is taking English, Music 2, Spanish, and bookkeeping.   Eyes and mind
                                                                        on copy
4   "The danger," an author said, "lies in giving up the chase."   as you type

5   Yes, I plan to go to the show, but I'll have to leave early.

6   The students of Westlake School saw a play at Ripon College.

| 1 | 2 | 3 | 4 | 5 | 6 | 7 | 8 | 9 | 10 | 11 | 12 |

Lesson 47

● *60-space line*

47a ■ Keyboard Review ● Each line three times

5 minutes

All letters   SS   Five or six Jersey cows grazed quietly back among the pines.

Symbol   Tom delivered my papers (Los Angeles Times) in half an hour.   Space quickly

Easy   Try using your head at a job before you try your hand at it.

| 1 | 2 | 3 | 4 | 5 | 6 | 7 | 8 | 9 | 10 | 11 | 12 |

Problem 2 ■ _Sentence Outline_

Directions—Set the margin stops for a 60-space line. Type the outline in the exact center on a half sheet.

The copy is set in problem form. Space and arrange the outline correctly.

SAFETY RULES FOR BICYCLES

I. WHAT ARE COMMON CAUSES OF ACCIDENTS?

  A. Two or more riders on a bicycle ranks first.
  B. Bicycle hitchhiking ranks second.
  C. Riding too closely behind other vehicles ranks third.

II. OBSERVE THESE COMMON-SENSE RULES.

  A. Obey all traffic laws.
    1. Make all necessary arm signals.
    2. Use lights for night riding.
  B. Do not be a show-off trick rider.
  C. Avoid riding in heavy traffic.
  D. Do not make sudden turns or stops.

Lesson 88

● _70-space line_

88a ■ Keyboard Review ● Each line at least three times   _5 minutes_

All letters   **SS**   Dozens of bombs exploded high over the quaint city just as dawn broke.

Figure-Symbol   Robin could have purchased a Model 27F-205 for less than $314 in 1978.

o, i   The anxious seniors outside noticed commotion coming from the offices.   Space quickly

Easy   We can do good work if we have a goal for each bit of work that we do.

| 1 | 2 | 3 | 4 | 5 | 6 | 7 | 8 | 9 | 10 | 11 | 12 | 13 | 14 |

88b ■ Speed Stretcher ● As directed in 78b, page 134   _10 minutes_

GWAM
    1'   5'

All letters   **DS**   It is such a simple matter these days to hop on a giant jet and   13 | 3 35

¶ 1
54 words
1.4 si   zip from coast to coast in just a few hours. The vast plains, rushing   27 | 5 38

rivers, and rocky peaks below provide majestic views. Flying along   41 | 8 41

at top speeds, one can easily forget the hardships of early travel.   54 | 11 44

A century ago these wonders of nature caused major problems that   13 | 13 46

¶ 2
55 words
1.3 si   had to be solved if the country was to be linked by the iron horse. In   27 | 16 49

fact, many said the task of tying east to west with a ribbon of rails   41 | 19 52

was too great. Squabbles over the proposed route hindered progress.   55 | 22 55

The bulk of the work began after the Civil War. The job of laying   13 | 24 57

¶ 3
55 words
1.4 si   track across the vast expanse of land was finished in less than three   37 | 27 60

years. Thousands labored diligently for their meager dollar a day by   41 | 30 63

All ¶'s
1.3 si   struggling over mountains and toiling in heat, cold, rain, and snow.   55 | 33 66

1' | 1 | 2 | 3 | 4 | 5 | 6 | 7 | 8 | 9 | 10 | 11 | 12 | 13 | 14 |
5' | 1 | 2 | 3 |

47b ■ Typing from Dictation and Spelling Checkup

Directions—Your teacher will dictate the words in 46b, page 79. Type the words from dictation. Check for correct spelling. Retype words in which you made an error.

47c ■ Continuity Practice from Rough Draft

Directions—At least twice. Make the corrections as you type. Listen for the bell to know when to return your carriage.

Words

DS   The personal letters *you* write should # look neat and fresh.   12

[make them ~~them~~ look as smart as you your self would like   22

48 words
1.2 si

to look *when* you meet your friends face to face.   write _c_learly   35

and correctly, of course, *but* keep the ~~the~~ wording warm and   46

friendly.   48

Typing Personal/Business Letters

- *The most commonly used form for a personal/business letter is illustrated on page 82. The typewritten name of the sender below the complimentary close is optional.*

Step 1—Set the machine for single spacing.

Step 2—Set the margins. (The margins vary according to the length of the letter.)

Step 3—Start typing the return address on the 18th line space. (The number of line spaces varies with the letter size. The longer the letter, the fewer the number of spaces.) For a modified block style letter, start the return address at the center point of the paper. For a block style letter, start the return address at the left margin.

Step 4—Space down 4 times for the address.

Step 5—Type the salutation a double space below the address.

Step 6—Start the body a double space below the salutation. Double-space between paragraphs.

Step 7—Type the complimentary close a double space below the body. For a modified block style letter, start at the center point. For a block style letter, type it at the left margin.

Step 8—Type the name of the writer on the 4th line space from the complimentary close.

47d ■ Problem Typing

Problem 1 ■ Personal/Business Letter in Modified Block Style

Full sheet
50-space line
Open
    punctuation

Directions—Type the letter on the next page. Follow the directions given for typing personal/business letters. Type the address on the 4th line space from the date.

- *ZIP Code numbers are typed one space after the state name or abbreviation.*

Problem 2 ■ Modified Block Style with Paragraph Indentions

Full sheet
50-space line
Open punctuation

Directions—Type the letter in Problem 1 again. Use today's date in the heading. Indent the first line of each paragraph 5 spaces. Listen for the bell to know when to return your carriage.

LESSON 47 ■ PAGE **81**

Lesson 87

87a ■ Keyboard Review • Each line at least three times

All letters **SS** Few know Blanca Munoz has very little equity in that adjoining duplex.

Figure   Ted Williams, who hit .406 in 1941, was the last player to reach .400.

Double letters   Bill succeeded in getting the committee's message to the office staff.

Type without pauses

Easy   We should not spend so much time asking others to do this and do that.

| 1 | 2 | 3 | 4 | 5 | 6 | 7 | 8 | 9 | 10 | 11 | 12 | 13 | 14 |

87b ■ Paragraph Skill Builder

Directions—1. Type a 1-minute writing. Remember the last word you typed; it is your goal word.

2. Type a 5-minute writing on the same material. At the end of each minute, the return will be called. Try to reach the goal word at each 1-minute goal signal.

DS   Many folks are filled with a desire to get ahead. Some of them
get over the feeling in thirty minutes or less. Some of them have it

60 words
1.3 si
for thirty days, or perhaps a little longer. Those who want to get
ahead for thirty years, though, are the ones who become successful.
They find that patience pays.

Quick carriage return

87c ■ Problem Typing

Problem 1 ■ Topic Outline

Directions—1. Set the margin stops for a 60-space line. Type the main points at the left margin. Set and use tabulator stops for subpoints.

2. Use a standard 2-inch top margin.

3. Indent, space, capitalize, and punctuate exactly as shown in the problem. Two spaces follow the period after all numbered or lettered divisions.

• *Align Roman numerals in the outline at the period.*

TYPING BOUND MANUSCRIPTS

I. MARGINS
- A. Left margin of 1 1/2 inches
- B. Right margin of 1 inch
- C. Top margin of first page of 2 inches
- D. Top margin of subsequent pages of 1 inch
  1. At least 2 lines of paragraph at bottom of page
  2. At least 2 lines of paragraph carried forward to new page

II. SPACING
- A. Double spacing of contents
- B. Single spacing of quoted materials of 4 lines or more, footnotes, and bibliographical items
- C. Triple spacing after the title

III. PAGE NUMBERS
- A. Centered 1/2 inch from bottom of first page
- B. Aligned with right margin 1/2 inch (4 line spaces) from top for pages following the first

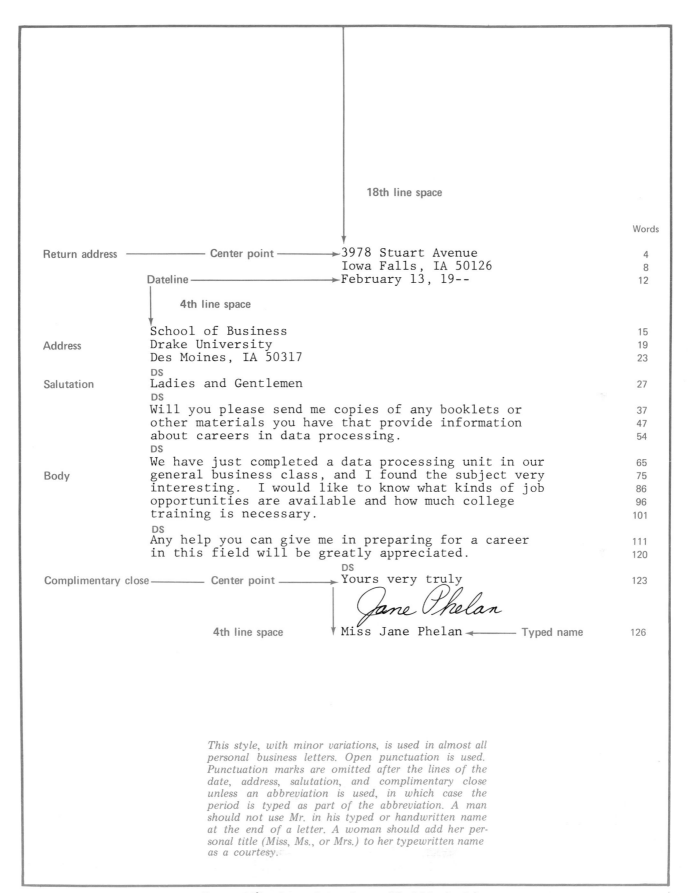

		Words
Return address ——————— Center point ———→	3978 Stuart Avenue	4
	Iowa Falls, IA 50126	8
Dateline ————————————→	February 13, 19--	12

4th line space

Address	School of Business	15
	Drake University	19
	Des Moines, IA 50317	23
	DS	
Salutation	Ladies and Gentlemen	27
	DS	
	Will you please send me copies of any booklets or	37
	other materials you have that provide information	47
	about careers in data processing.	54
	DS	
	We have just completed a data processing unit in our	65
Body	general business class, and I found the subject very	75
	interesting. I would like to know what kinds of job	86
	opportunities are available and how much college	96
	training is necessary.	101
	DS	
	Any help you can give me in preparing for a career	111
	in this field will be greatly appreciated.	120
	DS	
Complimentary close ——— Center point ———→	Yours very truly	123
	Jane Phelan	
4th line space	Miss Jane Phelan ←——— Typed name	126

*This style, with minor variations, is used in almost all
personal business letters. Open punctuation is used.
Punctuation marks are omitted after the lines of the
date, address, salutation, and complimentary close
unless an abbreviation is used, in which case the
period is typed as part of the abbreviation. A man
should not use Mr. in his typed or handwritten name
at the end of a letter. A woman should add her personal title (Miss, Ms., or Mrs.) to her typewritten name
as a courtesy.*

Personal/business letter in modified block style

86d ■ Speed Ladder Paragraphs • As directed in 71c, page 124

	G W A M
	1'	5'

All letters **DS**

¶ 1
36 words
1.3 si

    Dune buggies are one of the latest fads to bloom in the desert   13 | 3 46
sunshine. The frisky new sport of piloting a homemade jalopy over hill   27 | 5 49
and dale can put some added zip in your life.   36 | 7 51

¶ 2
40 words
1.3 si

    Buggies are put together from odds and ends of other vehicles.   49 | 10 54
Some of them are long and pointed in shape. They may have fat airplane   63 | 13 56
tires on the rear with extra-thin motorcycle tires in the front.   76 | 15 59

¶ 3
43 words
1.4 si

    Drivers include youngsters as well as folks in their sixties.   89 | 18 62
Many dune buggy buffs bring their families to roam the sandy hills.   103 | 21 65
Every buggy carries a flag on a pole to make it easy for drivers to   116 | 23 67
spot each other.   119 | 24 68

¶ 4
48 words
1.3 si

    The buggies come in quite a number of sizes, shapes, and colors.   133 | 27 70
Their events include dune climbing and drag racing. Many provide jump   147 | 29 73
seats in back of the driver so others can scream in joyful terror as   161 | 32 76
the bug roars down a steep dune.   167 | 33 78

¶ 5
52 words
1.3 si

    Lovers of the new sport claim it's an ideal way to cure freeway   180 | 36 80
frustrations. There are no traffic jams nor signal lights. It's safe   194 | 39 83
too. The major danger is a collision with another bug, but this is   208 | 42 85

All ¶'s
1.3 si

unlikely as the flag pole can be seen even behind a dune.   219 | 44 88

1'	1	2	3	4	5	6	7	8	9	10	11	12	13	14
5'		1			2			3		

86e ■ Continuity Practice from Script • Type as many times as possible in the time that remains

	Words

All letters **DS**

60 words
1.3 si

What does it take to keep major league baseball teams going these   13
days? It requires top players, of course, and good fields on which   27
to play. But the teams need even more than that. They must also have   41
zealous fans who get excited and really provide support with their   54
attendance and their cheers.   60

LESSON 86 ■ PAGE 149

Lesson 48

48a ■ Keyboard Review ■ Each line three times   *5 minutes*

All letters   **SS** How can Bud mix five quarts of gray paint for Jack and Liza?

Symbol   We may wish to type "c/o" for the abbreviation "in care of."   Quick, sharp strokes

Easy   Wait for your ship to come in only if you have sent one out.

| 1 | 2 | 3 | 4 | 5 | 6 | 7 | 8 | 9 | 10 | 11 | 12 |

48b ■ Paragraph Guided Writings   *10 minutes*

Directions—1. Set a speed goal for a 1-minute writing. Type three 1-minute writings. Try to type your goal word just as time is called. Type no faster or no slower than the goal you select.

2. Raise your goal by 8 words. Type three additional 1-minute writings. Try to reach your new goal as time is called. Your teacher may call the quarter- or half-minutes to guide you.

All letters   **DS**   We know that sizable numbers of people hold more than   Read words

41 words   one job these days. Two in ten say they do this because they

1.2 si   like the work. The need for extra cash is given as a reason   Think words

far more frequently, though.   Type words

48c ■ Problem Typing   *30 minutes*

Directions—Type the return address on the 18th line space. Use your address in the return address. Sign the letter.

• *When you supply the information, 11 words are counted for the heading, which includes the return address and date.*

Problem 1 ■ *Personal/Business Letter in Modified Block Style*

Full sheet
50-space line
Current date
Open punctuation

	Words
Your address	8
Current date	11
Ms. Susan Barger	14
1295 Vista Drive	17
Your city, state, and ZIP Code	22
Dear Ms. Barger	25
As chairperson of Career Day, I want to thank you for coming to	38
Roosevelt School to speak on the subject of "Pharmacy as a	50
Career."	52
We especially appreciated learning about the educational re-	64
quirements for becoming a pharmacist and hearing your de-	75
scription of the trials and rewards of owning your own business.	88
I'm sure all of us now have a much greater understanding of the	101
field of pharmacy than we did before you talked to us.	112
Yours very truly	115

BIBLIOGRAPHY

Triple-space ——————————

5-space ——————→ Fillmer, H. Thompson, <u>et al</u>. <u>Patterns of Language</u>. New York:
indention   American Book Company, 1974.

                                                        ←——————— Double-space

Laughlin, R. M. "Fun in the Word Factory: Experiences with
    the Dictionary." <u>Language Arts</u>, (March, 1978), pp. 319-21.

Maxwell, John C. <u>Ginn Elements of English</u>. Lexington: Ginn
    and Company, 1974.

Pollock, Thomas Clark, and Richard L. Loughlin. <u>The Macmillan</u>
<u>English Series</u>. New York: Macmillan, Inc., 1973.

~~~~~~

Bibliography

Lesson 86

● *70-space line*

86a ■ Keyboard Review ● Each line at least three times

5 minutes

All letters **SS** The king and queen brought dozens of expensive jewels from the colony.
Figure   Charles Lindbergh crossed the Atlantic in 33 hours 39 minutes in 1927.   *Type steadily*
4th finger   lamp palm quiz zipper pail lap soap group pupil people palace pit quit
Easy   The officers thought it was their duty to visit with the past members.

   | 1 | 2 | 3 | 4 | 5 | 6 | 7 | 8 | 9 | 10 | 11 | 12 | 13 | 14 |

86b ■ Correcting Errors—Squeezing Letters

5 minutes

> ● *If a letter has been omitted from the end of a word*
> *and no space has been allowed for it, you may*
> *make the correction by squeezing letters.*

Directions—1. Type the line just as it appears below.

2. Move the carriage to the space following *bee*.

3. Depress the backspace key half way. Hold it. Type *n*.

4. Repeat the problem.

Error: A letter has bee omitted at the end of a word.

Correction: A letter has beenomitted at the end of a word.

86c ■ Number Expression Guides—Review

5 minutes

Directions—Type each sentence twice. The first line
gives the rule. The remaining lines apply it.

1   **SS**   You must type in full all numbers used at the beginning of a sentence.
2   Thirty-six of our states now grow choice eating apples for the market.   *Even stroking*
3   Twenty-five thousand carloads are shipped from Washington in one year.

   | 1 | 2 | 3 | 4 | 5 | 6 | 7 | 8 | 9 | 10 | 11 | 12 | 13 | 14 |

Problem 2 ■ Addressing Small Envelope

Directions—Address a small envelope for the letter on page 82. Fold the letter, insert it. Refer to the illustration below.

● *Use paper cut to envelope size (6½- by 3⅝-inches) if envelopes are not available.*

Addressing a Small Envelope

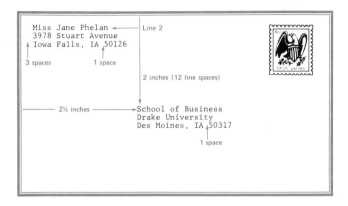

1. Type the writer's name and return address in the upper left corner as shown in the illustration. Begin on the second line space from the top edge and 3 spaces from the left edge.

2. Type the receiver's name about 2 inches (12 line spaces) from the top of the envelope. Start about 2½ inches from the left edge.

3. Use the block style and single spacing for all addresses. City and state names and ZIP Code (see p. 116) must be typed on one line in that order.

4. The state name may be typed in full, or it may be abbreviated by using the 2-letter state abbreviation or the standard abbreviation.

FOLDING LETTERS FOR SMALL ENVELOPES

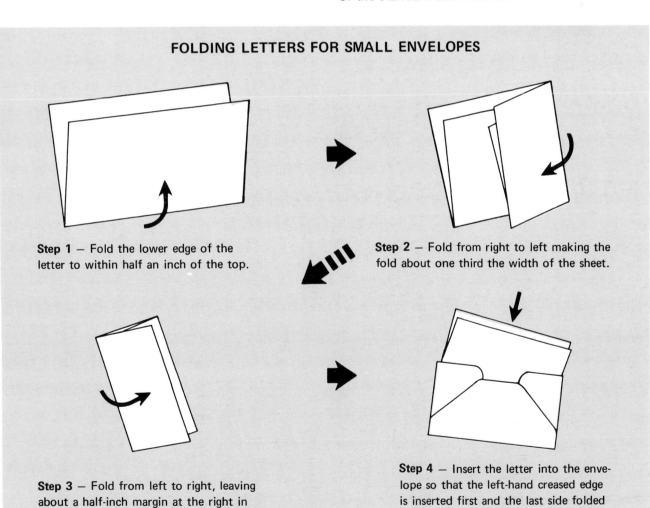

Step 1 — Fold the lower edge of the letter to within half an inch of the top.

Step 2 — Fold from right to left making the fold about one third the width of the sheet.

Step 3 — Fold from left to right, leaving about a half-inch margin at the right in order that the letter may be opened easily.

Step 4 — Insert the letter into the envelope so that the left-hand creased edge is inserted first and the last side folded is toward the backside of the envelope.

Lesson 85

85a ■ Keyboard Review • Each line at least three times

5 minutes

All letters **SS** Julie knew by the quizzical expression on my face that I had given up.

Figure Can Edward locate the state capitals on the maps on pages 434 and 435?

Home row Older hardware dealers definitely declined to indicate delivery dates.

Easy Turn your book so that it is at the right angle for you when you type.

Cut out waste movements

| 1 | 2 | 3 | 4 | 5 | 6 | 7 | 8 | 9 | 10 | 11 | 12 | 13 | 14 |

85b ■ Timed Writings

10 minutes

Directions—Type a 1- and a 5-minute writing on 81d, page 140. Circle errors. Compute *gwam*.

85c ■ Problem Typing

30 minutes

Problem 1 ■ *Title Page*

Directions—1. Type the title page in the illustration at the right. It is a title page for the report that you typed in Lesson 84.

2. Follow the directions given on the illustration at the right. The data on the title page are given in larger print below. Type from the larger print.

• *Remember to move the center point 3 spaces to the right.*

THE DICTIONARY

By

Your name
Typewriting II

Current date

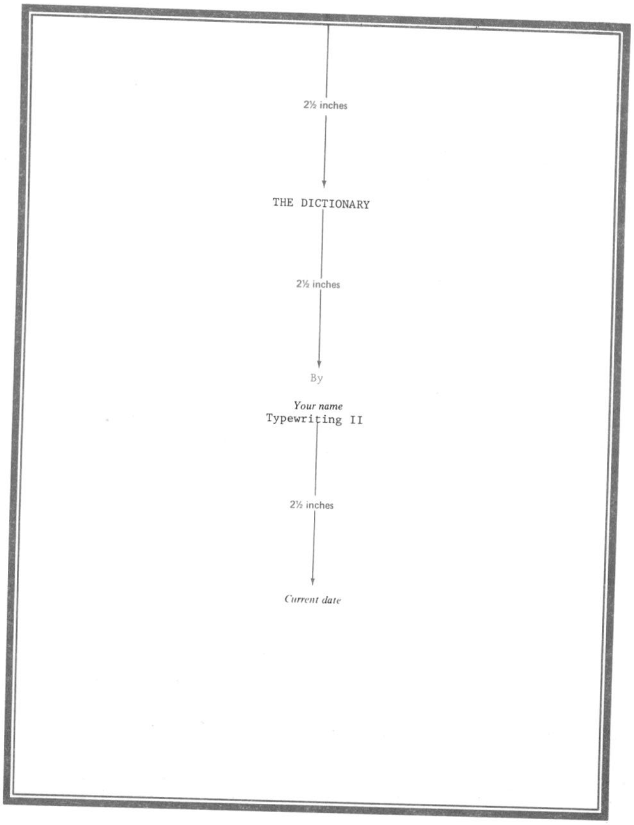

Title page

Problem 2 ■ *Bibliography*

Directions—1. Type the bibliography shown on the next page. Use the same margins used in the body of the report. Start typing 2 inches from the top.

• *Remember to move the center point 3 spaces to the right.*

2. This is the bibliography for the report you typed in Lesson 84. Number this page as page 3. Place the title page you prepared in Problem 1 on top. Staple the entire report at the left.

Problem 3 ■ Addressing Small Envelopes

Directions—1. On six envelopes or paper cut to envelope size (6½- by 3⅝-inches), type the addresses below.

2. Follow spacing directions given on page 84.

3. Type your name and address as the sender.

Miss Dottie Davis
5588 Gulf Shores
Corpus Christi, TX 78411

Ms. Gloria Guerra
14 Cactus Court
Tucson, AZ 85706

Mr. James Hosler
15 Griffith Avenue
Memphis, TN 38107

Dr. Margaret Schaffer
15293 Holland Drive
Brooklyn, NY 11212

Leger Galleries, Ltd.
13 Old Bond Street
London WIX 3DB
ENGLAND

Foothills Sportswear
1200 First Street, S.W.
Calgary, Alberta
CANADA
T2G 3G8

Lesson 49

● 60-space line

49a ■ Keyboard Review ● Each line three times

5 minutes

All letters **SS** Four experts quickly amazed the crowd by juggling five axes.

Figure-Symbol Many of Kim's ancestors moved west in the 1880's and 1890's.

Easy He has to learn to handle those kinds of problems right now.

| 1 | 2 | 3 | 4 | 5 | 6 | 7 | 8 | 9 | 10 | 11 | 12 |

Type with your fingers

49b ■ Paragraph Guided Writings ● As directed in 48b, page 83

10 minutes

All letters **DS** Some may not realize that the first flight attendants
were not women but were the co-pilots on the planes. They
served cold box lunches and poured drinks from thermos jugs.
After quite a long time, men are now hired for this type of
work.

48 words
1.2 si

Quick, crisp, short strokes

49c ■ Problem Typing

30 minutes

Problem 1 ■ *Personal/Business Letter in Modified Block Style, Paragraph Indentions, and Mixed Punctuation*

Full sheet
50-space line

Directions—1. Type the letter on the next page in modified block style. Type return address on Line 15 and inside address on 4th line space after date.

2. Address an envelope. Fold and insert the letter.

● *In mixed punctuation, a colon follows the salutation; a comma follows the complimentary close. Other parts are punctuated as they are in open punctuation.*

Problem ▪ *Two-Page Report to Be Bound at the Left*

Directions—1. Type this two-page report using the directions given on page 145. Number both pages.

2. Type the footnotes at the bottom of the first page of your typed report.

Words

THE DICTIONARY

3

Triple-space ────────────────────────────▶

Throughout our lives the one book all of us will probably refer to more often than any other is the dictionary. This invaluable reference book has to be consulted again and again by everyone who speaks and writes English. It is one of our most vital books for communicating ideas effectively.

17
32
47
61

While the English language dates back more than 1,500 years, the dictionary we take for granted today has a considerably shorter history. The first English dictionary was not written until the early 1600's. It was more than 200 years later, in 1828, when Webster published his two-volume American Dictionary of the English Language.[1]

75
90
105
119
137

Although some people believe that dictionaries dictate rules for using words correctly, such is not exactly the case. The dictionary describes how words are used, not necessarily how they should be used. Before writing the entry for a word, dictionary writers look at all the places the word has been used--in books, newspapers, and speeches--and from these contexts determine the various ways a word is used most often by most people.[2]

151
167
182
198
212
225

The major function of the dictionary, of course, is to promote accuracy in spelling, pronunciation, and word division. It provides a reliable way of getting answers to many different kinds of questions about words.

239
255
268

In addition to helping us spell, pronounce, and divide words properly, the dictionary offers much other valuable information. The derivation of a word is often given, telling from which language the word comes. If the object being looked up cannot easily be described, an illustration may be shown. When words are not considered appropriate for good usage, they are referred to as slang; when words are to be used only in conversation or informal writing, they are noted as colloquial; when words are no longer in common use, they are considered obsolete.

283
299
314
329
342
358
375
385

Single-space ───────▶

Double-space ───────▶

389

[1]Thomas Clark Pollock and Richard L. Loughlin, The Macmillan English Series (New York: Macmillan, Inc., 1973), p. 23.

407
418

[2]John C. Maxwell, Ginn Elements of English (Lexington: Ginn and Company, 1974), p. 214.

437
441

Biltmore Junior High School   6
Sacramento, CA 95821   10
November 18, 19--   13

Dr. Mary Lyons, Chairperson   19
Christmas Fund Drive   23
2814 Celeste Boulevard   28
Sacramento, CA 95828   32

Dear Dr. Lyons: 35

This is an offer on the part of the Teen-Age   44
Club of our school to help you in the Christmas   53
Fund Drive this year.   58

We are aware of the fine reputation the Drive   67
has earned under your leadership. There is a lot of   78
hard work involved, and our club can do a great deal   88
to ease the burden of busy people such as yourself.   99

Perhaps we could best serve in the sorting and   108
packaging phase of the drive since we could not take   119
part in soliciting funds. However, we shall do what-   129
ever you think we could best do.   136

Please let me know if we can help you.   144

Very truly yours,   148

Douglas Simpson, President   153
Teen-Age Club   156

Problem 2 ■ *Personal/Business Letter from Unarranged Copy*

Full sheet
50-space line
Indented ¶'s
Mixed punctuation
Current date

Directions—Type the letter in modified block style. Type the return address on Line 16. Address an envelope. Fold and insert the letter.

• *The lines in the problem are not set line-for-line the way you will type them. Set the margin stops properly; return your carriage with the bell.*

Return Address—Emerson School / Dallas, TX 75243

Address—Mr. Larry Glandon / President, Hi-Y Club / Clark School / Dallas, TX 75229

Dear Larry:

Plans are going ahead for the Hi-Y Conference to be held at Bragg Park next weekend.

Will you please send me the name of the person in charge of the luncheon and the names of those who will be helping with the games and other events planned for the afternoon. We need this information for the printing of the program.

Six schools are now signed up to send delegates. Each one will have at least eight members in attendance. It looks like a good conference, and we all appreciate the time and work you are putting into this meeting.

Sincerely,

Ms. Donna Nelson

Lesson 84

84a ■ Keyboard Review • Each line at least three times

5 minutes

All letters SS Jack got zero on his final exam simply because we gave hard questions.

Figure-Symbol Attendance at all their home games increased 5% between 1976 and 1979.

Long reach numb debit sum any zebra hunt myself nut nurse mystery style zany mute

Easy If they spend their time working in the right way, they can type more.

| 1 | 2 | 3 | 4 | 5 | 6 | 7 | 8 | 9 | 10 | 11 | 12 | 13 | 14 |

Elbows in

84b ■ Skill Comparison

10 minutes

Directions—Type two 1-minute writings on each sentence. Try to type all sentences at the rate set on the first one.

Easy SS It is said by many that I have but to start a job to get it half done.

Figure-Symbol Yashchenko now has the world's record high jump (7 feet 7 3/4 inches).

Shift Marcia MacMillan visited the Smithsonian Institute in Washington, D.C.

Rough draft Only the ~~man~~ ones who ~~is~~ are ab(e)l t(o) see t(h)e invisible ~~will~~ can do the impossibl(e).

| 1 | 2 | 3 | 4 | 5 | 6 | 7 | 8 | 9 | 10 | 11 | 12 | 13 | 14 |

Think as you type

Directions for Typing Bound Manuscripts

• *The directions given here apply to typing theses, formal reports, and other manuscripts bound at the left. Use these directions in typing the reports and compositions that follow.*

1. Set margin stops for a 1½-inch left margin (pica, 15 spaces; elite, 18 spaces) and a 1-inch right margin (pica, 10 spaces; elite, 12 spaces).

• *Move the center point 3 spaces to the right to allow for the wider left margin.*

2. On all but the first page, leave 1-inch top and bottom margins.

3. Type the title in all capital letters 2 inches from the top of the first page. Triple-space after it.

4. Long quotations (4 line spaces), footnotes, and bibliographical items should be single spaced. Long quotations should be indented 5 spaces from each margin. Double-space the remainder of the report.

5. If the first page is numbered, center the number ½ inch from the bottom. The following pages are numbered ½ inch (4 line spaces) from the top of the page and aligned with the right margin. Triple-space after typing the page number; type the body of the report.

6. At least 2 lines of a paragraph must appear at the bottom of a page, and at least 2 lines of a paragraph should be carried forward to a new page.

Lesson 50

50a ■ Keyboard Review ● Each line three times

5 minutes

All letters   **SS**   Ava Mudge will quickly explain the fire hazards of this job.

Figure-Symbol   All our girls ran the 100-yard dash in less than 15 seconds.   Type steadily

Easy   Terry thinks they would be smart to visit that island today.

| 1 | 2 | 3 | 4 | 5 | 6 | 7 | 8 | 9 | 10 | 11 | 12 |

Addressing A Large Envelope

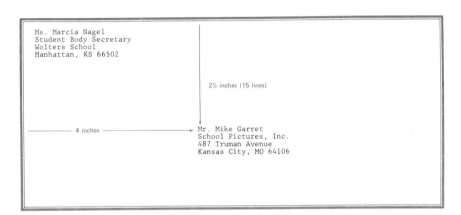

```
Ms. Marcia Nagel
Student Body Secretary
Wolters School
Manhattan, KS 66502


                              2½ inches (15 lines)



  ————— 4 inches —————→ Mr. Mike Garret
                         School Pictures, Inc.
                         487 Truman Avenue
                         Kansas City, MO 64106
```

A large envelope (9½- by 4⅛-inches) is usually typed for business letters or for letters of more than one page. Type the address 2½ inches from the top and 4 inches from the left edge of the envelope. Directions for spacing the address and using abbreviations for the state name and the ZIP Code are given on page 84.

FOLDING LETTERS FOR LARGE ENVELOPES

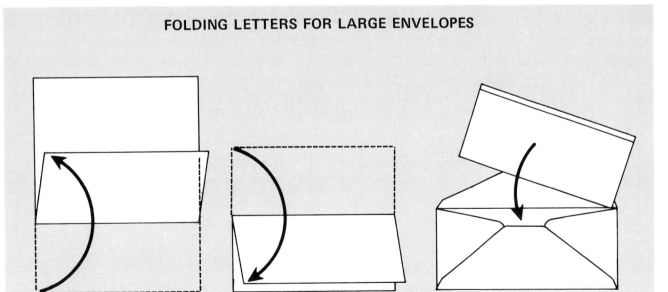

Step 1 — Fold from bottom to top, making the fold slightly less than one third the length of the sheet.

Step 2 — Fold the top down to within one half inch of the bottom fold.

Step 3 — Insert the letter into the envelope with the last crease toward the bottom of the envelope and with the last fold up.

2 inches
(13th line space)

LEARNING TO LISTEN

Triple-space

The fact that communication is a two-way process means both people in a conversation must listen as well as talk before real understanding can be achieved.

Experts in the field remind us that we spend more of our waking hours listening than we spend in any of the other basic communication activities. According to Miller, each of us can expect to spend more of our lives hearing and listening than doing anything else except breathing.[1]

1 inch
left margin

1 inch
right margin

Listening is much more than just hearing, however. Hearing involves only the ears; listening requires the use of both the ears and the mind. Unless our minds are tuned in to what the other person is saying, communication will not take place.

One of the keys to good listening is to learn to concentrate on the ideas the speaker is trying to convey and not be distracted by other sounds or thoughts. Because our minds are capable of going much faster than anyone can talk, we have to work at keeping our attention focused on what the other person is saying.

We can help keep our minds from wandering off the subject by speaking to the point occasionally or by asking questions which will help the other person expand on some point which may not have been clear.

Single-space

Double-space

[1]Dorothy Miller, Ginn Elementary English (Lexington: Ginn and Company, 1972), p. 55.

Approximately 1 inch

Theme with footnotes

50b ▪ Problem Typing

25 minutes

Problem 1 ▪ *Personal/Business Letter in Block Style*

50-space line
Open punctuation

Directions—Type the return address on Line 16. Address a large envelope with the return address in the upper left corner as shown on page 87.

● *The symbol (¶) stands for a new paragraph.*

Return Address—Wolters School / Manhattan, KS 66502 / April 24, 19--
Address—Mr. Mike Garret / School Pictures, Inc. / 457 Truman Avenue / Kansas City, MO 64106

Dear Mr. Garret

Ms. Taylor, our vice-principal, asked me to write to you regarding the arrangements for taking our school identification pictures. (¶) As we understand it, our school will be able to use the pictures for school records, the yearbook, and the student body cards. Students may also buy a large packet for themselves by paying $4 at the time the pictures are taken. (¶) We have scheduled students whose names begin with A-L for Tuesday, May 5, and students whose names begin with M-Z for Wednesday, May 6. Students will report to the gym beginning promptly at 9 a.m. each day.

Sincerely yours / Ms. Marcia Nagel / Student Body Secretary

```
Wolters School
Manhattan, KS 66502
April 24, 19--


Mr. Mike Garret
School Pictures, Inc.
487 Truman Avenue
Kansas City, MO 64106

Dear Mr. Garret

Ms. Taylor, our vice-principal, asked me to write
to you regarding the arrangements for taking our
school identification pictures.

As we understand it, our school will be able to
use the pictures for school records, the yearbook,
and the student body cards.  Students may also buy
a large packet for themselves by paying $4 at the
time the pictures are taken.

We have scheduled students whose names begin with
A-L for Tuesday, May 5, and students whose names
begin with M-Z for Wednesday, May 6.  Students will
report to the gym beginning promptly at 9 a.m. each
day.

Sincerely yours

Marcia Nagel
Ms. Marcia Nagel
Student Body Secretary
```

Personal/business letter in block style

Problem 2 ▪ *Personal/Business Letter in Block Style*

Block style
50-space line
Open punctuation

Directions—Type the return address on Line 16. Address a large envelope. Type the return address on the envelope. Fold and insert the letter.

Return Address—406 Marks Street / Sioux Falls, SD 57103 / May 10, 19--
Address—Mrs. Ruth Carr / 1634 Cornell Way / Sioux Falls, SD 57106

Dear Mrs. Carr

I am applying for a job at Woman Lake in Brainerd, Minnesota, for the summer months and need three letters of reference. Will you please write one of these letters for me. (¶) Mr. Packard, manager of the lodge, said I should try to get someone to recommend me who was familiar with my dependability. Since I have been delivering the Sioux Falls News to your home for the past two years and have also been taking care of your yard during this time, I thought you would be well qualified to judge me. (¶) The letter should be sent to Mr. Ron Packard, Manager, Woman Lake Lodge, Brainerd, MN 56501. Thank you very much for your help.

Yours very truly / Bob Beckley

G W A M

    1' | 5'

All letters   **DS**   Perhaps you don't think you could ever be tempted by a bargain   13 | 3   38

that seems just too good to pass up or be deceived by a fast-talking   26 | 5   40

¶ 1

60 words   salesclerk. Do not be too sure about it. Neither did thousands of   40 | 8   43

1.3 si

others who each year have had to make complaints to better business   54 | 11   46

bureaus or chambers of commerce.   60 | 12   47

How can you keep from becoming the victim of a gyp artist? The   13 | 15   50

most important rule is to deal only with persons or stores which are   26 | 17   52

¶ 2

60 words   familiar to you, your neighbors, or your friends. If you don't know   40 | 20   55

1.3 si

those who call on you, question what they say. Be extremely wary if   54 | 23   58

your questions go unanswered.   60 | 24   59

You should also realize the dangers in buying or in signing for   13 | 27   62

¶ 3

55 words   something before you have had time to check out the firm with which you   27 | 29   64

1.3 si

are dealing. Try not to take needless chances. A good plan is not to   41 | 32   67

All ¶'s

1.3 si   buy until you have compared prices for the same kind of merchandise.   55 | 35   70

1' | 1 | 2 | 3 | 4 | 5 | 6 | 7 | 8 | 9 | 10 | 11 | 12 | 13 | 14 |

5' | 1 | 2 | 3 |

Directions for Typing Footnotes

● *All important statements of fact or opinion and all direct quotations that are taken from books or articles for use in a theme must have footnotes. Footnotes give complete information about the references from which materials were taken.*

1. Make a light pencil mark in the margin to indicate where the divider line will be typed.

2. After typing the last line of a full page of copy, change from double spacing to single spacing. Space once, then use the underscore key to type a 1½-inch divider line.

3. After typing the divider line, space twice; then type the footnote reference.

4. Single-space footnotes; double-space between them.

● *Although footnotes vary in length, in general the following system works well for determining where the divider line should be typed: (a) make a light pencil mark for the 1-inch bottom margin, (b) from this pencil mark space up 3 line spaces for each footnote and once for the divider line, (c) make a second light pencil mark—the point at which the divider line should be typed.*

● *On a page only partially full, the footnotes appear at the bottom of the page.*

83d ■ Problem Typing   *25 minutes*

Problem ■ First Page of Theme with Footnotes

Directions—Type the first page of the theme illustrated on page 144. Use theme style. Follow the form shown in the illustration.

50c ■ Timed Writings

Directions—1. Type a 3-minute writing. Compute your *gwam*.
2. Type two 1-minute writings on each paragraph; the first for speed, the second for control.

3. Finally, type another 3-minute writing on all paragraphs. Compute your *gwam*. Compare the *gwam* and number of errors for the two 3-minute writings.

			GWAM	
			1'	3'
All letters	DS	Being courteous does not mean that you must always agree	11	4 45
¶ 1		with others. You have a mind, and you are expected to use it.	24	8 49
36 words		Keep in mind though that others must enjoy the same chance.	36	12 53
1.3 si		You must learn to state your own views correctly. Do	11	16 57
¶ 2		not call another who does not see things as you do a zany	22	19 61
42 words		fool, a bully, or a liar. That's the quickest way to declare	35	24 65
1.2 si		a war and the surest way to lose it.	42	26 67
¶ 3		Learn to admit that the ideas of others may have some	11	30 71
46 words		merit. Be willing to listen to them. Don't quibble over	22	33 75
1.3 si		moot points. If you have some facts to support your ideas,	35	37 79
All ¶'s		give them. Few will ever question your right to be heard.	46	41 83
1.3 si				

1'	1	2	3	4	5	6	7	8	9	10	11	12
3'		1			2			3			4	

50d ■ Extra-Credit Typing

Problem 1

Directions—1. Type the timed writing in 50c as a short report. Provide a title; type it in all capital letters.

2. Use a 60-space line; double-space the body.
3. Center the entire report vertically on a full sheet.

Problem 2

Directions—1. Assume that you are Ruth Carr in the letter in Problem 2, page 88. Write the kind of letter about Bob Beckley (the writer of the letter in the problem) that you would like to have written about you if you were applying for the job.

2. Type the letter in modified block style, blocked paragraphs, mixed punctuation. Date it for May 15, 19--. Use personal titles as needed.
3. Address a small envelope. Fold and insert the letter.

Problem 3

Directions—1. Address large envelopes for each of the addresses given in Problem 3, page 85.

2. Type your name and address as the sender on all the envelopes.

Problem 2 ■ *Short Report with Indented Items*

Directions—Set the margin stops for a 60-space line. Double-space the report; single-space numbered paragraphs. Indent numbered paragraphs 5 spaces from each margin and double-space between them. Spread the heading.

IMPROMPTU SPEAKING

You will be called upon many times to give a talk on the spur of the moment. You might be asked to give a short report on a book, trip, or play. You might be called upon to make an announcement or present a gift to a teacher. If you found yourself on one of these spots, could you deliver?

A plan for an impromptu talk is always helpful. Here is such a plan:

1. Make a statement that gets attention. If you can't think of anything else, tell your group that you are glad to tell them about your subject. Being glad in this situation is unique enough to draw some attention.

2. Explain why your subject is important to the group.

3. Make two or three general statements about your subject. Illustrate each with a few examples. Cite interesting cases. Describe them vividly.

4. Summarize your ideas. Do this quickly. Don't let your talk drag--especially at the end.

The ability to give a brief talk on almost any subject on short notice can be very profitable to you. You will be envied by everyone. Practice giving this type of talk. Collect your wits; think fast; organize your ideas. Prepare your talk along the lines suggested in the plan just described.

Lesson 83

• *70-space line*

83a ■ Keyboard Review • Each line at least three times

5 *minutes*

All letters **SS** One excited gazelle jumped the river before us and quickly raced away.

Figure-Symbol My projector has an f/1.2 lens, 406-foot take-up reel, and costs $375. Quick, crisp,

Balanced and one-hand We saw them there. Read my theme at noon. We saw them work and rest. short strokes

Easy Without question, I should drive my car on the right side of the road.

| 1 | 2 | 3 | 4 | 5 | 6 | 7 | 8 | 9 | 10 | 11 | 12 | 13 | 14 |

83b ■ Correcting Errors—Squeezing Letters

5 *minutes*

• *This problem shows you how to add an omitted letter to the beginning of a word when no space has been allowed for it.*

Directions—1. Type the line just as it appears below.
2. Move the carriage to the *m* in *mitted*.

3. Depress the backspace key half way. Hold it. Type *o*.
4. Repeat the problem.

Error: A letter has been mitted at the beginning of a word.

Correction: A letter has beenomitted at the beginning of a word.

Unit 8 ■ Typing Themes and Outlines

General Directions ■ Lessons 51 - 60

Machine Adjustments—Except as otherwise directed, use a 60-space line. Single-space lines of words and sentences, but double-space between repeated groups of lines. Double-space paragraph copy.

Correcting Errors—Your teacher will tell you if you are to correct errors on problem typing.

Lesson 51

● *Use a 60-space line for all lessons in this unit.*

51a ■ Keyboard Review ● Each line three times   5 minutes

All letters   SS   Gail required me to fix every brown jacket with new zippers.

Figure-Symbol   Asia's Mount Everest (5 1/2 miles high) was climbed in 1953.   Type steadily

Easy   Most of us show what we are by what we do with what we have.

| 1 | 2 | 3 | 4 | 5 | 6 | 7 | 8 | 9 | 10 | 11 | 12 |

51b ■ Spelling and Proofreading Aid ● Each line three times   5 minutes

1   SS   decision parcel ordinary maintenance canceled serious choose

2   belief familiar across wholly experience responsible visible   Wrists and elbows still

3   absence eighth congratulate immediate committee incidentally

51c ■ Technique Builder—Stroking ● Each line three times   5 minutes

One-hand   SS   Barb gave Lynn Waters a red scarf. John Holly was defeated.

Balanced-hand   Have them sign the form if they have done all of their work.   Quick, sharp strokes

Long reach   Brad Browne hunted in the humid brush for a mysterious bird.

| 1 | 2 | 3 | 4 | 5 | 6 | 7 | 8 | 9 | 10 | 11 | 12 |

51d ■ Paragraph Guided Writings   10 minutes

Directions—1. Set a speed goal for a 1-minute writing. Type three 1-minute writings. Try to type your goal word just as time is called. Type no faster or no slower than the goal you selected.

2. Raise your goal by 4 words. Type three additional 1-minute writings. Try to reach your new goal as time is called. Your teacher may call the quarter- or half-minutes to guide you.

All letters   DS   One health hazard some of you can expect to face more

44 words
1.2 si   now than in years past is that of noise. As workers insist   Flowing, rhythmic stroking

on peace and quiet at their jobs, firms may have to give

them earmuffs and muffle sounds of loud machines.

Lesson 82

* *70-space line*

82a ■ Keyboard Review ● Each line at least three times

5 minutes

All letters   SS   We couldn't give any excuse for most of the crazy quips and bad jokes.

Figure   While Maury Wills stole 104 bases in 1962, he was thrown out 13 times.

Adjacent keys   Some seventh graders dashed madly for class seconds ahead of schedule.

Easy   When the road on which you go is straight, it is not easy to get lost.

Fingers deeply curved

| 1 | 2 | 3 | 4 | 5 | 6 | 7 | 8 | 9 | 10 | 11 | 12 | 13 | 14 |

82b ■ Control Ladder Paragraphs

10 minutes

Directions—Type 1-minute writings on the paragraphs in 81d, page 140. When you can type a paragraph without error, move to the next one. Type with control.

82c ■ Problem Typing

30 minutes

Problem 1 ■ One-Page Report

Directions—Type the report in regular theme style. Set the margin stops for a 60-space line.

A BOOK TO SETTLE ARGUMENTS

You may find it hard to believe that the fastest time for demolishing an upright piano and passing the entire wreckage through a ring nine inches in diameter is only 2 1/2 minutes. Believe it or not, this considerable feat was accomplished way back in 1968.

Such interesting, if somewhat impractical, bits of information are contained in the GUINNESS BOOK OF WORLD RECORDS, a publication that lists almost every conceivable type of record that might have been set anywhere by anybody.

According to this book, somebody from Coon Rapids, Minnesota, once talked nonstop for 144 hours and 4 minutes. Interestingly enough, the longest political speech on record required less than 30 hours; and, luckily for the diners, the longest after-dinner talk was delivered in a mere 3 hours.

Since the record book was first published, more than two million copies have been sold. Because records change so often, many revised editions have had to be printed. One of the editions, for example, listed the world showering record as a mere 174 hours. Three years later the entry was changed to 200 hours for the most prolonged continuous shower bath on record.

One-page report

LESSON 82 ■ PAGE **141**

51e ■ Timed Writings

15 minutes

Directions—Type 1-, 2-, and 3-minute writings on the copy below. Repeat. Try to equal your 1-minute rates on the longer writings.

Technique Goals—Feet on the floor; body relaxed, but erect. Fingers deeply curved; wrists low and still. Keep your eyes on the copy.

• *For the 2-minute rate, divide the 1-minute gwam by 2.*

		GWAM	
		1'	3'

All letters DS

¶ 1
51 words
1.3 si

No matter whether it is a trip of several miles or just a jaunt to the local grocery store, many people are traveling by bike these days. While kids still account for the greatest share of all bike sales, quite a few adults now whiz around on two wheels.

1'	3'
11	4 46
24	8 50
36	12 54
48	16 58
51	17 59

¶ 2
43 words
1.4 si

In a commuter race staged in one major city a few years back, a bicycle rider covered a distance of four miles in less time than two competitors. The cyclist beat a sports car by one minute and a city bus by five.

62	21 63
75	25 67
87	29 71
94	31 73

¶ 3
33 words
1.3 si

All ¶'s
1.3 si

Bicycle riding is one of the best ways to stay healthy too. Some doctors prefer this type of exercise to jogging, at least for those folks who are past middle age.

105	35 77
117	39 81
127	42 84

1'	1	2	3	4	5	6	7	8	9	10	11	12
3'		1		2		3		4				

51f ■ Control Practice

5 minutes

Directions—1. Type the last paragraph of 51e, above, as many times as you can in the time that remains.

2. Circle your errors. Place a check mark (√) in the margin of each paragraph in which you made no more than one error.

Lesson 52

• 60-space line

52a ■ Keyboard Review • Each line three times

5 minutes

All letters SS May Dick will give the puzzle to Jess Quinn for the old box.

Figure-Symbol Since the tickets sell for $3.50 each, two will cost you $7.

Easy If we do not stand for something, we will fall for anything.

	1	2	3	4	5	6	7	8	9	10	11	12	

Fingers
deeply
curved

52b ■ Typing from Dictation and Spelling Checkup

5 minutes

Directions—Type the words in 51b, page 90, from your teacher's dictation. Check for correct spelling. Retype any words in which you made an error.

| | GWAM |
| | 1' \| 5' |

All letters DS   Today it seems quite natural for us to shake hands when we greet   13 \| 3 47

a person. Like lots of things that we do without thinking, such an   27 \| 5 49

¶ 1
36 words   action at one time likely symbolized something.   36 \| 7 51
1.3 si

In primitive life the hand was probably a symbol of power. It   49 \| 10 54

¶ 2
40 words   was used to fight enemies and to make spears. When extended, the hand   63 \| 13 57
1.3 si

might have meant goodwill by showing that a person was not armed.   76 \| 15 59

We know that the hand played a major role in early religions. The   89 \| 18 62

¶ 3   Greeks prayed to their gods with raised hands. Presenting the hands,   103 \| 21 65
44 words
1.3 si   palm to palm, was at one time how an inferior person paid homage to a   117 \| 23 67

superior one.   120 \| 24 68

In these days there are still a number of different ways to shake   133 \| 27 71

hands throughout the world. Certain groups of people rub their palms   147 \| 29 73

¶ 4
48 words   together. There are chiefs in some African tribes who snap the middle   161 \| 32 76
1.3 si

finger three times when greeting.   168 \| 34 78

We can easily see that the hand, and what was done with it, has   181 \| 36 80

¶ 5
52 words   been full of meaning all through the ages. Although today it is very   195 \| 39 83
1.3 si

common for most of us to shake hands without even thinking, we are   208 \| 42 86

All ¶
1.3 si   really carrying on a custom handed down from ancient times.   220 \| 44 88

```
1' | 1 | 2 | 3 | 4 | 5 | 6 | 7 | 8 | 9 | 10 | 11 | 12 | 13 | 14 |
5' |       1       |        |       2       |        |      3       |
```

81e ■ Continuity Practice from Script • Type the paragraph as many times as you can in the time that remains.   *10 minutes*

Words

DS   *A sign in a big city zoo informs visitors that it would be possible*   14

to build one more needed monkey house with the money it takes just to   28

60 words   *pick up litter. This sum is peanuts compared to the millions of dollars*   42
1.3 si

it costs to scoop up litter from our streets, parks, beaches, and public   57

areas each year.   60

52c ■ Paragraph Skill Builder from Rough Draft
5 minutes

Directions—Type the paragraph once for practice; then type three 1-minute writings on it. Circle your errors; figure the *gwam*. Compare your best rate with the highest rate reached on 51d, page 90.

			Words
All letters **DS**	Schools often play not only for the victory but for	11	57
45 words	unique trophies that go to the victors. one well-known prize	24	70
1.2 si	is the little brown jug. Two famous football teams vie	36	82
	each year for a price of steel called the axe.	45	90

(handwritten edits: games^, # winners, Also, two)

Vertical Centering Shortcut

1. Insert paper to Line 33, the vertical center. Roll the cylinder back (toward you) once for each two lines in the copy to be typed. This will place the copy in *exact vertical center*.
2. To type a problem in *off-center* or *reading position*, roll the cylinder back three more times.

3. If you wish, you can square the edges of the paper from top to bottom and make a slight crease at the right edge. The crease will be at the vertical center (Line 33). Insert the paper to the crease, roll back once for each two lines to the position for typing.

52d ■ Problem Typing
30 minutes

Trees

Triple-space

I think that I shall never see
A poem lovely as a tree.

Double-space

A tree whose hungry mouth is pressed
Against the earth's sweet flowing breast;

A tree that looks to God all day,
And lifts her leafy arms to pray;

A tree that may in summer wear
A nest of robins in her hair;

Upon whose bosom snow has lain;
Who intimately lives with rain.

Poems are made by fools like me,
But only God can make a tree.

Double-space

-- Joyce Kilmer

Problem 1 ■ *Poem Typed in Centered Position*

Directions—1. Full sheet. Center the poem vertically. Double-space after each 2 lines. Center the poem horizontally by the 4th line, which is the longest.

2. Type the author's name to end at the right margin with the longest line.

Problem 2 ■ *Poem Typed in Reading Position*

Directions—Type the poem in Problem 1 again. This time type it in *reading position*.

LESSON 52 ■ PAGE 92

Unit 11 ■ Typing School Reports

General Directions ■ Lessons 81 - 95

Machine Adjustments—For the lessons in this unit, use a 70-space line. Single-space lines of words and sentences, but double-space between repeated groups of lines. Double-space paragraph copy.

Correcting Errors—Your teacher will tell you whether or not you are to correct errors on the problems in this unit and if you are to follow the suggestions presented in this unit for correcting errors by "squeezing" and "spreading" letters and typing insertions.

Lesson 81

• *Use a 70-space line for all lessons in this unit.*

81a ■ Keyboard Review • Each line at least three times

5 minutes

All letters SS The jovial banquet speaker excited and amazed a large crowd of youths.

Figure In an 1895 car race, the winner drove 53 miles in 10 hours 23 minutes.

Right hand In my opinion you only imply I pull my plump lion puppy up Union Hill.

Quick, sharp strokes

Easy Your smile is one thing that is worth more when it is given to others.

| 1 | 2 | 3 | 4 | 5 | 6 | 7 | 8 | 9 | 10 | 11 | 12 | 13 | 14 |

81b ■ Alignment of Paper—Horizontal and Vertical

5 minutes

Directions—1. Type the following sentence.

This job requires high skill.

2. Note the relationship of the top of the aligning scale to the bottom of the letters. Note also how the white lines on the scale line up with the letters "l" and "i" in the typewritten matter.

3. Remove the paper from the machine and reinsert it in position to type over the first typing.

4. Align horizontally first by using the paper release lever and moving the paper to the left or right until the lines on the scale are brought into alignment with the letters "l" and "i."

5. Align vertically using the variable line spacer.

6. Retype the sentence over the first writing.

7. Repeat the problem.

81c ■ Typing "Spread" Headings

5 minutes

Directions—Spread and center each heading given at the right. The first line is typed in correct form.

1. Backspace from the midpoint once for each letter, except the last one in the line, and once for each space between words.

2. Type the heading. Space once between letters and three times between words.

S P R E A D   H E A D I N G S

WORKING WITH WOOD

TRAVELING THROUGH EUROPE

AIR POLLUTION

Lesson 53

• 60-space line

53a ■ Keyboard Review • Each line three times   5 minutes

All letters   SS   Joy Brave will squeeze six big limes for the drink of punch.

Figure-Symbol   John typed a 5-minute writing on page 127 with 98% accuracy.   Space quickly

Easy   We bought some more land down the road from their old house.

| 1 | 2 | 3 | 4 | 5 | 6 | 7 | 8 | 9 | 10 | 11 | 12 |

53b ■ Paragraph Guided Writings • As directed in 51d, page 90   10 minutes

All letters   DS
                   Many health experts have a low opinion of what they

45 words   call junk food. They say that things like pop and chips   Quick
1.2 si   carriage
                   or crackers are a real health hazard because they fill us   return

                   up quickly and tend to crowd out good foods from our diet.

53c ■ Problem Typing   30 minutes

Problem ■ One-Page Report or Theme

Directions—1. Type the report on page 94. Use a 60-space line. Indent paragraphs five spaces.   **2.** Double-space the body of the report. Center the report vertically on a full sheet.

Lesson 54

• 60-space line

54a ■ Keyboard Review • Each line three times   5 minutes

All letters   SS   Fred Vasquez again explained why he objected to the remarks.

Symbol   Joanne told us to read The Hobbit and The Lord of the Rings.   Elbows in

Easy   Fix the handle so tight that he will not be able to turn it.

| 1 | 2 | 3 | 4 | 5 | 6 | 7 | 8 | 9 | 10 | 11 | 12 |

54b ■ Technique Builder—Stroking • Each line three times   10 minutes

Hyphen   SS   The left-handed pitcher can be sure-footed and clear-headed.

One-hand   saw him, refer you, we are, look upon, as you are, my grades

Weak fingers   Zane Pepper will acquire the apparatus for the player piano.

Balanced-hand   they may, with them, for the, and then, if she, and did work   Type with
                                                                                         your fingers
Combination   and see, the case, with only, for him, may look, she saw the

Double letters   I shipped the books to the committee that equipped the room.

| 1 | 2 | 3 | 4 | 5 | 6 | 7 | 8 | 9 | 10 | 11 | 12 |

Lesson 80

80a ■ Keyboard Review • Each line at least three times

All letters SS The objective was to organize and make plans for an exquisite display.

Figure-Symbol Dan's note for $3,270 (due June 1) bears interest at the rate of 8.5%.

Left hand We saw brave crews steer fast craft as great westward breezes started.

Easy Signs of rising profits will be found in most firms during the spring.

| 1 | 2 | 3 | 4 | 5 | 6 | 7 | 8 | 9 | 10 | 11 | 12 | 13 | 14 |

80b ■ Timed Writings

Directions—Type a 1- and a 5-minute writing on 76d, page 131. Circle errors. Compute *gwam*.

80c ■ Problem Typing

Problem ■ Club Schedule

Directions—Type the following club schedule on a half sheet. Center the main heading one inch from the top. Use double spacing. Leave eight spaces between columns.

• You may need to review the steps in arranging tables, page 108, and the steps for centering columnar headings, page 117.

CURRENT EVENTS CLUB SCHEDULE

Month	Speaker	Topic
October	Angelina Cruz	Crisis in Education
November	F. Lee Hull	The Middle East
December	Kelly Black	Solar Energy
January	Jean Acevedo	Health Care
February	Irving Davis	A New China
March	Barbara Dodds	An Electronic Age
April	Ann Silveira	The Third World
May	G. L. Johnson	Nuclear Power

80d ■ Extra-Credit Typing

Problem 1

Directions—Assume that you were a weekend guest in a friend's home. On 4¼- by 5½-inch stationery, write a "bread and butter" note to your friend's parents.

Problem 2

Directions—Type the letter in Problem 1, page 135, in modified block style with indented paragraphs and mixed punctuation on 8½- by 11-inch paper. Arrange the letter neatly.

Problem 3

Directions—Type the letter in Problem 1, page 133, in modified block style with indented paragraphs and mixed punctuation on a full sheet. Arrange it neatly.

TYPING A SHORT REPORT OR THEME   6

Triple-space ⟶

    Short reports or themes of one page or less may be typed   18
with a 60-space line. If the number of lines can be counted   30
easily, center the copy vertically; if not, use a standard   42
margin of 2 inches (12 line spaces) at the top.   51

    Double spacing is usually used in themes and reports.   62
Class notes, book reviews, and minutes are usually single-   74
spaced to provide better groupings of information.   84

    Every report should have a title which is typed in all   95
capital letters. It is always separated from the body by a   107
triple space.   110

    Longer reports or papers are usually typed with side   121
margins of 1 inch. When the paper is to be bound at the   132
left, however, an extra one-half inch must be provided in   144
the left margin for binding.   150

    The heading is typed 2 inches from the top of the first   161
page. All pages after the first have a top margin of 1 inch.   174
The bottom margin should not be less than 1 inch. The copy   186
usually looks better if this margin runs an extra one-half   198
inch.   199

⟵ 60-space line ⟶

One-page theme

Problem 2 ■ Order Letter in Modified Block Style

Directions—1. Type in modified block style the personal business letter shown below. Begin the return address on Line 15; leave 4 spaces between the date and the inside address.

2. Type the ordered items as a table, using a 40-space line. (Merely set each margin stop in 5 spaces. To determine the tab stop for the second column, backspace 6 spaces from your new right margin.).

Full sheet
50-space line
Indented ¶'s
Mixed punctuation

● *An enclosure notation is used when a paper (or papers) is sent with the letter. Type the notations at the left margin a double-space below the name of the sender or the title. Use the plural* **Enclosures** *if two or more items will be enclosed.*

Return address--450 Elwood Drive / Moorhead, MN 56560 / November 5, 19--

Address--Weber and Byde, Inc. / 3819 Herndon Avenue / St. Paul, MN 55110

Ladies and Gentlemen:

Please send me the following tools you have advertised in the December issue of Shop News. I understand that by ordering now I can be sure of having them in time for Christmas.

Crosscut saw	$14.95
Keyhole saw	5.65
Curved claw hammer	8.40
Deluxe hand drill	9.85
Total	$38.85

Enclosed is a check for $38.85. According to your advertisement, the postage on these items will be prepaid.

Sincerely yours,

Andy Houtz

Double-space ———————➤

Enclosure

The Attic Shop
3724 Vine Street Cincinnati, OH 45217
513- 242-3905

To: Ceramic Supply House
2304 5th Avenue West
Chicago, IL 60612

Order No. 102
Ship via Express

Quantity	Cat. No.	Description	Price		Total	
24	A106-F	Mugs	1	69	40	56
24	A107-F	Candleholders	2	49	59	76
36	G801	Glaze		89	32	04
					132	36

Date 4/21/--   Purchasing Agent *Sandra Lee*

Order form

Problem 3 ■ Order

Directions—1. Using the order form included in your workbook, type a copy of the order shown above exactly as it appears in the illustration.

2. Use the variable line spacer and the top of the alignment scale to adjust the paper correctly for each line of copy.

Alternate Suggestion—If a workbook is not available, order the items in Problem 3 by order letter similar to the one typed for Problem 2.

1   SS   accept independent liable promptly appearance column fulfill

2   occasion explanation affect color vehicle budget unnecessary   *Think as you type*

3   summary guidance temporary favorable possibility approximate

Carbon Copies

To make carbon copies, place the carbon paper (with glossy side down) on a sheet of plain paper. The paper on which you will prepare the original is then laid on the carbon paper, and all the sheets are inserted into the typewriter. The *dull* surface of the carbon sheet should be toward you when the sheets have been rolled into the typewriter. Erasing on carbon copies is explained on page xv.

● *Carbon copies are called for in this lesson. Your teacher will tell you if you are to prepare carbon copies in any other lessons in this unit.*

54d ■ **Problem Typing**   *25 minutes*

Problem ■ *Short Report or Theme*

60-space line
Double spacing

Directions—Use a standard 2-inch top margin (12 line spaces). Make one carbon copy.

	Words
HOW TO GET HIGHER GRADES IN YOUR CLASSES	8

Ask questions. If you don't understand an explanation, get help | 21
from your teacher, either in class or after classes are over. Teachers | 36
often wonder why students don't ask for help when they need it. | 49

Raise your hand. Take an active part in class discussions. You may | 62
not always be right, but it is better for you to test your views than it | 77
is to sit in complete silence. | 83

Get assignments straight. Teachers are always amazed at the number | 97
of students who turn in wrong assignments. Write them down. If you have | 112
any doubts, check with your teacher. | 119

Make up missed work. Teachers are always puzzled by the great num- | 132
ber of students who don't turn in late assignments or those that are missed | 148
during an absence. A few zeros are bound to pull a grade down quickly. | 162

Do a little more than is required. Read ahead; work extra problems. | 176
Bring in outside reports about the topics you are discussing. These | 190
small extras pay off in higher grades. | 198

Do these hints help students earn higher grades? The students who | 211
have tried them say they do. Why don't you try them too? | 223

Lesson 79

79a ▪ Keyboard Review • Each line at least three times

All letters **SS** Lee knew my expensive habits jeopardized chances for making the quota.

Figure-Symbol The admission for adults was $1.50; children 5-11, 75¢; under 5, free.

Think letters

Adjacent keys Terry wrote three other letters reporting the threats to their resort.

Think words

Easy They who spend their leisure time in the right way are sure to profit.

| 1 | 2 | 3 | 4 | 5 | 6 | 7 | 8 | 9 | 10 | 11 | 12 | 13 | 14 |

79b ▪ Punctuation Guides—Comma • Each sentence twice

10 minutes

Line 1—Use a comma after each item in a series, except the last.

Line 2—Use a comma to separate consecutive adjectives when the *and* has seemingly been omitted. Do not use the comma when the adjectives do not apply equally to the noun they modify.

Line 3—Use a comma to separate a dependent clause that precedes the main clause.

Line 4—Use a comma to separate the independent parts of a compound sentence joined by *and, but, for, or, neither, nor.*

Line 5—Use a comma to prevent misreading or confusion.

Line 6—Use a comma to set off a direct quotation from the rest of the sentence.

Line 7—Do not set off an indirect quotation from the rest of the sentence.

1   **SS** Most of our players can hit, catch, and throw the ball extremely well.

2   You will enjoy this new, useful book. I like its light blue sketches.

Sit erect

3   Whenever you type personal papers, you will want to type with control.

4   Gayle worked the problems he assigned, but she did not write the poem.

5   In 1979, 364 were sold. Compared to Ruth, Amy cannot dance very well.

Feet on the floor

6   I thought it was Franklin who said, "A penny saved is a penny earned."

7   Mrs. Brock said I could leave when I had finished the math assignment.

| 1 | 2 | 3 | 4 | 5 | 6 | 7 | 8 | 9 | 10 | 11 | 12 | 13 | 14 |

79c ▪ Problem Typing

30 minutes

Problem 1 ▪ *Typing on Ruled Lines*

Half sheet
40-space line
Triple spacing
2″ top margin

Directions—1. Using the underline, type three lines across the page. Note the position of the line in relation to the top of the alignment scale.

2. Remove the paper; then reinsert it.

3. Align the paper, using the variable line spacer, to type on the first line.

4. Type the lines shown at the right.

     Mr. Vincent P. Lucero

     8642 Magnolia Drive

     Memphis, TN 38117

Lesson 55

55a ■ Keyboard Review • Each line three times

5 minutes

All letters   **SS**   Jacqueline amazed everyone by fixing these packages of bows.

Figure-Symbol   Type distances in figures: I drove 837 miles in 1 3/4 days.

Easy   Both of them asked to take their autos to the new body shop.

Type without pauses

| 1 | 2 | 3 | 4 | 5 | 6 | 7 | 8 | 9 | 10 | 11 | 12 |

55b ■ Timed Writings • As directed in 51e, page 91

15 minutes

	GWAM	
	1'	3'

All letters   **DS**

¶ 1
42 words
1.2 si

Have you ever noticed that busy people are the ones who   11 | 4 48
are asked to do important jobs? That's because they have   23 | 8 52
learned how to organize their work, lay out a plan, and stick   35 | 12 56
to it. When they work, they work.   42 | 14 59

¶ 2
44 words
1.3 si

Thinking and studying go hand in hand. If you want to   53 | 18 62
cut down the time you spend doing homework, you can surely   65 | 22 66
do this. The formula is quite simple. Give your mind the   77 | 26 70
chance to think by closing out everything else.   86 | 29 73

¶ 3
48 words
1.3 si

Have a definite time for study. When that time comes,   97 | 32 77
plunge right in. Do not find excuses for doing something   109 | 36 81
else. Keep your attention on the task at hand. Close out   120 | 40 85
confusion. Ideas will come to you only when you give them   132 | 44 89

All ¶'s
1.3 si

a chance.   134 | 45 90

| 1' | 1 | 2 | 3 | 4 | 5 | 6 | 7 | 8 | 9 | 10 | 11 | 12 |
| 3' | | 1 | | 2 | | 3 | | 4 | | | | |

55c ■ Problem Typing

25 minutes

Problem ■ Two-Page Theme

Directions—1. Type the theme on page 97. Use theme style, double spacing.

2. Top margins—
First page: 2 inches (13th line space).
Second page: 1 inch (7th line space).

3. Set stops for 1-inch side margins.

● *As is illustrated on page vi, there are 10 spaces per inch on a pica typewriter and 12 spaces per inch on an elite typewriter.*

● *For pica typewriters, the side margins should each contain 10 horizontal spaces. For elite typewriters, the side margins should each contain 12 spaces.*

78d ■ Problem Typing

Problem 1 ■ *Personal/Business Letter in Block Style with Quoted Paragraphs*

Full sheet
60-space line
Open punctuation

Directions—1. Type the letter below as a personal/business letter in block style. Start typing the return address on the 12th line space from the top of the paper. Type the address on the 4th line from the date. Indent the quoted paragraphs 5 spaces from each margin.

2. Address a small envelope. Fold the letter; insert it into the envelope.

2579 Wilson Road
Council Bluffs, IA 51501
October 18, 19--

Miss Kristi Sakamoto
Student Body President
Pyle Intermediate School
Omaha, NE 68128

Dear Kristi

The two paragraphs quoted below were taken from the brochure Mr. Taylor left at our school:

The student from whom you receive this note is engaged in a school project intended to earn money for a worthy purpose. This project will help the student develop poise, confidence, and good manners. It provides a work experience that can be valuable in later life.

You can make an important contribution to the success of our project by choosing from this list of magazines and by encouraging the student to call on other prospects.

The remainder of the brochure contains the price list as well as a sample order form. If you will let me know how many you need, I can get a supply from Mr. Taylor next week.

Sincerely yours
Miss Robin Peterson

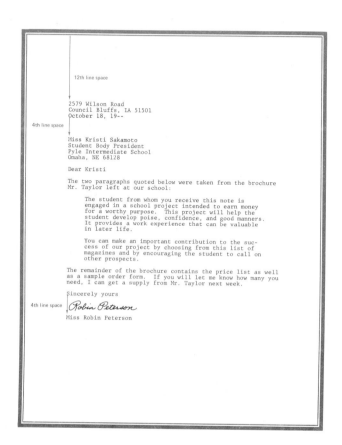

Personal/business letter in block style

Problem 2 ■ *Personal/Business Letter in Block Style*

Directions—1. Type the letter in Problem 1 again. This time, however, address the letter to Ms. Barbara Harris, Student Body Vice-President. Start typing the return address on the 12th line space from the top of the paper. Type the address on the 4th line space from the date.

2. Use your own address and today's date in the return address. Type your name at the end of the letter; sign it.

Miniature models of both pica and elite solutions of the first page are shown. Do not type from the models; work from the copy at the bottom of the page.

Leave a margin of at least one inch at the bottom of the first page. A bottom margin of 1½ inches is preferred. Before inserting your paper, draw a light pencil line in the horizontal center of your paper, 1½ inches from the bottom edge as a warning.

For the page number on the second page, type 2 on the 4th line space from the top, at the right margin.

Pica

Elite

THROWING OUT THE FIRST BALL

Each April in cities across the land, somebody stands up, cocks an arm, takes aim at the catcher's mitt, and lets go with the first toss of the baseball season. As sure a sign of spring as the sighting of a crocus or a robin, this ritual of throwing out the first ball has become an annual event enjoyed by sports enthusiasts everywhere.

No one is quite sure when the practice of having someone other than the pitcher heave the first pitch began, but we know it was being done in the early 1900's. One story has it that President William Howard Taft started the tradition at a 1910 Washington Senators game. In any event, he was the first of a long line of Presidents who can say they threw at least one pitch in the big leagues.

While Presidents, mayors, and various politicians have been favored for the honor over the years, people from all walks of life have gotten into the act. Opening day hurlers for the California Angels, for example, have included Richard Nixon, Ronald Reagan, and Disneyland's Mickey Mouse. Famous ex-players and even the fans have all taken part in the ceremony.

Bill Veeck, the Chicago White Sox owner famous for his promotional stunts in baseball, once handed out foam-plastic balls to all those in the crowd so everyone could have an opportunity to throw out the first ball.

In San Diego, the Padres also devised a system whereby fans could be involved in the action. They allowed the person who purchased season ticket No. 10,000 to be the favored ball tosser.

Some of the most innovative opening day antics have been staged by the Philadelphia Phillies. In 1971, the ball was dropped from a helicopter. The next year they attempted to get the ball to the field by fastening a kite to a roller skater, who then zoomed down a ramp in the upper deck. In 1975, a trapeze artist dropped the baseball to the pitcher, and two years later someone brought it in by parachute.

Lesson 78

78a ▪ Keyboard Review • Each line at least three times

5 minutes

All letters **SS** Juan B. Ramirez has received a plaque for his exceptionally good work.

Figure   Two men rowed a boat from New York to England in just 54 days in 1896.

Long reach   debt bet batter bury tub tumble gamble stumble mumble bench turn curve

Easy   It is tough for us to keep our minds and mouths open at the same time.

Eyes on
this copy

| 1 | 2 | 3 | 4 | 5 | 6 | 7 | 8 | 9 | 10 | 11 | 12 | 13 | 14 |

78b ▪ Speed Stretcher • Speed Stretchers may be used for 5-minute writings, or each paragraph may be used separately for 1-minute writings.

10 minutes

G W A M
1'   5'

All letters **DS** A new era began when one of our astronauts made the first step on   13 | 3 37

¶ 1
60 words
1.3 si

the moon. Many who saw the televised image of a foot being placed on   27 | 5 39

lunar soil had a feeling their lives would never again be quite the   41 | 8 42

same. Today, the moon is no longer merely a subject of myth in the   54 | 11 45

sky. Instead, it's a place.   60 | 12 46

¶ 2
55 words
1.3 si

From early times the moon has been one heavenly body many have   13 | 15 48

aspired to visit. The sun appeared a searing ball of fire. The stars   27 | 17 51

and planets were nothing more than points of light. Those who imagined   41 | 20 54

we might some day fly, however, often dreamed of zooming to the moon.   55 | 23 57

¶ 3
54 words
1.3 si

Of what use is the moon? No one knows for sure, of course, but   13 | 26 59

some believe it has potential value for many things. Perhaps it will   27 | 28 62

All ¶'s
1.3 si

be used as a space lab or as a base for further explorations. Possibly   41 | 31 65

it can serve as a refueling stop and launching site for rockets.   54 | 34 68

1' | 1 | 2 | 3 | 4 | 5 | 6 | 7 | 8 | 9 | 10 | 11 | 12 | 13 | 14 |
5' | 1 | 2 | 3 |

78c ▪ Skill Builder • Two 1-minute writings on each sentence

5 minutes

1 **SS** It is better to know where you are going than to get there in a hurry.

Quiet wrists
and arms

2   When you work in the right way, your typing skill is bound to improve.

| 1 | 2 | 3 | 4 | 5 | 6 | 7 | 8 | 9 | 10 | 11 | 12 | 13 | 14 |

Lesson 56

56a ■ Keyboard Review • Each line three times
5 minutes

All letters | SS | Major Philips could give the first quiz in botany next week.

Figure-Symbol | She paid $14.50 for the books and another $7.98 for pencils.

Easy | It was almost light enough for us to get going there by six.

| 1 | 2 | 3 | 4 | 5 | 6 | 7 | 8 | 9 | 10 | 11 | 12 |

Quick, firm reach to the shift key

56b ■ Paragraph Guided Writings • As directed in 51d, page 90
10 minutes

All letters | DS

52 words
1.3 si

The best thing about the future is that it comes only
one day at a time. Keep this simple text in your quest for
typing speed. Just add a word a day to your speed, and very
soon you will have the ability to whiz through copy on your
typewriter in record time.

Read words

Think words

Type words

56c ■ Timed Writings
15 minutes

Directions—Type 1-, 2-, and 3-minute writings on the copy below. Repeat. Try to equal your 1-minute rate on the longer writings.

Technique Goals—Fingers deeply curved; wrists low and still. Use quick, short, sharp strokes. Type at a steady pace—without pauses.

		GWAM 1'	3'

All letters | DS

¶ 1
42 words
1.2 si

¶ 2
65 words
1.3 si

All ¶'s
1.3 si

	1'	3'
Most of us require a certain amount of physical activity	11	4 39
if we are to do our best in school or on the job. We need	23	8 43
some moderate exercise every day, and we should have a real	35	12 47
workout two or three times a week.	42	14 50
The benefits of a good fitness program are many. You	53	18 53
can improve your strength and build your endurance. You can	65	22 57
count on exercise to provide a release valve for stress and	77	26 61
to put new zip in your step. There are social benefits, too,	89	30 65
since many others will be around to keep you company in the	101	34 69
gym or on the playing field.	107	36 71

1' | 1 | 2 | 3 | 4 | 5 | 6 | 7 | 8 | 9 | 10 | 11 | 12 |
3' | 1 | 2 | 3 | 4 |

77c ■ Problem Typing

Problem 1 ■ *Personal/Business Letter in Modified Block Style*

Directions—1. Type the letter below as a personal/business letter in modified block style. Type the address on the 18th line space.
2. Address a small envelope. Fold the letter; insert it into the envelope.

Full sheet
50-space line
Blocked paragraphs
Open punctuation

642 Howard Street
Davenport, IA 52806
Current date

Ms. Ellen Medley
Federal Savings and Loan
3948 East Ashland Avenue
Davenport, IA 52802

Dear Ms. Medley

My social studies teacher, Mr. Wayne Snell, suggested that I write to you for help with our class project. We are studying the various types of savings plans suitable for people who can save only a limited amount of money each month.

Will you please send me any materials you have that will help us understand the investment opportunities available at Federal Savings. My classmates and I are looking forward to hearing from you soon.

Sincerely yours

Miss Judy Miller

● *See page 81 for directions on typing personal/business letters.*

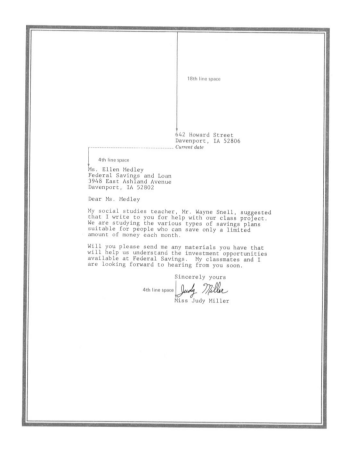

**Personal/business letter
in modified block style**

Problem 2 ■ *Personal/Business Letter in Modified Block Style*

Directions—1. Follow the directions given in Problem 1. Type the return address on the 18th line space.

2. Use your own address and today's date in the return address.

Fay's Fabric Supply / 29 Erie Lane / Topeka, KS 66684 / Ladies and Gentlemen / Ms. Ellen Smith, Manager of the Modern Fabric Center in Salina, suggested that I write and explain to you our urgent need for orange fringe. Ms. Smith sent an order to you on August 23, but she says shipments sometimes take as long as two weeks. (¶) We will have to receive the material by September 2 if we are to complete making our pep team uniforms in time for orientation. If you can possibly speed up delivery of Ms. Smith's order for the additional fringe, the pep team at Washington School will be grateful. We hope you won't let us down! / Sincerely yours / Miss Kathy Burcell

Problem 3 ■ *Personal/Business Letter in Modified Block Style*

Directions— Type the letter in Problem 2 again. This time, use mixed punctuation. Indent the paragraphs 5 spaces.

56d ▪ Composing at the Typewriter

5 minutes

Directions—Type answers to as many of these questions as time permits. Use complete sentences.

1. Name a nationally prominent person in politics and the office that person holds or has held.

2. Name one of the United States senators from your state.

3. Name the capital city of the state in which you are now living.

4. What nationally prominent person would you most like to meet in person? Why?

56e ▪ Capitalization Guides

10 minutes

Directions—Read the explanation carefully; type the line to which it applies twice.

Line 1—Capitalize days of the week, months of the year, and holidays, but not seasons.

Line 2—Capitalize names of rivers, oceans, and mountains.

Line 3—Capitalize *North, South,* etc., when they name particular parts of the country, but not when they refer to directions.

Line 4—Capitalize names of religious groups, political parties, nations, nationalities, and races.

Line 5—Capitalize all proper names and the adjectives made from them.

Line 6—Capitalize the names of stars, planets, and constellations, except *sun, moon, earth,* unless these are used with other astronomical names.

Line 7—Capitalize a title when used with a person's name.

1   SS   The Fourth of July falls on Monday this summer, does it not?

2   Ralph crossed the Columbia River and soon saw Mount Rainier.

3   From Tacoma, I drove east on the Northwest's newest highway.

4   The Norwegian people gave the French books to the Democrats.

Quick, firm reach to the shift key

5   I bought a Swiss watch, a Hawaiian shirt, and an Indian rug.

6   I saw Mercury and Mars in relation to the Earth and the Sun.

7   Senator Jones, Governor Brown, and Judge King spoke briefly.

| 1 | 2 | 3 | 4 | 5 | 6 | 7 | 8 | 9 | 10 | 11 | 12 |

Lesson 57

▪ *60-space line*

57a ▪ Keyboard Review ▪ Each line three times

5 minutes

All letters   SS   Tammy Planck will squeeze five or six juice oranges by hand.

Figure-Symbol   At 9% Dan's monthly payments are $191; at 12% they are $199.

Eyes on this copy

Easy   The greatest of all faults is to believe that you have none.

| 1 | 2 | 3 | 4 | 5 | 6 | 7 | 8 | 9 | 10 | 11 | 12 |

76e ■ Punctuation Guides—Period, Question Mark, and Exclamation Point

10 minutes

Directions—Read the explanation carefully; type each line to which it applies twice.

● *A space follows each period after initials. No space is needed after a period within an abbreviation. Space once after a period that ends an abbreviation unless that period also ends a sentence, in which case, space twice.*

Line 1—Use a period after a sentence making a statement or giving a command.
Line 2—Use a period after each initial.
Line 3—Nicknames are not followed by periods.
Line 4—Use a period after most abbreviations.

Line 5—Use a question mark after a question.
Line 6—After requests and indirect questions, use a period.
Line 7—Use an exclamation point to express strong or sudden feeling.

1 SS Frank told the class that we bought Alaska for only two cents an acre.

2 The new members were J. L. Austin, Sally G. Costis, and Betty J. Dodds.

3 Ed told me that he and Al would get together with Mary later that day.

4 We will leave at 11:15 a.m. and arrive in Washington D.C. at 1:10 p.m. *Cut out waste movements*

5 How many tickets have been sold for the variety show on Tuesday night?

6 I asked Fran how she remembered. Will you please let me know at once.

7 Hurrah! Your team won the game! Congratulations! What a great gang!

| 1 | 2 | 3 | 4 | 5 | 6 | 7 | 8 | 9 | 10 | 11 | 12 | 13 | 14 |

Lesson 77

● *70-space line*

77a ■ Keyboard Review ● Each line at least three times

5 minutes

All letters DS Mickey won big prizes for diving in the last exciting junior aquatics.
Figure-Symbol The Dodgers' Koufax walked only 71 men while striking out 382 in 1965.
4th finger was upon saw polite warm zone zeal police quake quack quit pay pad paw
Easy Our city papers are rushed to neighboring towns when they are printed.

Resume typing at once

| 1 | 2 | 3 | 4 | 5 | 6 | 7 | 8 | 9 | 10 | 11 | 12 | 13 | 14 |

77b ■ Speed Builder

10 minutes

Directions—1. Type a 1-minute writing. The last word typed will be your goal word.

2. Type a 5-minute writing. At the end of each minute, the return will be called. Try to reach your goal.

| | | . | 4 | . | 8 | . | 12 | Words |

DS Many will not know that the typical neckties we wear today are 13

often called four-in-hand. They received this name from a group of 26

60 words
1.3 si

nineteenth century carriage drivers who were noted for holding the 40

reins of four horses in one hand. When most people were wearing bow 53

ties, the drivers wore long ones. 60

57b ■ Spelling and Proofreading Aid • Each line three times   *5 minutes*

1   SS statue preparation foreign already quality listen economical

2   occupy receive piece dining judgment grateful emphasis loose   Wrists and
                                                                           elbows still

3   freight surprise competent weather language succeed campaign

57c ■ Skill Comparison •   1-minute writing on each   *5 minutes*
                               sentence. Compare gwam.
                                                                           Words

Goal sentence SS Truth has to change hands but a few times to become fiction.   12

One hand   Fred Polk erected seats in a vast cave. Jill Lyn ate beets.   12

Script   *Write out the chief ideas of a lesson, using your own words.*   12

Rough draft   Ar̂ange the ~~ideas~~ points of a les⌒son in and ŝorder ~~they~~ that makeŝ senŝe.   12

               | 1 | 2 | 3 | 4 | 5 | 6 | 7 | 8 | 9 | 10 | 11 | 12 |

57d ■ Problem Typing   *30 minutes*

Problem 1 ■ *Sentence Outline*

Directions—1. Set margin stops for a 60-space line. Type the main points at the left margin. Set and use tabulator stops for subpoints.
2. Type the outline in reading position on a full sheet.

3. Indent, space, capitalize, and punctuate exactly as shown in the problem. Two spaces follow the period after all numbered or lettered divisions in an outline.

• *Note that complete sentences are used. Each is followed by a period.*

~~~~~~

```
                        GUIDES FOR STUDYING
                                                        ←————— Triple-space

         I.   STUDYING IS A SKILL, LIKE READING AND WRITING. ————— Double-space

4-space  ———→ A.   Learn how to study.
indention     B.   Develop correct study habits through practice.

Align Roman ——→
numerals at  II.   OBSERVE THESE GUIDES IN DEVELOPING STUDYING SKILLS.
right
              A.   Set up a schedule with definite study periods.
8-space  ————————→ 1.   Do not let anything change this schedule.
indention         2.   Find a quiet place to study.
                  3.   Have needed materials available before you start.
                  4.   Start at once; don't find excuses for delaying.
              B.   Study with a purpose.
                  1.   Copy your assignments accurately; know what you
                       are to do.
                  2.   Search for ideas; think as you read or solve
                       problems.
              C.   Practice remembering the main points of a lesson.
                  1.   Ask yourself questions on what you have studied.
                  2.   Take brief notes.
```

~~~~~~

Sentence outline

76c ■ Technique Builder—Stroking

5 minutes

Directions—Type each line three times.   **Technique Goal**—Finger-action stroking.

1 SS   Try never to confuse keeping your chin up with sticking your neck out.

2   Remember to borrow from pessimists as they think they won't be repaid.

3   Someone once said that most hard-boiled people are usually half-baked.

4   It doesn't pay to brood--after all, only the chickens get paid for it.

Resume typing at once

| 1 | 2 | 3 | 4 | 5 | 6 | 7 | 8 | 9 | 10 | 11 | 12 | 13 | 14 |

76d ■ Speed Ladder Paragraphs ● As directed in 71c, page 124

15 minutes

GWAM

		1'	5'

¶ 1
36 words
1.3 si

DS   Edison once said that everything comes to those who hustle while   13   3 46
they wait. Time alone can bring you little. All gain requires some   27   5 49
effort. Know what you want; then work for it.   36   7 51

¶ 2
40 words
1.3 si

Experts claim that the reason we dislike some people is that we   49 10 54
see in them our defects. We dislike them for our weaknesses. If this   63 13 56
be true, we can use others as a mirror to uncover our own faults.   75 15 59

¶ 3
44 words
1.3 si

Many people want to improve the world, but few think of improving   88 18 62
themselves. The world is the people who live in it. What you do in   102 20 64
a small way, the world does in a big way. Begin with yourself if it   116 23 67
needs improving.   119 24 68

¶ 4
48 words
1.3 si

The trouble with being a good sport is that one has to lose to   131 26 70
prove it. Nobody likes to lose; everybody likes to win. We must remem-   146 29 73
ber, however, that all winners lose at times. Thus, good winners must   160 32 76
know how to take a loss in stride.   168 33 77

¶ 5
52 words
1.3 si

In the long history of law and order, early human beings took a   180 36 80
big step forward when the tribes to which they belonged sat down in a   191 39 83

All ¶'s
1.3 si

circle and permitted just one person to talk at a time. Almost any   208 42 85
group would get more done if it adopted this kind of rule.   219 44 88

| 1' | 1 | 2 | 3 | 4 | 5 | 6 | 7 | 8 | 9 | 10 | 11 | 12 | 13 | 14 |
| 5' | | | 1 | | | | 2 | | | | 3 | | |

Problem 2 ■ Topic Outline

Directions—1. Set margin stops for a 40-space line. Type the problem in reading position on a full sheet. **2.** The outline is set in two columns. Type it in a single column. Space between parts as illustrated in Problem 1.

● *Topic statements are used; omit ending periods.*

LEARNING TO WRITE SUMMARIES

I. REASONS FOR SUMMARIZING
   A. Getting ideas from your lessons
   B. Expressing ideas concisely
II. GUIDES FOR WRITING SUMMARIES
   A. Reading the lesson
   B. Finding the central idea
   C. Finding supporting ideas
   D. Writing down ideas
      1. Writing briefly
      2. Using nouns and verbs
      3. Using your own words
   E. Editing your first draft
      1. Eliminating minor details
      2. Arranging ideas in logical order
      3. Omitting your own opinions
   F. Writing summary in final form
      1. Using proper form
      2. Writing or typing neatly

Lesson 58

● 60-space line

58a ■ Keyboard Review ● Each line three times

5 minutes

All letters **SS** Jack Walder bought five exquisite topaz pins in Mexico City.

Figure-Symbol   We ordered 25 bicycles; 16 are 10-speeds and 9 are 3-speeds.

Easy   They said she should get a bid from more than one rock band.

Resume typing at once

| 1 | 2 | 3 | 4 | 5 | 6 | 7 | 8 | 9 | 10 | 11 | 12 |

58b ■ Paragraph Guided Writings

10 minutes

Directions—Three 1-minute writings on each paragraph. Try for no more than two errors on the first writing; one error on the second; no errors on the third. Compute *gwam* on the three writings.

		GWAM	
		1'	3'
All letters **DS**	One sure method people can use to save both gasoline and	11	4 41
	money is to crowd extra miles per gallon into their driving.	24	8 46
¶ 1 60 words 1.3 si	Good mileage depends on more than just the make and model of	36	12 50
	a car. It is also a direct result of the grade of gas used,	48	16 54
	the way the car is driven, and the condition of the engine.	60	20 58
	Those who pay heed to these hints will be amazed at the	11	24 61
	results. Avoid quick starts and jerky driving. Have the	23	28 65
¶ 2 53 words 1.3 si	engine tuned at regular intervals. Check tire pressure at	34	31 69
	least once a month and watch the pattern of wear to see if	46	35 73
All ¶'s 1.3 si	your wheels are properly aligned.	53	38 75

| 1' | 1 | 2 | 3 | 4 | 5 | 6 | 7 | 8 | 9 | 10 | 11 | 12 |
| 3' | | 1 | | 2 | | 3 | | 4 | |

Problem 2 ■ Personal Letter in Semibusiness Form

Directions—Follow the directions given in Problem 1.

847 Holland Drive
Miami, FL 33155
April 21, 19--

Dear Mrs. Potter

Congratulations to you upon your election as president of the North Miami Sunshine League.

One of my final responsibilities as outgoing president is to make arrangements for our annual joint board meeting. This year we have scheduled a dinner meeting to be held at The Breakers on Tuesday, May 10, at 7:00 p.m.

I know you will have a most successful year. Please feel free to call upon me whenever you think I might be of assistance to you.

Sincerely

Mrs. Roberta Potter
2195 Ocean Avenue
Miami, FL 33155

Lesson 76

● 70-space line

76a ■ Keyboard Review • Each line at least three times

5 minutes

All letters **SS** Don is explaining why he believes I must acquire a jackal for the zoo.

Figure-Symbol In the period 1951-1974, Lucille Ball starred in 495 television shows.

Even stroking

Balanced and one-hand if it is to pull, if it is to trace, if it is to join, if it is to get

Easy Remember that you can't be blamed for advice which you have not given.

| 1 | 2 | 3 | 4 | 5 | 6 | 7 | 8 | 9 | 10 | 11 | 12 | 13 | 14 |

76b ■ Speed Ladder Sentences

10 minutes

Directions—Type each sentence for 1 minute. Your teacher will call the guide at 15-, 12-, or 10-second intervals. Return the carriage quickly. Start typing immediately. Repeat sentences on which you were not able to type a complete line with the call of the guide.

			G W A M		
			15″	12″	10″
1	SS	You should think about the future today.	32	40	48
2		It will pay you to build strong study habits.	36	45	54
3		Choose all your classes with a great deal of care.	40	50	60
4		See if you can find where your own special talents lie.	44	55	66
5		Every student is a problem in search of some good solutions.	48	60	72
6		Learn all you can about those fields which interest you the most.	52	65	78
7		When you are older, you will be very glad that you heeded this advice.	56	70	84

| 1 | 2 | 3 | 4 | 5 | 6 | 7 | 8 | 9 | 10 | 11 | 12 | 13 | 14 |

58c ■ Problem Typing

30 minutes

Problem ■ Typing Class Notes in Final Form

Directions—1. Assume that the following notes have been prepared from those taken sketchily in class. They appear here in final form. Prepare a typewritten copy of them.

2. Use regular theme style. Type the date 1 inch from the top of the page and the heading 2 inches from the top.

3. Assume, too, that these notes are to be placed in a notebook; thus, the copy requires a wider left than right margin so that it will have a centered appearance when placed in the notebook.

   a. Set the margin stops for a 1½-inch left margin and a 1-inch right margin.

b. Because of the wider left margin, the center point will be 3 spaces to the right of the point normally used.

● *As is illustrated on page vi, there are 10 spaces per inch on a pica typewriter and 12 spaces per inch on an elite typewriter.*

● *For pica typewriters, the left margin should contain 15 horizontal spaces; the right margin, 10 horizontal spaces. For elite typewriters, the left margin should contain 18 horizontal spaces; the right margin, 12 horizontal spaces.*

● *In setting the right margin stop, 5 to 8 spaces are added for the bell.*

Today's date

TAKING NOTES

Notes on What You Hear

   1. Don't try to write everything down. Get only the important facts and ideas.

   2. Relate what you know to what you hear. In this way you will get a better understanding of the topics discussed.

   3. If the speaker says something is important, put it down.

   4. If the speaker dwells on a fact or point, put it down.

Notes on What You Read

   1. Get the major points in mind by reading an article that gives you a broad view of the subject in which you are interested.

   2. Summarize. Don't try to copy everything you read.

   3. If a statement is made that you wish to quote, put quotation marks around it. Get the complete source.

Preparing Notes in Final Form

   1. If you have taken the notes hurriedly, the sooner you type them in final form, the better.

   2. Type your notes in complete sentences. Add details that you remember from your reading or from listening to a discussion so that your notes will be meaningful to you when you read them later.

   3. Type your notes in good form. Space them so they will be easy to read. Put a heading on them. Date them.

Lesson 75

75a ■ Keyboard Review • Each line at least three times

5 minutes

All letters **SS** Lema organized a very expert quartet with banjo for my new show.
Figure-Symbol During that day--May 29, 1962--the market average rose over 27 points.
Adjacent Keys Only a long look below the surface will help you locate their problem.
Easy They liked to sit by the side of the lake and throw rocks at the fish.

Feet on
the floor

| 1 | 2 | 3 | 4 | 5 | 6 | 7 | 8 | 9 | 10 | 11 | 12 | 13 | 14 |

75b ■ Timed Writings

10 minutes

Directions—Type a 1- and a 5-minute writing on 71c, page 124, Circle errors, Compute *gwam*.

75c ■ Problem Typing

30 minutes

Problem 1 ■ *Personal Letter in Semibusiness Form*

Directions—1. Type the letter below as illustrated at the right on half-size stationery (5½- by 8½-inches).

2. Start typing the return address on the 7th line space from the top.

3. Use a 40-space line. Type the salutation on the 8th line space from the date. Paragraph indentions: 10 spaces.

8416 Crawford Street
Bloomington, IN 47401
April 28, 19--

Dear Mr. Anderson

You will be happy to learn that our program plans for the coming school year are now complete. Two evening meetings are planned in addition to the annual Back-to-School Night in October. Afternoon meetings will be held in November and March.

Mrs. Kathleen Moore has done an outstanding job as head of the program committee. Her enthusiasm for the work of the Franklin School PTA should help make this our best year ever.

Sincerely

Mr. David Anderson
437 Noakes Avenue
Bloomington, IN 47401

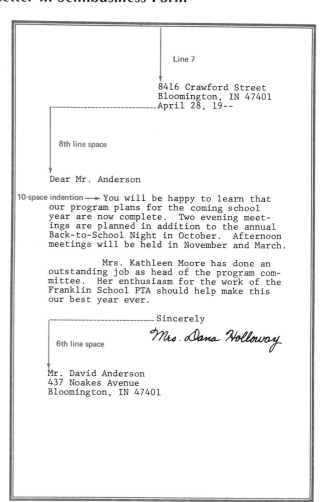

Line 7

8416 Crawford Street
Bloomington, IN 47401
April 28, 19--

8th line space

Dear Mr. Anderson

10-space indention ⟶ You will be happy to learn that our program plans for the coming school year are now complete. Two evening meetings are planned in addition to the annual Back-to-School Night in October. Afternoon meetings will be held in November and March.

Mrs. Kathleen Moore has done an outstanding job as head of the program committee. Her enthusiasm for the work of the Franklin School PTA should help make this our best year ever.

Sincerely

Mrs. Dana Holloway

6th line space

Mr. David Anderson
437 Noakes Avenue
Bloomington, IN 47401

Personal letter in semibusiness form

• *Note the placement of the address at the left margin on the 6th line space below the complimentary close.*

Lesson 59

59a ■ Keyboard Review • Each line three times

5 minutes

All letters   SS   Ken Gumpy will acquire a deluxe razor just before he leaves.

Figure-Symbol   The club's meeting dates are March 30, April 17, and May 24.

Instant release

Easy   See if they can do most of their work on these new machines.

| 1 | 2 | 3 | 4 | 5 | 6 | 7 | 8 | 9 | 10 | 11 | 12 |

59b ■ Typing from Dictation and Spelling Checkup

5 minutes

Directions—Type 57b, page 100, from your teacher's dictation. Check for correct spelling. Retype any words in which you made an error.

59c ■ Skill Comparison

5 minutes

Directions—Type a 1-minute writing on each sentence. Compare *gwam* rates. Try typing all sentences at the rate made on the first one.

Words

Easy   SS   We prove what we really are by what we do with what we have.   12

Long reach   My young brother may bring the play money that Brenda needs.   12

Script   *The best prizes go to those who learn to do their jobs well.*   12

Rough draft   the print ing money does n't create the wealth of nation .   12

| 1 | 2 | 3 | 4 | 5 | 6 | 7 | 8 | 9 | 10 | 11 | 12 |

59d ■ Problem Typing

30 minutes

Problem 1 ■ Assignment Paper

Directions—1. Assume that you are preparing this problem as an assignment for a class. Use a 60-space line, a 2-inch margin, and double-spacing.

2. As you type the sentences, capitalize the words that should be capitalized. Capitalization rules are summarized on page xxi. Refer to them if necessary.

APPLYING THE CAPITALIZATION RULES

they plan to spend this fall and winter in phoenix, arizona.
robert visited miami junior high school on thursday morning.
she saw senator kennedy in a school in chicago on labor day.
three indians from asia stayed at the hilton hotel in omaha.
the danish reporters attended a noon meeting of republicans.
she will read a paper on venus and mars in my english class.
the mayor may tour the damaged areas of the south this fall .
after leaving tulsa, i drove east until i crossed the river.
luis and anna banuelos belong to the national honor society.
the meeting is set for friday in the first methodist church.
several senators will study pollution of the atlantic ocean.
only the irish and french teams will meet on tuesday, may 1.

Lesson 74

74a ■ Keyboard Review • Each line at least three times

5 minutes

All letters **SS** I know it is an expensive job to organize and equip the men carefully.

Figure   Approximately 1,074 girls and 875 boys were enrolled there after 1978.

Long reach   The builders in Illinois had only a minimum of light aluminum numbers.

Easy   Always keep your goal in view, and you can reach the top in your work.

Space quickly

| 1 | 2 | 3 | 4 | 5 | 6 | 7 | 8 | 9 | 10 | 11 | 12 | 13 | 14 |

74b ■ Control Builder

5 minutes

Directions—Use Speed Stretcher 73b, page 126, for four 1-minute writings. Type at your control rate.

74c ■ Number Expression Guides—Time of Day

5 minutes

Directions—Type each sentence three times. The first line gives the rule; the remaining lines apply it.

1   **SS**   With "o'clock," spell out the hour. Use figures with "a.m." or "p.m."

2   Our Glee Club will sing in the library at eleven o'clock this morning.

Think as you type

3   When it is 10:15 a.m. in Long Beach, it is 1:15 p.m. in New York City.

| 1 | 2 | 3 | 4 | 5 | 6 | 7 | 8 | 9 | 10 | 11 | 12 |

74d ■ Problem Typing

30 minutes

Problem 1 ■ *Postal Card Announcement*

Directions—**1.** Start typing on the third line space from the top. Triple-space between the date and the salutation. Double-space between parapraphs.

2. Address the card to Mr. Paul Lange / 736 Grand Street / Scottsdale, AZ 85251.

• *A postal card address and message are illustrated on page 77.*

• *Use paper cut to postal card size (5½- by 3¼-inches) if cards are not available.*

May 21, 19--

Dear Mr. Lange,

The Boosters Club will hold its final meeting of the year on Thursday, June 1, in the Hoover multi-purpose room. Dinner will be served promptly at 7:00 p.m. The program will begin at 8:15 p.m. (¶) Please make your reservation by calling Ray Harrison at 439-0759 before next Friday.

Ms. Ruth Carr, President

Problem 2 ■ *Postal Card Announcements*

Directions—Type the message in Problem 1 to the names at the right. Address the cards. Use appropriate salutations.

Ms. Charlotte Erb
118 Rural Road
Scottsdale, AZ 85252

Dr. Joan Schroeder
2476 West Alamos Avenue
Scottsdale, AZ 85264

Problem 2 ■ Outline of Directions for Typing Book Reviews

Directions—Set the margin stops for a 60-space line. Use a standard 2-inch top margin. Indent, space, capitalize, and punctuate the outline correctly.

Directions for Writing a Book Review)all caps

Triple space ⟶

I. Items to ~~be~~ Included in Review)all caps

   A. Title ∧and name of author ∘ the
   B. central theme of ∧book characters
   C. Some of the important ~~people~~
D.   D. Setting for the story interesting
   E. Brief summary of some ∧incidents ∘
   F. comments on and opinion of the book ~~itself~~

II. General Guides ~~which are~~ to ~~be~~ Followed)all caps
   #

   A. Should arouse reader's interest
   B. Should be well written support
   C. Should contain examples to ∧comments

III. Typing Guides to ~~be~~ Observed)all caps
   style

   A. Typed in regular theme ∧ ~~form~~
   B. Single-spaced with double spacing between par ⌐#
   C. Extra spaces in left margin for binding ∘
   D. heading typed in off-center ~~ed~~ position

Lesson 60

• *60-space line*

60a ■ Keyboard Review • Each line three times

5 minutes

All letters   **SS**   I'm amazed Dave Kowing expects to qualify in the broad jump.

Figure-Symbol   Janie replied, "Please meet me at Pat's house after school."   Elbows in

Easy   The students wanted to visit all the towns shown on the map.

| 1 | 2 | 3 | 4 | 5 | 6 | 7 | 8 | 9 | 10 | 11 | 12 |

60b ■ Timed Writings

10 minutes

Directions—Type two 3-minute writings on 58b, page 101. Compute *gwam*. Submit the better of the two writings.

60c ■ Problem Typing • *Book Review*

30 minutes

Directions—Type the book review on page 105. Use regular theme style with the heading typed 2 inches from the top. Single-space the copy, but double-space before and after capitalized headings and between paragraphs. As this book review is to be placed in a notebook, use a 1½-inch left margin and a 1-inch right margin.

• *Directions for 58c, page 102, explain how to set 1½-inch left and 1-inch right margins.*

Invitations, Acceptances, and Thank You Notes

Invitations, acceptances, "bread and butter" notes, thank you notes, and similar letters vary greatly in wording and form. Formal notes are usually printed. Informal notes may be handwritten or typewritten.

As a rule, they are written without an address on personal-size stationery (usually 5½- by 8½-inches or 4¼- by 5½-inches). Only a handwritten signature is used.

73c ▪ Problem Typing

30 minutes

Problem 1 ▪ *Informal Invitation*

Directions—1. Type the informal invitation shown in the model illustration at the right. Use 4¼- by 5½-inch stationery. Allow a margin of about 1 inch at the top and ¾ inch in each side margin.

2. Begin the return address, date line, and complimentary close at the horizontal center of the paper.

3. Allow from 2 to 4 line spaces between the date and the salutation.

Problem 2 ▪ *Informal Acceptance*

Directions—1. Type the informal acceptance below.
2. Follow the directions given for Problem 1.

1906 Poplar Avenue / **Canton, OH 44701** / **April 8, 19--**

Dear Sharon

Charles and I are delighted to accept your thoughtful invitation to attend the concert with you and Jim next Friday evening. We're especially anxious to hear the Philharmonic in the new convention center theater.

Thank you so much for thinking of us. We shall plan to meet you in the foyer before eight.

Very sincerely

```
                    258 Cedar Drive
                    Akron, OH 44308
                    April 2, 19--

Dear Virginia

     Jim and I are planning to attend
the spring concert of the Cleveland
Philharmonic on Friday evening, the
fifteenth, at eight o'clock. Will
you and Charles be able to join us
as our guests?

     We know how busy both of you
are at this time of year, but we
hope you will enjoy taking a break
for a fine musical performance.

                    Very sincerely

                    Sharon
```

Typewritten informal invitation

Problem 3 ▪ *"Bread and Butter" Note* • As directed in Problem 1

37 East Shaw / **Austin, TX 78744** / **May 9, 19--**

Dear Marilyn

Thank you for a most relaxing weekend in your lovely new home. All of us thoroughly enjoyed the chance to talk over old times again.

Please don't forget your promise to visit us next year. We'll certainly do our best to repay your many kindnesses. Thanks again.

Sincerely

BOOK REVIEW: THE HOBBIT

THE AUTHOR

J. R. R. Tolkien

THE STORY AND ITS SETTING

J. R. R. Tolkien (1892-1973) is probably best known for writing a series of three books called THE LORD OF THE RINGS.

A prelude to this famous fantasy trilogy, THE HOBBIT is a story of little people who inhabit a land located in the Middle Earth. It is a story of delightful creatures who love peace and quiet, have sharp ears and eyes, are handy with tools, like to laugh and eat, and are inclined to be fat.

IMPORTANT CHARACTERS

The main character is Bilbo Baggins, a Hobbit who is talked into helping a group of dwarves regain their kingdom in a far-off land. Another interesting character in the story is a magical wizard named Gandalf. His major role is to help Mr. Baggins and his friends whenever they get into trouble, which is most of the time.

INTERESTING INCIDENTS

During their journey, while trying to escape from a creature called Gollum, Bilbo finds a ring which has the amazing power to make him invisible. With the help of this mysterious ring, he gets his friends out of several dangerous situations. Once, when spiders entrap them in their webs, Bilbo sets them free. Another time he uses the powers of the ring to help his friends slay a fierce dragon.
184
198
211
225
239
251

COMMENTS

THE HOBBIT is both interesting and exciting. It is one big adventure with no dull moments. Anyone who likes suspense is bound to enjoy this book.

60d ■ Extra-Credit Typing

Problem 1

Directions—Type the two paragraphs in 58b, page 101, in theme style as directed in the problem on page 94. Supply an appropriate title.

Problem 2

Directions—Type the two paragraphs in 56c, page 98, in regular theme style, following the guides for typing reports stressed in this unit. Supply an appropriate title.

Problem 3

Directions—Prepare the manuscript of a short article from a current magazine. Type your paper in regular report form, following the guides for typing reports stressed in this unit.

Problem 2 ■ Invitation

Half sheet   Triple spacing   Exact vertical center

DELEGATES TO STUDENT COUNCIL
you are invited to the advisor's home
for tea
Thursday, November 19, 4:15 p.m.
9900 Riverside Drive, Van Nuys

Problem 3 ■ Announcement

Full sheet   Triple spacing   Reading position

KIWANIS CLUB PICNIC
Sunday, July 15--2:30 p.m.
Swimming and Games for Everyone
Hot Dogs, Potato Salad, Lemonade
Don't Miss the Fun!

Lesson 73

● *70-space line*

73a ■ Keyboard Review ● Each line at least three times

5 minutes

All letters **SS** We all realized that even an expert jockey must qualify before racing.

Figure   Our nation ranked fourth in production in 1860; we were first by 1894.

Shift   Don Ruiz and Lucy Wong saw both Mickey and Minnie Mouse at Disneyland.

Easy   It is better to get in the first thought than to get in the last word.

Fingers
deeply
curved

| 1 | 2 | 3 | 4 | 5 | 6 | 7 | 8 | 9 | 10 | 11 | 12 | 13 | 14 |

73b ■ Speed Stretcher ●

Speed Stretchers may be used for 5-minute writings, or each paragraph may be used separately for 1-minute writings.

10 minutes

	GWAM
	1' 5'

All letters **DS**   Some students and their parents seem to take it for granted today   13 | 3 35

¶ 1
54 words
1.3 si
that after high school comes college. This is quite sensible because   27 | 5 38

there is no doubt that a need exists for many students who have been   41 | 8 41

college trained. We need them in key jobs throughout the nation.   54 | 11 43

¶ 2
53 words
1.3 si
Should everyone go to college? The answer to such a question is   13 | 13 46

clear. Many will realize that this is the last and perhaps worst place   27 | 16 49

for them to be. College is a place for people with good reasons for   41 | 19 51

wanting to be there and with sufficient talents to succeed.   53 | 21 54

¶ 3
55 words
1.3 si
Are you college material? You are if you're going to college for   13 | 24 56

the right reasons and if you have what it takes to succeed there. Go   27 | 27 59

All ¶'s
1.3 si
because you want to go. Go to prepare yourself for a career. College   41 | 30 62

may be a place where you will discover what you really want in life.   55 | 32 65

| 1' | 1 | 2 | 3 | 4 | 5 | 6 | 7 | 8 | 9 | 10 | 11 | 12 | 13 | 14 |
| 5' | | 1 | | | 2 | | | 3 | | | | | | |

UNIT 9 ■ Learning to Type Tables

General Directions ■ Lessons 61 - 70

Machine Adjustments—Single-space sentences and drill lines. Double-space between repeated groups of lines. Double-space paragraph copy. Set a tabular stop for a 5-space paragraph indention.

Correcting Errors—Your teacher will tell you if you are to correct errors in the problems in this unit.

Lesson 61

• *Use a 60-space line for all lessons in this unit.*

61a ■ Keyboard Review • Each line three times

5 minutes

All letters	SS	Pamela gave Nick exquisite old jewelry for the bazaar today.
Figure-Symbol		In 1978, the prices ranged from $395.50 to more than $1,200.
Easy		The profit you can make depends on both labor and materials.

Quick, firm reach to the shift key

| 1 | 2 | 3 | 4 | 5 | 6 | 7 | 8 | 9 | 10 | 11 | 12 |

61b ■ Fluency Practice

5 minutes

Directions—Type each line three times.   **Technique Goal**—Think the words as you type.

• *The vertical lines indicate brief reading stops.*

1	SS	and he | and if he | and if he is | and if he is to do the work
2		and go | with us | and go with us | and go with us to the right
3		if they | and if they | and if they go | and if they go to this
4		and show | and to show | and to show it | and to show it to the

Even stroking

61c ■ Technique Builder—Stroking • Each line three times

10 minutes

Hyphen	SS	This well-known actor-singer won the coast-to-coast contest.
Double letters		The assessor called a committee meeting on the small matter.
Long reach		Myrtle Bray may bring a number of jumpers to my annual hunt.
One-hand		Jump up, Barbara Reed! Look at my car race on Cascade Hill.
Balanced-hand		Is this the form she is to sign so that she can do the work?
Balanced- and one-hand		Jo West is to sign the form so that she can enter the races.

Wrists and elbows quiet

| 1 | 2 | 3 | 4 | 5 | 6 | 7 | 8 | 9 | 10 | 11 | 12 |

61d ■ Skill Comparison • Type 57c, page 100, as directed

5 minutes

71d ■ Spacing Guides—Review

Directions—Type each line twice. Read the explanation for each line before you type it.

Line 1—Space twice after the period at the end of a sentence.

Line 2—Space once after a semicolon or comma.

Line 3—Space twice after a question mark at the end of a sentence.

Line 4—Space twice after a colon except in stating time.

Line 5—Space twice after an exclamation point that ends a sentence.

Line 6—Type the dash with hyphens, without spacing before or after.

1 SS Please pay attention. Directions are not repeated. Listen carefully.

2 Tomorrow is the assembly; remember that your schedule will be changed.

3 What time is it? Can I get there in an hour? Who will drive the bus?   *Think as you type*

4 Please bring these materials: baseballs, gloves, mitt, and mask.

5 Heads up! Be alert! To learn anything, you must have a zealous mind.

6 Many things can be done in a day--if you don't make that day tomorrow.

| 1 | 2 | 3 | 4 | 5 | 6 | 7 | 8 | 9 | 10 | 11 | 12 | 13 | 14 |

Lesson 72

• *70-space line*

72a ■ Keyboard Review • Each line at least three times

5 minutes

All letters SS Five or six big jet airliners flew quickly overhead at amazing speeds.

Figure-Symbol We hope to hold the 1980 meetings on March 29-31 instead of April 4-6.   *Reach with your fingers*

Adjacent keys Sandra has always assumed that all necessary assistance was available.

Easy Some nations of the world used quantities of such coal for their fuel.

| 1 | 2 | 3 | 4 | 5 | 6 | 7 | 8 | 9 | 10 | 11 | 12 | 13 | 14 |

72b ■ Control Ladder Paragraphs

10 minutes

Directions—Type 1-minute writings on the paragraphs in 71c, page 124. When you can type a paragraph within the error limit specified by your teacher, move to the next one. Type with control.

72c ■ Problem Typing

30 minutes

Problem 1 ■ Announcement

FEBRUARY MEETING OF GIBSON SCHOOL PTA

Thursday, February 23, 7:30 p.m.

School Cafeteria

Discussion of Plans for Career Education Day

Mrs. Janet Pelton, President

Half sheet
Triple spacing
Exact vertical center

61e ■ Paragraph Guided Writings

15 minutes

Directions—1. Type a 3-minute writing. Circle errors. Note your *gwam*.
2. Type each circled word 3 times along with the words preceding and following it.

3. Type two 1-minute writings on each paragraph. Try to add 4 words to your 3-minute *gwam* each time.
4. Type another 3-minute writing. Note your *gwam* and compare it with that of the first writing.

GWAM

		1'	3'
All letters DS	The subject of energy is now one of the hottest topics	11	4 54
¶ 1	around. Most experts think we are on the edge of a new era,	23	8 58
39 words 1.3 si	a new stage of history in which our wasteful way of living	35	12 62
	will have to change.	39	13 63
	To put it bluntly, all of us have been on one big energy	50	17 67
	spree. As citizens, we have become used to a lifestyle which	63	21 71
¶ 2 56 words 1.3 si	consumes energy as though the supply will last forever. Our	75	25 75
	entire stock of goods requires more and more power while the	87	29 79
	sources of gas and oil are running low.	95	32 82
	Here are several things that may happen in the next few	106	35 85
	years. Our cars will be smaller, lighter in weight, and more	119	40 90
¶ 3 55 words 1.3 si	efficient. Houses will be built so as to reduce heating and	131	44 94
	cooling costs. A shift from gas and oil to coal, nuclear, or	143	48 98
All ¶'s 1.3 si	solar energy will need to be made.	150	50 100

```
1' |  1  |  2  |  3  |  4  |  5  |  6  |  7  |  8  |  9  | 10  | 11  | 12  |
3' |     1     |        2        |       3       |      4      |
```

61f ■ Control Practice

5 minutes

Directions—1. Type the last paragraph of 61e as many times as you can in the time that remains.

2. Circle your errors. Place a check mark in the margin of each paragraph in which you made no more than one error.

Lesson 62

• 60-space line

62a ■ Keyboard Review • Each line three times

5 minutes

All letters SS Jeff expects to have two dozen big aprons made very quickly.

Symbol Fifty-nine votes were cast for vice-president--a new record!

Flowing rhythm

Easy At least eight of their members work there in the same firm.

```
|  1  |  2  |  3  |  4  |  5  |  6  |  7  |  8  |  9  | 10  | 11  | 12  |
```

71b ■ Technique Builder—Stroking • 1-minute writing on each line   *10 minutes*

Weak fingers **SS** Pam was quite amazed by the political opinions expressed in the paper.

Weak fingers   Paul Quintana always gave pop quizzes in his sixth period law classes.

First row   We can't exactly blame them for not moving the boxes back into my van.

Third row   It is quite true that they were to report to you right after our trip.

Quick, sharp stroking

One-hand   I stated we were aware my extra baggage was carried by nonunion crews.

One-hand   We think we can get him to look after my puppy and my pony after noon.

| 1 | 2 | 3 | 4 | 5 | 6 | 7 | 8 | 9 | 10 | 11 | 12 | 13 | 14 |

71c ■ Speed Ladder Paragraphs   *20 minutes*

Directions—Type as many 1-minute writings as time permits. When you can type the first paragraph at the rate specified, type the next one. Climb the speed ladder. See if you can reach the top.

Alternate Procedure—Type a 1-minute writing on the first paragraph. Move to the succeeding paragraphs only when you have completed each one within the error limit specified by your teacher.

			GWAM	
			1'	5'
All letters **DS** ¶ 1	Stick to a job until it is completed. This is the thing that		12	2 36
36 words 1.3 si	people who reach the top in art, music, flying, or education have in		26	5 39
	common. They do not quit; they stick to the job.		36	7 41
	The biggest room in the world, we are told, is the room for improve-		50	10 44
¶ 2 40 words 1.3 si	ment. This being the case, why not study the way you are stroking the		64	13 46
	keys? You can eliminate errors by using quick, sharp strokes.		76	15 49
	One frequently hears that the world is like a jigsaw puzzle. The		89	18 52
¶ 3 44 words 1.3 si	job you do, no matter how small, is related to other jobs. The puzzle		104	21 54
	would never be complete without it. That is exactly why you must do		118	23 57
	your job well.		121	24 58
	Not a single one of us knows how hard others work until we try to		134	27 60
¶ 4 48 words 1.3 si	do their jobs. We envy those who seem to get high grades so easily.		147	29 63
	The fact is they have learned how to study. Even natural talents have		162	32 66
All ¶'s 1.3 si	to be developed through practice.		168	34 67

1' | 1 | 2 | 3 | 4 | 5 | 6 | 7 | 8 | 9 | 10 | 11 | 12 | 13 | 14 |
5' | 1 | 2 | 3 |

10 minutes

● *The rates at which you will be typing are given in the first column at the right.*

			GWAM 15" Guide	12" Guide
1	SS	Time will not wait for anyone.	24	30
2		Every day gives you another chance.	28	35
3		You are worth what you make of yourself.	32	40
4		Every time you speak, your mind is on parade.	36	45
5		Do not look for jobs that are equal to your skill.	40	50
6		Look, instead, for skills that are equal to your tasks.	44	55
7		The only time people dislike gossip is when it's about them.	48	60

| 1 | 2 | 3 | 4 | 5 | 6 | 7 | 8 | 9 | 10 | 11 | 12 |

Steps In Arranging Tables

Horizontal Placement

1. Center the paper in the machine.

2. Move the left and right margin stops to the ends of the scale. Clear all tab stops.

3. Find how many spaces are to be used between the columns. The directions for the problems that follow tell how many spaces to use.

4. Move the carriage to the center of the paper.

5. Spot the longest word or entry in each column.

6. Backspace once for each two spaces in the longest word or entry in each column. If one letter is left over, do not backspace for it.

7. Backspace once for each two spaces *between* the columns. If one space is left over, do not backspace for it.

8. Set the left margin stop at the point at which you stop backspacing. This is the point where the first column will start.

9. From the left margin, space forward once for each letter, digit, symbol, and space in the longest entry in the first column and once for each space between Columns 1 and 2. Set a tab stop for the second column. Continue in this way until stops have been set for all columns.

10. Return the carriage. Operate the tab bar or key to determine whether or not all the tab stops have been set.

Vertical Placement

Vertical placement of material is not new to you. See directions given on page 61.

62c ■ Problem Typing

30 minutes

Problem 1 ■ Short Trial Table

Directions—1. Type the table on a half sheet of paper as it appears on page 109.

2. Leave 12 spaces between columns. Set the left margin stop for the first column and a tab stop for the second column, as directed above.

3. Vertical placement directions for this problem are given in the table. This table is placed in exact vertical center. In the problems that follow, you will have to plan the vertical placement yourself.

● *A half sheet of paper contains 33 line spaces.*

CYCLE 3 ■

Preparing Personal Papers

Problem Summary—Using the following summary, look at some of the problems you will prepare in Cycle 3 before you begin your typing:

Announcements, invitations, and thank you notes, pages 125-128.

Letters in semibusiness form, pages 129-130.

Personal/business letters, pages 133-135.

Orders and order letters, page 137.

Themes and reports, including outlines, footnotes, title pages, bibliographies, and note cards, pages 141-161.

Agenda and minutes, pages 164-166.

Club tickets and membership cards, page 167.

Postal cards, pages 168-170.

Bar graphs, pages 171-172.

School organization budget, page 173.

Programs of meetings, pages 175-176.

Bulletin board notices, pages 178-179.

Articles and stories for the school newspaper, pages 180-183.

Student-writer's style guide, pages 184-187.

Improving Your Basic Skills—In addition to the problems, every lesson provides materials for improving your typing accuracy and speed. One lesson in each group of five lessons is entirely devoted to technique refinement and skill building. Continue to improve your speed and accuracy through these drills and lessons.

Emphasis on Related Learnings—Drills stressing capitalization, punctuation, and number expression guides appear throughout the lessons of this cycle. Use these drills to improve the quality of your written work in typewriting and in your other classes.

Measurement—Timed writings to check your progress in typing are scheduled in each group of five lessons. In addition, Unit 14 includes problems typical of those typed earlier in the cycle. Use this unit to check up on your understanding of the different types of problems covered in Cycle 3.

Extra-Credit Assignments—Problems are given at the end of each unit for students who finish assignments ahead of schedule. Type these problems as time permits. Extra credit will be given for them.

Unit 10 ■ Typing Papers and Reports for Your Family

General Directions ■ Lessons 71 - 80

Line Length—Use a 70-space line for drills and timed writings. Much of the problem copy that you will type will be set in lines either longer or shorter than those for which your margins are set. It will be necessary for you to listen for the bell, to use the right margin release, and to divide long words coming at the ends of lines.

Spacing—Single-space sentences and drill lines. Double-space between repeated groups of lines. Double-space paragraph copy. Space problem copy as directed.

Identifying Papers—Your teacher will tell you how to identify the papers you prepare.

Correcting Errors—Your teacher will tell you if you are to correct errors made on problem copy.

Margin Stop Reminder—Set the right margin stop 5 to 8 spaces beyond the desired right margin.

Lesson 71

● Use a 70-space line for all lessons in this unit.

71a ■ Keyboard Review ● Each line at least three times

5 minutes

All letters   **SS**   We have just realized Gib's black picture frame is not exactly square.

Figure   The largest fish ever caught by rod was a shark weighing 2,536 pounds.   Wrists low

Opposite hand   Kate Dark had a knack for finding all kinds of kindling on their dike.   and still

Easy   It is a shame that more folks are not able to laugh at their problems.

| 1 | 2 | 3 | 4 | 5 | 6 | 7 | 8 | 9 | 10 | 11 | 12 | 13 | 14 |

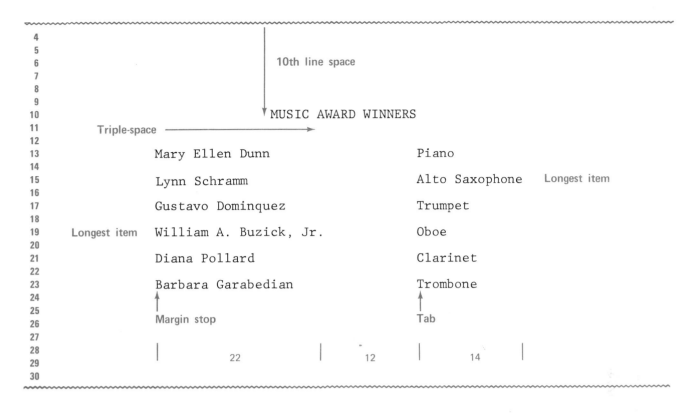

4		
5		
6	10th line space	
7		
8		
9		
10	↓ MUSIC AWARD WINNERS	
11	Triple-space ————————→	
12		
13	Mary Ellen Dunn	Piano
14		
15	Lynn Schramm	Alto Saxophone Longest item
16		
17	Gustavo Dominquez	Trumpet
18		
19	Longest item William A. Buzick, Jr.	Oboe
20		
21	Diana Pollard	Clarinet
22		
23	Barbara Garabedian	Trombone
24	↑	↑
25		
26	Margin stop	Tab
27		
28	│ 22 │ ¨ 12 │ 14 │
29		
30		

Simple two-column table

Problem 2 ▪ *Two-Column Table*

Directions—1. Retype the table in Problem 1, but add Mary Ann Wang, who plays the flute, to the list of award winners.

2. This time type the table on a full sheet in *reading position*. Leave 16 spaces between the columns.

- *Use the vertical centering shortcut explained on page 92. Remember to place the table in reading position.*

Lesson 63

• *60-space line*

63a ▪ Keyboard Review • Each line three times

5 minutes

All letters	SS	We might require five dozen packing boxes for our July crop.
Figure-Symbol		Only 24 of the 95 students who completed the test passed it!
Easy		They thought there should be goals at each end of the field.

Cut out waste movements

| 1 | 2 | 3 | 4 | 5 | 6 | 7 | 8 | 9 | 10 | 11 | 12 |

Cycle 3

Preparing
Personal Papers

63b ■ Skill Comparison

Directions—Type two 1-minute writings on each sentence. Compare *gwam*. Try typing all sentences at the rate of the first one.

Words

Easy	**SS**	Say what you will, those who learn to study earn top grades.	12
Figure-Symbol		The 14 1/2-foot boat crossed the mighty Atlantic in 84 days.	12
Script		*It is a simple fact of life that we do far less than we can.*	12
Rough draft		Bel(e)ive it *or* not, learn(C)ing how(u)to st(y)dy in ~~the~~ school(s) pays(s)off.	12

| 1 | 2 | 3 | 4 | 5 | 6 | 7 | 8 | 9 | 10 | 11 | 12 |

63c ■ Spelling and Proofreading Aid

Directions—Type each line twice. Study the words carefully as you type them.

1	**SS**	bureau February partial forty governor miscellaneous process
2		between niece participate battery ceiling graduate permanent
3		address lose recognize nephew courteous family exceed memory

Type letter by letter

63d ■ Problem Typing

Problem 1 ■ Two-Column Table

Directions—**1.** *Center* this table vertically on a half sheet of paper. Leave 20 spaces between columns. **2.** Single-space the columnar entries. Triple-space between the heading and the columns.

LEADERS IN PRODUCTION OF FOOD CROPS

Triple-space ────────▶

Barley	Soviet Union
Cacao Beans	Ghana
Coffee	Brazil
Corn	United States
Oats	United States
Peanuts	India
Potatoes	Soviet Union
Rice	China
Rye	Soviet Union
Sugar	Soviet Union
Wheat	Soviet Union

Problem 2 ■ Two-Column Table

Directions—**1.** Retype the table in Problem 1. Use a full sheet; type the table in *reading position*. **2.** Double-space the columnar entries. Leave 24 spaces between columns.

70d ■ Problem Typing

Problem ■ Report with Short Table

Full sheet
60-space line
Double spacing
Single-space
the table

Directions—Have a top margin of two inches (12 spaces). Allow eight spaces between the columns of the table.

● In double-spaced copy, a triple space should precede the table and a triple space should follow it.

THE AUTOMOBILE IN AMERICA

Today more than 1 million cars compete for space on our nation's streets and highways. We have become so dependent upon automobiles that they now provide about 90% of our personal transportation needs.

Many different people have played important roles in the development of the auto industry in the United States. Here are just a few of them.

Triple-space ⟶

AUTOMOBILE INDUSTRY LEADERS

Triple-space ⟶

David Buick	Charles Kettering
Charles Duryea	George Selden
Henry Ford	Alfred Sloan

Triple-space ⟶

While the earliest cars were powered by steam, their major source of power has been the gasoline engine. In recent years, however, scarcity of oil and increasing concern over pollution have rekindled an interest in finding other types of fuel. Experiments with electric, atomic, and solar power will undoubtedly have to be speeded up if America's love affair with the automobile continues.

Another problem generated by the steadily increasing number of automobiles is that of finding places to park them. There are now more than 6 million spaces in 8,000 American cities where paid parking is available.

70e ■ Extra-Credit Typing

Problem 1

Directions—Type the names of students in your typing class by rows. Provide main, subheadings, and columnar headings. Arrange the columns and center the table on a full sheet.

Problem 2

Directions—Type a summary of the report in 70d. Do not use a table, but use the ideas in it. Use the directions in 70d for typing your summary.

Problem 3

Directions—Use the first paragraph in 70c, page 120. Type as many copies of this paragraph as you can in the time that remains.

Lesson 64

64a ■ Keyboard Review • Each line three times   5 minutes

All letters   SS   Jack Howd can mix five quarts of gray paint for Liz and Bev.

Figure-Symbol   All 30 of my students had seen Star Wars more than one time.   Quiet wrists
                                                                                        and arms

Easy   He knows you can locate all eight of the islands on the map.

| 1 | 2 | 3 | 4 | 5 | 6 | 7 | 8 | 9 | 10 | 11 | 12 |

64b ■ Typing from Dictation and Spelling Checkup   5 minutes

Directions—Type the words in 63c, page 110, from dictation. Check for correct spelling. Retype any words in which you made an error.

64c ■ Sentence Guided Writings • Turn to 62b, page 108   10 minutes

Directions—1. Type each sentence for one minute. Try typing each four times in the minute without error.

2. Your teacher will call the return of the carriage each 15 seconds to guide you.

64d ■ Problem Typing   25 minutes

Problem 1 ■ Table with Subheading

Full sheet   Exact vertical center
Double-space column   18 spaces between
  entries   columns

• Space the main heading and subheading as shown in the table.

Problem 2 ■ Table with Subheading

Full sheet   Reading position
Double-space column   12 spaces between
  entries   columns

• Space main and subheading as you did in Problem 1.

NATIVE STATES OF PRESIDENTS

←—— Double-space

Since 1900

←—— Triple-space

Theodore Roosevelt	New York
William H. Taft	Ohio
Warren G. Harding	Ohio
Calvin Coolidge	Vermont
Herbert C. Hoover	Iowa
Franklin D. Roosevelt	New York
Harry S. Truman	Missouri
Dwight D. Eisenhower	Texas
John F. Kennedy	Massachusetts
Lyndon B. Johnson	Texas
Richard M. Nixon	California
Gerald Ford	Nebraska
Jimmy Carter	Georgia

STATE NICKNAMES

(14 Largest States)

California	Golden
Florida	Sunshine
Illinois	Prairie
Indiana	Hoosier
Massachusetts	Bay
Michigan	Wolverine
Missouri	Show Me
New Jersey	Garden
New York	Empire
North Carolina	Tarheel
Ohio	Buckeye
Pennsylvania	Keystone
Texas	Lone Star
Virginia	Old Dominion

70b ■ Sentence Guided Writings

Directions—1. Type each sentence for one minute. Try typing each at least four times in the minute.

2. Your teacher will call the return of the carriage each 15 seconds to guide you.

• *The rates at which you will be typing are given in the first column at the right.*

			GWAM 15" Guide	GWAM 12" Guide
1	SS	Do you sit poised and erect as you type?	32	40
2		Do you type without pauses between the words?	36	45
3		Do you strike each key with a quick, sharp stroke?	40	50
4		Do you think and type the short, easy words as a whole?	44	55
5		Do you hold the wrists low and quiet as you strike the keys?	48	60

| 1 | 2 | 3 | 4 | 5 | 6 | 7 | 8 | 9 | 10 | 11 | 12 |

70c ■ Timed Writings

Directions—1. Type two 1-minute writings on each ¶. Mark the one on which you made your best rate; then mark the one on which you made the fewest errors.

2. Type two 3-minute writings on the copy below. Circle errors. Compute *gwam*. Submit the better of the two writings.

		GWAM 1'	3'
DS	Do you know why many people fail in their jobs? Their	11	4	54
¶ 1 50 words 1.3 si	spelling, poor as it often is, is not the reason. They get	23	8	58
	by in figuring too. The reports of many studies show that	35	12	62
	they fail because they do not work with one another as well	47	16	66
	as they should.	50	17	67
	We ask much of other people but give little in return.	61	20	70
¶ 2 50 words 1.2 si	We stress their mistakes with the same zest we use in hiding	73	24	74
	our own. We are being neither fair to them nor honest with	85	28	78
	ourselves. When we do these things, we cannot work as well	97	32	82
	as we should.	100	33	83
	Good teamwork comes, first of all, from handling our	110	37	87
¶ 3 50 words 1.3 si	duties well. It comes, too, from using kind words when we	122	41	91
	refer to those with whom we work. Adopt the rule never to	134	45	95
All ¶'s 1.3 si	say anything about someone else that you would not like to	146	49	99
	have said about you.	150	50	100

| 1' | 1 | 2 | 3 | 4 | 5 | 6 | 7 | 8 | 9 | 10 | 11 | 12 |
| 3' | | 1 | | 2 | | 3 | | 4 |

Lesson 65

65a ■ Keyboard Review • Each line three times
5 minutes

All letters **SS** Kim required only five major exercises with the big trapeze.

Figure-Symbol A. Tangora (1923) typed 147 net words a minute--for an hour! Type steadily

Easy They came with the chain to see if we had made a first down.

| 1 | 2 | 3 | 4 | 5 | 6 | 7 | 8 | 9 | 10 | 11 | 12 |

65b ■ Technique Builder—Stroking • Each line three times
10 minutes

Home row **SS** Dashing Sir Galahad, with sword and half a flag, flashed by.

First fingers You can try to hunt with my gun if you cannot get a new one.

Second fingers Did Dick decide to check Cindy's deck to locate any defects? Center stroking in fingers

Third fingers Wilma Swanson with sixty-six others followed Lolita to Oslo.

Direct reach My brother expects to hunt for a diamond mine in the jungle.

Repeated letters We agreed to call a committee meeting to discuss the matter.

| 1 | 2 | 3 | 4 | 5 | 6 | 7 | 8 | 9 | 10 | 11 | 12 |

65c ■ Timed Writings
10 minutes

Directions—Type two 3-minute writings on the paragraphs. Circle errors. Compute *gwam*. Submit the better of the two writings.

	GWAM	
	1'	3'

All letters **DS** How many times have you heard people say that they just   11 | 4 49

¶ 1
42 words
1.2 si

could not write letters? You never hear these same people   23 | 8 53

say that they cannot talk to their friends. Still the two   35 | 12 57

remarks mean exactly the same thing.   42 | 14 59

Writing a friendly note or letter to someone is like   53 | 18 63

¶ 2
46 words
1.3 si

having a long cozy chat with him or her. If you find chat-   64 | 21 67

ting with someone pleasant, you should not find writing too   76 | 25 71

terrifying; for you can just write as if you were talking.   88 | 29 75

Begin your letter by typing the first thought that enters   100 | 33 78

¶ 3
48 words
1.2 si

your head. Write about what you did, whom you saw, or what   112 | 37 83

you read. Very quickly, you will find that one idea leads to   124 | 41 86

All ¶'s
1.3 si

another until the page is full of news that sounds like you.   136 | 45 91

| 1' | 1 | 2 | 3 | 4 | 5 | 6 | 7 | 8 | 9 | 10 | 11 | 12 |
| 3' | | 1 | | 2 | | 3 | | 4 | |

69c ▪ Problem Typing   *30 minutes*

Problem 1 ▪ *Table with Columnar Headings*

JOBS HELD BY FAMOUS PEOPLE

Full sheet
Reading position
Double-space
6 spaces between
columns

Name	Latest Job	Former Job
Edward Brooke	Senator	Lawyer
Jim Brown	Actor	Football Player
Carol Burnett	Comedian	Usher
Johnny Carson	TV Personality	Magician
Sean Connery	Actor	Bricklayer
Howard Cosell	Sports Announcer	Lawyer
Albert Einstein	Physicist	Patent Clerk
William Faulkner	Author	House Painter
W. C. Fields	Comedian	Juggler
Althea Gibson	Tennis Player	Teacher
Adolph Hitler	Dictator	Poster Painter
Bob Hope	Comedian	Boxer
Barbara Jordan	Representative	Judge
Dean Martin	Entertainer	Steelworker
Golda Meir	Prime Minister	School Teacher
Marilyn Monroe	Actor	Factory Worker
O. Henry	Author	Cowboy
Elvis Presley	Singer	Truck Driver
Babe Ruth	Baseball Player	Bartender
Harry S. Truman	President	Haberdasher

(Triple-space between heading row; Double-space below)

Problem 2 ▪ *Table with Columnar Headings*

Directions—1. Type the table in Problem 1 in the *exact vertical center* of a half sheet.
2. Single-space the column items.
3. Leave 8 spaces between columns.

Lesson 70   ● *60-space line*

70a ▪ Keyboard Review ● Each line three times   *5 minutes*

All letters   SS   Bea and Jacque Flam gazed transfixed through Clovis Parkway.

Figure-Symbol   My 12 accounts all pay 8.25% when held for an 8-year period.   *Quick, crisp, short strokes*

Easy   Their first goal is to make enough to own their own bicycle.

| 1 | 2 | 3 | 4 | 5 | 6 | 7 | 8 | 9 | 10 | 11 | 12 |

65d ■ Problem Typing   *20 minutes*

Problem 1 ■ Three-Column Table

Directions—1. Type the table in *reading position* on a full sheet of paper.
2. Double-space the columnar entries.
3. Leave six spaces between the columns.

● Use the directions on page 108 for setting the left margin stop for the first column and tab stops for the second and third columns.

GREAT INVENTIONS AND SCIENTIFIC DISCOVERIES

Selected Items

Air Conditioning	Carrier	1911
Airplane, Jet Engine	Ohain	1939
Engine, Automobile	Benz	1879
Meter, Parking	Magee	1953
Movie, Talking	Warner Brothers	1927
Pen, Fountain	Waterman	1884
Piano	Cristofori	1709
Radar	Taylor and Young	1922
Sewing Machine	Howe	1846
Soap, Hard–Water	Bertsch	1928
Telephone	Bell	1876

Problem 2 ■ Two-Column Table from Script

Directions—1. Type the table in *exact vertical center* on a half sheet of paper.

2. Single-space the columnar entries.

3. Leave 18 spaces between columns.

● Space the main and subheadings as you did in earlier problems.

LARGEST U.S. CITIES

In Order of Size

New York	New York
Chicago	Illinois
Los Angeles	California
Philadelphia	Pennsylvania
Detroit	Michigan
Houston	Texas
Baltimore	Maryland
Dallas	Texas
San Diego	California
San Antonio	Texas

Problem 2 ■ Table with Columnar Headings

Directions—1. Type this table in *exact vertical center* on a half sheet.

2. Single-space the columnar entries, as shown.
3. Leave 24 spaces between columns.

```
                    JEFFERSON CAMERA CLUB
Double-space ──────────────►
                    Program Assignments
Triple-space ──────────────►
              Date                    Chairperson
Double-space ──────►
           October 3            Jeff Herron
           October 17           Craig Johnson
           November 14          Rosemary Papagni
           November 28          Valerie Fender
           December 12          Orlando Gomez
           January 9            Susan Anderson
           January 23           Nancy Brock
```

Lesson 69

● *60-space line*

69a ■ Keyboard Review ● Each line three times

5 minutes

All letters **SS** Zelda expects to be in Quincy for a visit with Jack Goodman.

Figure-Symbol Single-space the lines from page 324; double-space the rest.

Easy Please have them fix the sign on the left side of the field.

```
|  1  |  2  |  3  |  4  |  5  |  6  |  7  |  8  |  9  |  10  |  11  |  12  |
```

Quick carriage return

69b ■ Composing at the Typewriter

10 minutes

Directions—Type answers to as many of these questions as time permits. Use complete sentences.

1. What is your favorite popular song?

2. Which popular singer do you like best?

3. What was the event that made Charles Lindbergh famous?

4. What is the capital city of your state?

5. What do you enjoy doing most in your spare time?

6. What event is celebrated on July 4?

7. If you start typing on the 13th line space from the top of your paper, how many inches are there in the top margin?

8. What is your favorite subject in school?

9. Who do you think is the greatest living American?

10. For what discovery is Madame Curie famous?

Lesson 66

• 60-space line

66a ■ Keyboard Review • Each line three times   5 minutes

All letters   **SS** Bud Roper may take this quiz next week if Jack will give it.

Figure-Symbol   Leave 18 spaces (elite) for the left margin of 1 1/2 inches.   Instant release

Easy   It will pay them to take some time to plan for their visits.

| 1 | 2 | 3 | 4 | 5 | 6 | 7 | 8 | 9 | 10 | 11 | 12 |

66b ■ Capitalization Guides—Typing Titles   5 minutes

• Capitalize first words and all other words in titles of books, articles, periodicals, headings, and plays, except words which are articles, conjunctions, and prepositions.

• The title of a book may be underscored or typed in all capital letters.

Directions—Type each line twice. The sentences illustrate the capitalization rule given above.

1   **SS** She will play a small part in the musical, "Sound of Music."

2   I took the notes from an article, "Africa's Garden of Eden."   Think as
                                                                                you type

3   DELOS is the name of Nelson's book on the islands of Greece.

4   Carol reviewed Durrell's book, <u>Birds, Beasts, and Relatives</u>.

| 1 | 2 | 3 | 4 | 5 | 6 | 7 | 8 | 9 | 10 | 11 | 12 |

66c ■ Control Ladder Sentences   15 minutes

Directions—Type 1-minute writings on each sentence. Try typing each four times without error. Your teacher may call the return of the carriage each 15 seconds to guide you.

• The rate increases 4 words a minute with each succeeding line.

GWAM 15" Guide

1	**SS**	Wear a smile and have friends.	24
2		Wear a scowl and have bad wrinkles.	28
3		You must believe in yourself, of course.	32
4		Great jobs are performed by sticking to them.	36
5		No problem we face is as big as the ones we dodge.	40
6		*Their teams have lost only three times this whole year.*	44
7		Do you keep your arms in and your wrists low and quiet?	44
8		*Our geography class will not meet at the regular time today.*	48
9		A smart person makes errors; a dull one goes on making them.	48

| 1 | 2 | 3 | 4 | 5 | 6 | 7 | 8 | 9 | 10 | 11 | 12 |

Lesson 68

68a ■ Keyboard Review • Each line three times

All letters   SS   Marvel Jackson was requested to pay a tax for the big prize.

Figure-Symbol   Judy scored 91% in English, 87% in history--and 98% in math!

Wrists and elbows still

Easy   I know for sure which items are on sale at the market today.

| 1 | 2 | 3 | 4 | 5 | 6 | 7 | 8 | 9 | 10 | 11 | 12 |

68b ■ Skill Comparison • 1-minute writing on each sentence. Compare gwam.

Easy   SS   The first rule of writing good copy is knowing your subject.

Script   *When you write papers, be brief; there is no weight to wind.*

Type without stopping

Rough draft   In the free countries there will always be a clash of of ideas.

| 1 | 2 | 3 | 4 | 5 | 6 | 7 | 8 | 9 | 10 | 11 | 12 |

68c ■ Typing from Dictation and Spelling Checkup

Directions—Type 67b, page 116, from dictation. Check for correct spelling. Retype any words in which you made an error.

Centering Columnar Headings

Follow these steps to center headings over the columns of a table:

1. Set the carriage at the point a column is to begin.

2. Space forward 1 space for each 2 spaces in the longest line in that column.

3. From that point, backspace once for each 2 spaces in the columnar heading.

4. Type the heading. It will be centered over the column.

68d ■ Problem Typing

Problem 1 ■ Practice Problem

Directions—1. Insert a sheet of practice paper. The two entries below are the longest in each of two columns of a table.

2. Plan the tabulation, allowing 24 spaces between the columns. Type the two entries.

3. A double-space above the items type the columnar headings. Center the headings over the entries.

• *To center the headings, follow the steps in the foregoing explanation.*

Columnar headings ⟶ Date   Chairperson

Longest entries ⟶ November 14   ⟵ Double-space   Rosemary Papagni

			GWAM	
			1'	3'

All letters   DS

¶ 1
48 words
1.3 si

We envy the batter who can hit the ball out of the park, — 11 | 4 52
the swimmer who has the title for fancy diving, or the artist — 24 | 8 56
who can give life to colors on canvas. What we fail to see — 36 | 12 60
is the long hours these experts spent acquiring their skill. — 48 | 16 64

¶ 2
48 words
1.3 si

How thrilling it must be for those who can sing the best, — 59 | 20 68
run the fastest, or jump higher than anyone else in the class. — 72 | 24 72
Talent like this does not just happen, however. The people — 84 | 28 76
who come out on top work hard for the honors they receive. — 96 | 32 80

¶ 3
48 words
1.2 si

Practice is a potent learning aid. All experts know this — 107 | 36 84
secret, and they use it to perfect their crafts. Why not use — 120 | 40 87
this secret too? Prize good work highly; practice. It is — 131 | 44 92

All ¶'s
1.3 si

great to have the power to learn; it is tragic not to use it. — 144 | 48 96

1' | 1 | 2 | 3 | 4 | 5 | 6 | 7 | 8 | 9 | 10 | 11 | 12
3' | 1 | | 2 | | 3 | | 4

66e ■ Control Practice   *5 minutes*

Directions—1. Type the last paragraph of 66d, above, as many times as you can in the time that remains.

2. Circle your errors. Place a check mark in the margin of each paragraph in which you made no more than one error.

Lesson 67

● *60-space line*

67a ■ Keyboard Review ● Each line three times   *5 minutes*

All letters   SS   Phil Singer wanted Liza to fly Jack to Quebec next November.

Figure-Symbol   The $3.50 tickets now cost $4, and the $4.50 tickets are $5.

Type with your fingers

Easy   I know she can see most of the fish if she sits on the dock.

| 1 | 2 | 3 | 4 | 5 | 6 | 7 | 8 | 9 | 10 | 11 | 12 |

1 SS machinery endeavor faculty assistant ninth necessity equally

2 appropriate ninety knowledge career truly pamphlet Wednesday *Type letter by letter*

3 doctor completely enthusiasm since occur accurate beneficial

67c ■ Paragraph Guided Writings — 5 minutes

Directions—1. Turn to ¶ 1, 66d, page 115.
2. Set a goal of 40, 44, or 48 words a minute on the paragraph.

3. Type three 1-minute writings. Try to hit your goal word just as time is called. The quarter- or half-minutes will be called to guide you.

67d ■ Problem Typing — 30 minutes

Problem 1 ■ Four-Column Table

Directions—1. Type the table in *reading position* on a full sheet of paper.
2. Single-space the columnar entries.
3. Leave six spaces between the columns.

● *Use the directions on page 108 for setting the left margin stop for the first column and tab stops for the second, third, and fourth columns.*

TWO—LETTER ABBREVIATIONS FOR THE STATES

Recommended by the U.S. Postal Service

Alabama	AL	Montana	MT
Alaska	AK	Nebraska	NE
Arizona	AZ	Nevada	NV
Arkansas	AR	New Hampshire	NH
California	CA	New Jersey	NJ
Colorado	CO	New Mexico	NM
Connecticut	CT	New York	NY
Delaware	DE	North Carolina	NC
Florida	FL	North Dakota	ND
Georgia	GA	Ohio	OH
Hawaii	HI	Oklahoma	OK
Idaho	ID	Oregon	OR
Illinois	IL	Pennsylvania	PA
Indiana	IN	Rhode Island	RI
Iowa	IA	South Carolina	SC
Kansas	KS	South Dakota	SD
Kentucky	KY	Tennessee	TN
Louisiana	LA	Texas	TX
Maine	ME	Utah	UT
Maryland	MD	Vermont	VT
Massachusetts	MA	Virginia	VA
Michigan	MI	Washington	WA
Minnesota	MN	West Virginia	WV
Mississippi	MS	Wisconsin	WI
Missouri	MO	Wyoming	WY